THE PRESS
AND POPULAR CULTURE

THE PRESS
AND POPULAR CULTURE

MARTIN CONBOY

SAGE Publications
London • Thousand Oaks • New Delhi

First published 2002

Reprinted 2003

SAGE Publications Ltd
6 Bonhill Street
London EC2A 4PU

SAGE Publications Inc
2455 Teller Road
Thousand Oaks, California 91320

SAGE Publications India Pvt Ltd
32, M-Block Market
Greater Kailash - I
New Delhi 110 048

British Library Cataloguing in Publication data

A catalogue record for this book
is available from the British Library

ISBN 0 7619 6660 9
ISBN 0 7619 6661 7 (pbk)

Library of Congress Control Number available

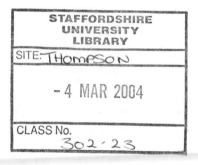
Typeset by SIVA Math Setters, Chennai, India
Printed and bound in Great Britain by Athenaeum Press, Gateshead

Ich lebe mein Leben in wachsenden Ringen,
die sich über die Dinge ziehn.
(Rainer Maria Rilke)

für Simone und Lara

CONTENTS

PREFACE

This book offers a much needed critical history of an underdeveloped area of journalism for examination – the popular press. Eschewing approaches to popular culture which restrict themselves to the contemporary, it proposes that the terrain of the popular has a history which must be understood if controversies about the current relationship between the popular and the press are to be fully engaged with. This historical critique is further distinguished by its cultural approach which centres on the use of language in constructing a rhetorical appeal to the people and how the popular press has been able to adapt that rhetorical call within different cultural paradigms.

Framed by discussion of the Western European popular print tradition and the role which the popular press played in revolutionary movements, the book concentrates on the contrasts and comparisons between the popular newspaper as it emerged in the United States and Britain from the 1830s and the role this played in the formation of widely accepted definitions of popular culture. This historical approach serves to develop an awareness of the very important alignment within the popular press of the issues of power and public knowledge which underpin the economic imperatives and questions of citizenship inherent in popular readerships.

Contemporary example and discussion drawn from Britain, Germany and the United States enables the debate to be located outside the narrow confines of national borders, as part of a debate about how the popular is being reconfigured in the popular press as a part of a global strategy while retaining its essential appeal to local readerships; meeting challenges by recombining aspects of its traditional rhetorical appeal.

There are certainly important newspapers and important popular print genres which have been omitted from this account. It is not that they have no place in this critical history, more that constraints of space have meant that a sample view has been taken to illustrate its central theses outlined above.

Any criticism of the fact that there is not enough attention paid to the specificities of the local, weekly, regional and evening variants of the popular press while undoubtedly true must be tempered by the book's primary aim which is to provide less a chronology of the popular press in its entirety and more an assessment of the themes and political debates attached to print journalism in general. This approach possibly favours an emphasis on the continuities within the popular press rather than on the differences to be found. This is a strategic decision taken in order to highlight the important political point made by the book that commercial popular culture has always depended on the rhetorical impression that it belongs somehow to the people and that this is nothing specific to the contemporary era.

Nevertheless, I would hope that all omissions and other decisions about content and approach may serve to generate vigorous debate about the range of issues raised throughout the book.

ACKNOWLEDGEMENTS

As this book charts several aspects of my developing professional interests over the last few years, it seems appropriate to acknowledge the people who have been instrumental and supportive on the way. My thanks go to Dr Heidrun Klemm who initially backed the inclusion of work on the British press into the curriculum at the University of Potsdam in the turbulent months after German Reunification and to Dr Wolfgang Petschan and Professor Wolfgang Wicht who subsequently encouraged and supported my Cultural Studies work there in the Institute for English and American Studies.

At my current place of work, Dr Andrew Darley, Dr Matthew Rampley and Dr Helen Davis have all been supportive, stimulating and most importantly, friendly partisans in their unstinting efforts to establish a research culture. Without them the process of this work would have been much lonelier. Gwynneth Wilkey and Lindsay Da Silva have exceeded mere efficiency in their processing of my copious requests for library support for the research. Above all, I owe a debt of gratitude to Jane Taylor who has been stalwart in her championing of fresh approaches to journalism here in Farnham and in securing and protecting the time necessary for me to pursue this project. The Surrey Institute of Art and Design University College Research Fund has been generous in providing financial assistance in the important final stages of publication.

In bringing an idea to fruition and in demonstrating the collegiality which can still prevail no matter how competitive the academic environment may become, Dr David Finkelstein and Dr Richard Keeble have helped more than they would appreciate through their encouraging support and timely textual interventions.

To newspaper reader, Erich Hausmann, and the postal services of Dieter and Bärbel Vick my thanks for assistance in securing a regular supply of the German newspapers used in the book.

Finally thanks to Julia Hall at Sage for her genuine enthusiasm and vision in enabling not only this book to see the light of day but the area of journalism to become opened up for broad intellectual enquiry.

INTRODUCTION
POPULAR PRESS: THEORY
AND HISTORY

The popular press has always claimed an allegiance with the people, the ordinary people. At some times it has claimed to represent their interests; at all times it has endeavoured to reflect the broader cultural patterns of their lives. Whether from a political standpoint or from the perspective of the breadth of its influence, the people are central to the popular press. This book will explore the complex and dynamic relationship between the popular press and popular culture as the culture of those ordinary people. In doing that it will attempt to bring to the attention of the reader the links between the practice of popular print journalism and cultural theory. The reason for this is as simple as it is obvious. If we do not explore this form of journalism through an engagement with ideas about how such things as popular readerships are formed and addressed, then we are left with a rather hollow notion of what popular culture is at work in the press and we are left also with a rather uncritical view of the popular press as disconnected from contemporary cultural debate. Neither is true. The popular press has always expressed a rich engagement with the dissemination of cultural norms and survives on its ability to maintain a dialogue with contemporary cultural trends.

Dahlgren and Sparks claim that there is a close relationship between the popular press and popular culture when they assert that 'cultural studies argues that journalism is something part of, rather than separate from, popular culture' rather than being a separate entity. (1991: 18). Such an observation generates problems for any easy assumption that contemporary popular newspapers can be marked off from the practices of an authentic popular culture because of the daily continuity of their mass-market appeal, relative to other media, and the fact that these newspapers are owned and controlled by powerful commercial concerns. To maintain that the popular press does form a legitimate area of popular culture for study is to understand these papers and their readers as part of the continuum which links economic structure to cultural consumption in all areas of contemporary cultural life. Successful popular newspapers, like their popular print predecessors, have always managed to articulate a real relationship between the reader and the commercial enterprise and at their most effective involved the reader symbolically in that venture. How the popular press has been successful in articulating the lifeworld of the majority of ordinary men and women excluded from the mainstream of political power is the focus of this book.

WHY THEORY?

We may begin by posing this simple question. Theory foregrounds the role of the popular press in the wide-ranging cultural debates around the definition of the popular it seeks to address. It assists in testing the claims of journalism down the years as to its location and political importance within popular culture. Theory allows the student of popular culture to challenge her/his assumptions about the ambiguities of the popular press and its influences. Theory allows an opportunity to assess common sense attitudes to these areas.

It is worth recalling in this context what Catherine Belsey has proposed concerning thoughtful engagement with any form of practice: '... there is no practice without theory, however much that theory is suppressed, unformulated or perceived as "obvious"'. (1993: 4).

WHY HISTORY?

Part of the fascination in assessing the appeal and success of the popular press is in seeing how it has been able to adapt to its cultural and political environments and sometimes provide the dynamism for a radical departure from them. These processes have always taken place in particular historical contexts. History allows us to examine the continuities which the popular press inherited from other popular printed forms and also to locate the periods in which major shifts in the representation of the people took place, fulfilling its role as: 'a continuous process of interaction between the historian and his facts, an unending dialogue between the present and the past'. (Carr, 1986: 30).

History can illustrate how popular culture emerged from the fifteenth century onwards along with the development of printing in Western Europe and was displayed in the early printed broadsides and ballads and how these became incorporated into early popular newspapers. In addition, historical perspectives allow an insight into considerations of power. As popular print culture becomes involved in the struggle over access to knowledge, who owns these channels of communication and how the people are addressed through them become central to questions of political representation. The popular press has realigned itself in different cultures and at different times to accommodate the conflicting interests of ordinary people and the commercial and political elites. As the political and economic status of these people shifts, within the dynamics of capitalism, the people take on a different perspective and become more included within the texts of popular print culture and are addressed more in a language which approximates to their daily speech. In fact, the whole theme of the developments within the popular newspaper from the nineteenth century, for instance, is redolent of the movement of the content of the popular press towards the daily experiences of the ordinary people. Up to the present day political power as inscribed in the popular press is of enormous importance. Even when it foregrounds entertainment and diversion, we will endeavour to explore how these enhance or obscure broadly political issues. History allows a long and critical view of these processes.

THE HISTORY OF A TRADITION

The popular press formed a channel which enabled the expansion and extension of popular culture from its secession with earlier forms of folk and common cultures. The subtle and reflexive relationship with popular culture that the popular press draws upon is an essential ingredient in its success.

In order for us to establish that the popular press has links with and represents elements of the culture of ordinary people, we must be able to demonstrate how it incorporated elements of the community of the folk culture which preceded it into the oppositional tendencies of a politically popular culture, directed against the powerful stakeholders in society and articulating an alternative vision more sympathetic to those outside the ranks of the powerful. This alternative may be via an overt political engagement or via utopian, escapist fantasies of a better world. A historical view can show how these elements have been grafted onto the institutions of the popular press and the political implications of this process.

The popular press needed to mould or refract the development of a distinct culture of the people if it were to be considered as having any direct relationship to popular culture or to claim that it constituted a part of that culture. The make-up of this press and its relationship to the culture of the ordinary people has had different emphases in over two centuries of an institutionalized popular press. Such a historical survey will highlight the ruptures as well as the consistencies as the starting point for discussions of the legitimacy of this press as a form of popular culture today.

The popular is not a recent category and the analytical and political challenges that it gives rise to are of equally long gestation. An exclusive concentration on the contemporary has led to a recent survey of the area being described '… as though culture had entirely lost its moorings from the bedrock of history' (Golding and Fergusson, 1997: xxi).

I will provide an account which blends an historical awareness with contemporary cultural debate so as to clarify the traditions which have maintained the dynamism of the popular press and its ability to speak to the common people. This will in turn allow a better understanding of the current challenges facing this particular area of the news and entertainment media. This combination of the historical and the contemporary gives the popular an important contextualization.

We will begin with an overview of approaches to popular culture but it is one which will be targeted towards a precise and historical account of the emergence and development of one area which claims to constitute a part of popular culture: the popular press. This examination will emphasize, in general terms, the rhetorical strategies that the popular press deploys to form part of popular cultural practice and, at the same time, the ways it acts as a vector of elements of a broader popular experience.

1

POPULARIZING THE PEOPLE

Raymond Williams expresses much of the complexity of the issues which intersect in defining 'popular' in his book *Keywords*. He avoids any simplistic celebration of the popular while at the same time refusing to be drawn into an elitist dismissal of the popular as trivial. His starting point is political and it is this insistence which enables him to maintain a perspective which keeps all the contradictory elements of the concept in play. He points out that the origins of the word denoted 'belonging to the people' but also carried implications of 'base or low'. Its extension in the sense of being well liked, he argues, was firmly established by the nineteenth century. By this point, he claims:

> **Popular** was being seen from the point of view of the people rather than from those seeking favour or power from them. Yet the earlier sense has not died. **Popular culture** was not identified by *the people* but by others, and it still carries two older senses: inferior kinds of work (cf. **popular literature, popular press** as distinguished from *quality press*); and work deliberately setting out to win favour (**popular journalism** as distinguished from *democratic journalism*, or **popular entertainment**); as well as the more modern sense of well-liked by many people, with which of course, in many cases, the earlier senses overlap. (Williams, 1976b: 19 original emphasis)

Drawing so often on the press as an example, as he does, illustrates how debates over the changing role and definition of the popular coincide within the popular press. A later commentator on these issues brings this range of definition into sharper focus by his refinement of Williams's observations into three aspects: the quantitative, the political and the aesthetic (Sparks, 1991).

The attraction of Williams's range of definition, and Sparks's leaner version, is that they do not attempt to close down popular culture prescriptively. Their multi-faceted nature suggests that the power of popular culture lies in its ability to be appropriated in any of these ways to a greater or lesser degree and still be able to claim legitimacy as representative of the people. The element of claiming is crucial in the effectiveness of this process and, in the case of the popular press particularly, is how it is achieved textually. Popular culture is necessarily a hybrid relationship between categories of definition rather than a pure category by itself. One consequence of this hybridity is that there is an uneven, unpredictable

(295)

Numb. 38. 7

Mercurius Britanicus.

Communicating the affaires of great

B R I T A I N E :

For the better Information of the People.

From *Monday* the 27. of *May*, to *Monday* the 3. of *June*. 1644.

I Shall pursue *Aulicus* as his *Excellency* doth his *Majestie*, I hope I shall **Britanicus**
now overtake him, for his *wit* marches like their train of Artillery in **pursuite.**
wet weather, very heavily, he begins thus :

   We told you last weeke of a notable sally made upon the Rebels, by the **Aulicus his**
most noble Countesse of Derby : Yes, you have told us every weeke of *her*, **first relation.**
you will not let the *Countesse* be quiet in her *Castle*, but fathers such *pro-*
digious, and masculine *Sallies* upon the *Countesse,* (that the Earle vowes)
if all be true I hear, never to appear for them again, for he sayes they give
the Lady all the *reputation,* and he was never so much as named, but at his
voyage into the *Ile of man,* where he was neither able to raise the Ile, nor
a man in it.

   But now sayes he we have received Letters of unquestionable credit; but **Aulicus re-**
where are these *Letters* so unquestionable ? no where but in *Oxford,* that **ceives strange**
I know on, or within their *Prelaticall line of Communication.* **Letters.**

   But sayes he, *we have Intelligence of another Sally :* Reader did you ever **Another Sally**
see such an *impudent Pamphlet* as this, to affirme the *Countesse* was in another *Sally,* when I know one that dare take oath, she hath not stirred out of
her *bed-chamber* since the Siege begun : *Aulicus,* I prethee do not trouble
a *Countesse* thus with thy continuall *Sallies,* thou woot do her more disho-
nour, for there is a little rumour wandring about, that the *Countesse* is not **The Coun-**
all of one *Sex,* but like the Earles *Principality,* she is suspected to be part **tesse not**
of the *Ile of man,* plainly, some thinke her an *Hermophrodite,* a Lady be- **thought to be**
twixt two genders. **of one Sex.**

   He sayes this Sally was on Sunday night last ; yes, it is very likely, if they
do any murder, or mischiefe, it is upon the *Lords day,* that is all the solem-
             P p   nity,

Mercurius Britanicus, 1644 – An early invocation of the people in print

overlap between these categories. For instance the popular can never be
considered as divorced from the economy. Even its precursors, folk culture
or the 'common culture', were as much the products of a feudal economy
as popular culture has become a constituent part of a capitalist economy.
In each genre of popular culture, at each point in its historical existence,
the combination and the relationship of Sparks's triadic is arranged differently. This is what makes it important to consider the popular newspaper
in all its historical complexity.

SPEAKING FOR THE PEOPLE? THE POPULAR AS DISCOURSE

Despite stressing the long tradition of the popular in printed form, as soon as we attempt to find a departure date for the emergence of a popular press we are set a series of questions. These questions indicate the problems which beset the core of the debate about the politics and 'popularity' of this variant of the popular press in Western Europe and the United States of America. Do we take the irregular, popular formats whose popularity was incorporated into later manifestations of the popular press, such as almanacs, gossip, tales of dread and wonder, melodrama? Do we take the French Revolutionary press from 1789 or the radical Unstamped of the English 1830s as a properly politicized manifestation of the desires of the people for social change? Do we take the first successful penny dailies in the United States or the Sunday papers of the mid-nineteenth century in England as the incorporation of people into Schudson's 'democratic market society' (1978: 57)? Do we wait until Pulitzer, Hearst and later Harmsworth bring technology, style, commerce and the reading public together with the first million-selling daily papers at the opening of the twentieth century? Do we extend our horizon and look at the million-selling dailies in Germany and Britain today?

Perkin has simply, yet perceptively, remarked: '... the origins of the popular press go back far beyond 1870 ... The origins of the popular press go back long before Northcliffe. They are to be found, in part at least, where the most casual reader of nineteenth-century newspapers would expect to find them – in the press itself' (1991: 47–51).

It becomes clear that, if one attempts to trace an institutional path of evolution, the question of a popular press is a complex one depending on definitions of its audience and its ambition. Does popularity depend on adherence to a political agenda that favours the people broadly defined or is it more a question of being sold to many people and reflecting the concerns of the day in a lively and contemporary fashion? A more productive approach would claim the popular press to be a set of discourses which establish elements of authenticity in part through its rhetoric and is thus able to establish an inclusivity based on its appeal to wide sections of ordinary people.

Popular culture, as we will see in more detail later, emerges alongside printing in the early modern period. Both textually and politically it is far from a uniform or stable set of practices. It cannot be regarded as an entity nor even as an evolution from one distinct cultural formation to another. It is not an object nor is it a fixed category which can be observed consistently across the miscellany of popular print culture. We need therefore to return to questions of definition. It would be more accurate to claim that its meaning lies in the ways in which it claims a power to legitimate its status as representative of 'the people', the majority, as opposed to the powerful, the elite minority within a society. Such claims to power have been described in analytical terms as discourses.

The concept of discourse needs clarification if it is to help us in coming to understand the importance of the interplay between popular culture and its claims to be a legitimate representative of the people's interests. Broadly speaking, linguists choose to use the term discourse as describing the co-existence of text and context, and the regularities present in any stretch of language longer than a sentence (Crystal, 1991: 106). It means that there can be, from the perspective of a discursive analysis, no utterance which can be divorced from the circumstances of its production and reception, beyond the utterance itself in its interconnections with other linguistic and non-linguistic phenomena, without losing an essential part of its meaning: its context.

Critical Discourse Analysis extends this point from a perspective informed by the thought of Michel Foucault (1974). This work, developed by theorists such as van Dijk, Fairclough and Fowler, Hodge and Kress, sees discourse as a set of practices which enable language and power to be combined in a powerful and persuasive rhetoric of common-sense.

Popular culture works as a discourse in that it provides a framework of expectations which allows an idealized version of the ordinary people to emerge. Popular newspapers are potent factors in this normative process as they build upon these discourses of the people and can target them emo-tionally, economically and politically, claiming to speak on their behalf. The popular precedes the popular newspaper but the legitimacy of the popular press is to a large extent drawn from the ways in which print culture moved the folk and oral traditions of Western Europe into a series of popular printed formats and discourses of the popular upon which the popular newspaper could build.

Viewing popular culture as a set of discourses which define and set limitations on the concept and the content of a culture claiming to represent the people therefore allows us to identify the definitions of popular culture as part of the discourse itself. The definitions themselves form part of the claim to legitimacy of a certain perspective on popular culture in that they do not make it any more specific – they simply make it more persuasive. There is a hole at the heart of popular culture we might say: the hole is the absence of real people. Popular newspapers have always exploited this absence, claiming to articulate the views of the people while in the main being owned by wealthy entrepreneurs. Discursive debates about popular culture implicitly restrict the potential of this area to forge genuine political change to the system with which it shares cer-tain coordinates. This is a point made by Schiach in her analysis: 'The ideological and practical struggles over definitions of popular culture are reproduced, or refought, in language, and not solved by it' (1989: 19). This suggests that it may not be possible nor worthwhile attempting a finite definition of popular culture simply because it is a process of argumentation and debate over values and symbols within society which are implicated in the constantly shifting relationship of the mass of people to the artefacts which claim to represent their interests. This argumentation is constant and framed by the power relationships of those involved.

John Street illustrates this in a discussion of various American authors on popular culture: '... radicals see popular culture as exploitative of the lower classes, conservatives see popular culture as debased and menacing, and liberals see all culture and all classes as equally valid and valuable' (1997: 5–6). This approach to popular culture as an ongoing sequence of arguments about the power implications each set of definitions is emphasizing has its uses. Considering popular culture as a discourse enables us to appreciate the extent to which any definition of the popular signals the political intent of the author.

If the meaning of popular print culture depends upon its claims to represent 'the people' in the broadest possible sense which incorporates, first, an ability to represent the political interests of the people excluded from the direct workings of power and, second, to represent qualitatively the views and life experiences of the people, then one of the chief problems in defining it precisely lies in the fact that the 'people' has little specific meaning. It is always a politicized term in that it depends upon who is invoking them and to what ends. Writing on behalf of the people and selling that writing to the people has always been a political process. The concept of 'the people' is inevitably bound up with 'an articulation of political discourse' (McGuigan, 1993: 12).

Morag Schiach also claims that popular culture's definition lies within the domain of discourse, which she defines as 'the continuities in the ways in which popular culture has been described and evaluated' (1989: 2). It follows from this that any claim that popular culture represents the people must be supported and legitimated within the practice itself, within the traditions of any popular genre. Therefore, the people have no real existence. As a term, its legitimacy depends on the credibility of its rhetorical appeal. A focus on popular culture as discourse will assist in understanding how the rhetorical processes at work within the practice of the popular press create its apparent legitimacy.

Another concept which recurs in attempts to define popular culture is that of process. This is of particular importance if we refute any notion of culture as a fixed entity. Popular culture may be manifest in specific practices and, for our purposes, in all the stability of printed artefacts, but the idea of process allows us to keep in view the flexibility of popular culture over time and, perhaps most importantly, its reception. This is what Fiske means when he writes: 'Popular culture is always in process; its meanings can never be identified in a text, for texts are activated, or made meaningful, only in social relations and in intertextual relations' (1994: 3).

The element of process also distinguishes popular culture from the relative stability of high culture. This is not to say that popular culture does not have its own traditions and characteristics, its own genres and rhetoric, but it is less likely that they will be formed into a canon as is the case with elite/high culture. Part of the explanation for this is that popular culture is a difficult space to own: difficult for the elite, because of the resistance it encounters from the people, and difficult for the people because of the encroachment of the political and commercial motives of the elite on what they perceive as their popular space.

HEGEMONY AND THE POPULAR TRANSACTION IN THE PRESS

A popular press does not only address the people themselves, but places that address within the dominant economic structures of society since to a large extent the categorization of the ordinary people takes place in terms of their relative economic marginalization. Any discursive approach to popular journalism must be located within a particular economic framework. The people are always defined within that economic pattern.

A purely discursive approach would seem to suggest that popular culture is a relatively enclosed set of practices aligning and realigning themselves to accommodate changing political/economic configurations. It leaves open the question of the participation of the people themselves and their ability to dissent from or re-create the practices they are presented with – in other words, to be active consumers and participants. It would be an outrageously patronizing and simplified view of the relationship between popular culture and its audience to suggest that these were passive observers of texts produced in their name or blindly naive to claim that they and their lives were the authentic and sole sources of these texts. One move to provide an explanatory framework to create a model of relative interchange between producer and consumer of popular culture comes to us through the work of Antonio Gramsci and the writers who in the last decades have appropriated his key ideas in an attempt to formulate a more positive, dynamic approach to these questions.

The main point that Gramsci brings to contemporary disussions of popular culture is his concept of hegemony. Many analyses of popular culture come from the Left but these analyses have little to tell us, other than negatively, of the sort of popular culture that might be applicable to the phenomenon of the popular press. Because of its ownership by capitalist entrepreneurs, the popular press is seen to be part of the problem of the disenfranchisement of ordinary people, rather than an interesting phenomenon in its own right. Indeed, Colin Sparks has written: 'The consequence of the classic left-wing view is that "popular" culture and journalism must necessarily be a contradictory term' (1992: 28).

An opposing account of the popular includes potential for social change to emerge from it. Mukerji and Schudson describe it thus: 'the radical mirror image of conservative cultural hierarchy is a response that assumes that popular culture can assist in mobilizing political action' (1986: 57). But even this account prevents us applying it to the popular press because the definition assumes that popular culture lies outside the realm of the market-capitalist model in which all popular newspapers function.

For Gramsci hegemony is the provisional stability achieved between the ruling class and its subordinates:

> ... the dominant group is coordinated concretely with the general interests of the subordinate groups, and the life of the state is conceived of as a continuous process

of formation and superseding of unstable equilibria ... between the interests of the fundamental group and those of the subordinate groups – equilibria in which the interests of the dominant group prevail, but only up to a certain point. (1971: 181–2)

Gramsci highlights, through his theory of hegemony, the crucial aspect of process in the formation of such a culture. Hegemony is not dominance pure and simple but a negotiation between groups in society of unequal power in which those in power manage to retain the overall strategic control while acknowledging partially the aspirations of the subordinate groups in ways in which the power base of the dominant group is relatively unaffected. Popular culture is a key area where this struggle takes place between the interests of two sections of society: those with direct access to power and capital and those without that direct access.

According to a Gramscian perspective, as articulated by Tony Bennett:

Such processes neither erase the cultures of subordinate groups, nor do they rob 'the people' of their 'true culture': what they do is reshuffle those cultures on to an ideological and cultural terrain in which they can be disconnected from whatever radical impulses which may (but need not) have fuelled them and be connected to more conservative or, often, downright reactionary cultural and ideological tendencies. (Bennett, 1986: 19)

Gramsci claims a central place for education, broadly defined, in this process. The subordinate groups are inducted into the interrelationships of their own impulses with the concerns of the powerful so that they recognize not only the authenticity of traditional aspects of their voice in the culture which claims to represent their ways of life but also the place of their voice in the greater schemes of economy and polity. Popular culture is at the same time a process of resistance and affirmation (Giroux and Simon, 1989: 8–9).

The dual nature of popular culture as a field of resistance and dominance is particularly relevant to the popular press and explains the ambiguity in its content and reception. It also enables the processes at work in constructing a popular imagery in the press to be viewed in a more reciprocal fashion than certain discursive approaches which seem merely to allow a shuffling of a deck of marked cards.

The principal challenge with popular culture is that it has two contradictory thrusts. It may claim to speak from the people or it may claim to speak on behalf of the people. This polarity is reflected in the connotations of the different forms of the popular. The first comes with an aura of authenticity, a qualitative aspect; the second, with a negative connotation of a commodified inauthentic, exploited mass. What I seek to do here is to examine the flow of influence between the two modes, inevitable within a capitalist economy of consumption, thus indicating the relational flow between these apparently exclusive claims, in particular in terms of the popular press.

OPEN READINGS AND THE POPULAR PRESS

One contemporary strand of assessment emerging from de Certeau (1988) and elaborated by Fiske (1994) acknowledges a more open argument than that of critics from the left working around the concept of hegemony. Its difference from the hegemonic dynamic is that whereas Gramsci implies at least a series of provisional closures dependent on dominant economic and political paradigms. Fiske sees popular culture as a constant, almost anarchic, continuum of ebb and flow with the people always able to appropriate on their own terms.

Fiske, foregrounding the active role that people play in the construction of their own meanings from textual evidence, claims 'Culture is the constant process of producing meanings of and from our social experience, and such meanings necessarily produce a social identity for the people involved' (1994: 1).

In the main, Fiske's approach to popular culture would appear to be of little relevance to the popular press since its texts must be commercially produced elsewhere than among the people and subsequently it must persuade from a distanced perspective that it does indeed form an authentic part of the popular sensibility. The way it achieves this is through its rhetoric of the popular. However, Fiske also blends the qualitative and the quantitative arguments concerning popular cultural texts in a way that does have implications for popular journalism since it is primarily an economic transaction which depends on being able to effect a cultural response from a readership which is specifically targeted textually through the rhetoric of the newspaper: 'If the cultural commodities or texts do not contain resources out of which people can make their own meanings of their social relations and identities, they will be rejected and will fail in the marketplace. They will not be made popular' (1994: 2).

This readership and the parameters within which the popular newspaper works alter over time and the newspaper must seek to negotiate its relationship between sales and rhetoric at particular moments in history. In contemporary Britain, we have no alternative but to acknowledge that a newspaper such as Rupert Murdoch's *Sun*, which sells over three million copies a day and is read by three times that number, is just as much a manifestation of popular culture, although produced by a global media company, as an independent fanzine or a local community newsletter produced on a word processor – but it is popular culture in different ways. The *Daily Mail*, *Daily Express*, *Mirror* and *Sun* all have been able to work that hegemonic transaction to become the leading popular voices of their respective eras (Engel, 1996), indicating once again the temporal and shifting nature of popular newspapers as sites of incorporation and resistance.

THE ECONOMICS OF MASS CULTURE AS POPULAR CULTURE

This section will start by indicating the linkage between the dynamics of hegemony and the ways in which the popular press is able to promote its inclusivity as part of popular culture as opposed to the exclusivity of the elite culture. Inclusivity is the strategy which the popular press employs to maintain a relationship which is hegemonically negotiated in favour of the dominant power structures within society while keeping its readers relatively happy that their views and interests are represented.

This inclusivity is expressed in two ways: first, in terms of its rhetoric; second, in terms of the scale of its popularity. The second is often taken as proof that the authenticity of the rhetorical claims can be substantiated. This perspective seeks to focus on the quantitative element in the definition of the popular. John Frow takes us to the heart of attempts to distinguish the mass from the popular when he distinguishes between quantitative and qualitative approaches to the popular, noting that the qualitative judgements would tend to preclude that which had gained mass appeal, while the quantitative argument sees it as a process of approval. He defines the popular inclusively: 'This is a processual and quantitative measure, as opposed to the directional and qualitative definitions that seek out originary, organic sites of the popular in the people themselves through "folk" culture' (1993: 3).

First and foremost, popular culture is a mass culture, especially with regard to the press. Yet such a mass culture involves a semantic allusion to homogenization of both audience and product which simply cannot be borne out by the evidence of the varieties of reader response to popular newspapers (Billig, 1992) nor any uniformity of content throughout their history. The economic success of the truly popular newspaper has always been based on a flexible and responsive relationship with its readership expressed in its mode of address and its rhetoric, combined with its ability to project this to a large audience.

From a more conservative position the popular is simply reacting to the needs of the people expressed in their consumer choice and cannot contain anything of true value or meaning. Nevertheless, even from this perspective, it does fulfil certain aspects of the tripartite demands of popular culture. It is liked by the many, must reflect a view of the world with which they can identify, for people will not voluntarily consume what they consider to be residual or second rate, and their contribution to it, as consumers, cannot be underestimated even if they are not literally the authors of the process or the product. This target audience must be inscribed in the text and be recognized as of relevance to that actual audience. This does not mean, however, that this process is not problematic nor downright contradictory.

The notion of inclusivity, the goal which any popular address seeks when involving its consumers actively in identifying with the products of popular culture, is one way of avoiding the pejorative traces in the term 'mass culture'. One of the benefits of historical analysis is to indicate how elements of folk culture have become incorporated into our contemporary notions of popular culture in ways which invigorate its claims to authenticity.

Agger finds that eliding mass and popular enables the focus to sharpen on the appeal at the heart of any popular culture:

> In this period of rethinking, 'popular culture' is a difficult term to define. We will side-step a great many terminological disputes with the inclusive claim that popular culture refers to the beliefs and practices, and the objects through which they are organized, that are widely shared among a population. This includes folk beliefs, practices and objects rooted in local traditions, and mass beliefs, practices and objects generated in political and commercial centers. (1992: 3)

In this definition, the scale of the audience indicates nothing of the quality of the product, simply that the process of appeal to a popular, non-elite audience is functioning and in that success of scale lies also the success of the cultural production laying its claim to the approval of the people in general through their market choice.

Geoffrey Nowell-Smith is also keen to stress the continuities within modern culture. His argument takes us once more away from a simplistic model of popular culture demarcated from culture in general by stressing complexity and reciprocity:

1. Modern culture is capitalist culture
2. Modern culture also takes the form of a single intertextual field, whose signifying elements are perpetually being recombined and played off against each other. (1987: 83)

Nowell-Smith's particular version of inclusivity also provides an extended perception of the production of popularity of particular relevance to students of journalism in that he acknowledges the flow between institution and consumption which enables a popular form to retain its viability: 'the term popular culture retains its value when one is talking about the people who make it popular – that is, when one is talking about the people who keep a particular cultural form going by being the public for it or its producers' (1987: 83).

Grounding his discussion in the primary facts of capitalist economic life, Nowell-Smith illustrates how this political economy plays itself out in relation to cultures participated in by the majority of the population. His interpretation works against any organicist theory of pure, authentic cultural practices existing outside the matrices of the political/economic system. Once again we may observe the interpretation of popular culture as a process, a process of inclusion within the acceptable parameters of a capitalist economy.

Writing in *The Rhetorics of Popular Culture*, Root also takes this approach of broadest application, defining popular culture as those activities and artefacts among the intellectual and social components of a civilization or society which are 'generally dispersed and approved... accessible intellectually and logistically to the broadest spectrum of the society' (1987: 10).

Despite the fact that all popular culture is mediated through economic considerations, the success of those mediations can only be sustained if they do articulate something of what the majority of the people identify as in their interest and reflecting their views of the world. The fact that certain artefacts are consumed and continue to be liked by a substantial number of people in a society at a particular time can be taken as indicative that they refract and construct at least part of their authentic view of the world. Popular culture represents a symbolic relationship between people in the world of the imaginary and the tastes and views of people in the real world. The link of the imaginary/real-life elements of popular culture here is a very important part of the negotiation: that important normative function of the popular in constructing views of society acceptable to the people.

The fact that these popular artefacts are bound up with an economic system that may not share the interests of the consumers of these artefacts is part of an altogether more complex operation. We do not wish to fall into a simple celebration of consumer popularity but simply to state that for all practical purposes the quantitative view of popular culture insists that we look at questions of authenticity and appropriation as second to the economic fact of the success of certain products. This is a materialist account of the popular which seeks to explore the reasons why it is popular rather than define the 'popular' from the outset as necessarily hostile to the prevailing political/economic orthodoxy.

RHETORIC AS AUTHENTICITY

One aspect which traverses all discussions of popular culture is that of authenticity. In fact it is such an essential claim for the popular that it needs to be considered as a category which transcends the three interconnecting categories of Sparks. Older, pre-capitalist folk artefacts and practices may have been isolated from any other section of society except the common people but the pervasive nature of capitalism means that popular culture no longer claims an authenticity in the sense of products or practices which are either manufactured by the people themselves or solely representative of their interests. It is a commercially negotiated transaction between a product, in our case the popular newspaper, which represents aspects of the lived experience of broad sections of the people.

Yet there are important reasons why the popular press often claims allegiance to these folk traditions. These might include reference to continuities in the lives of ordinary people, memories of past glories, national iconography, identification with the concerns of the 'little people' on money matters, not to mention the single most important element, the printed press itself as a conduit for these common cultural concerns. They are traditional discourses which can be employed as a short cut to popular memory, sense of place and notions of tradition which are important in binding a sense of place into questions of identity.

In order to explore the nature of the appeal of the popular press we need to question the relationship between the popular and its authenticity, between the interests of the consumers of popular culture and their producers, and to see how this becomes manifest in printed texts. This will enable us to consider the contradictory elements between the readerships of popular newspapers and the political and economic motives of the owners of these newspapers. It will also shed light on how those apparently irreconcilable differences are prevented from breaking apart.

The popular press has always managed to put the people into a form of popular culture. To explore how the popular press legitimates its connections to the ordinary people, we must go beyond the simple statement that a popular product must be liked by the many and get closer to the processes by which 'the people' as distinct to the elite or ruling classes of a society and their culture are articulated. They are principally formulated, I will argue, through the imaginary/symbolic representative power of rhetoric.

A rhetorical approach may help in understanding the flows and restrictions in these processes within one area of popular culture: the popular press. Indeed one is tempted to argue that rhetoric may indeed be considered as a political balm which eases the friction inherent in hegemonic processes between the powerful and the powerless. This would mean rhetoric plays an important part in maintaining that strategic superiority; it allows the hegemonic process its proper reciprocity.

Rhetoric was the ancient Greeks' term for the persuasive strategies of speech-making perfected by the Sophists. Critics, such as Plato, thought it dwelt too much on the techniques of persuasion and not enough on the ends it brought about. It became in time a series of formulae which could be learnt and practised to maximize one's chances of having one's argument accepted. In an attempt to bring rhetoric away from mere textual analysis or linguistic virtuosity and into analyses of how popular culture is structured to persuade, Brummett defines rhetoric as: 'the social function that influences and manages meaning' (1991: xii). Such a view insists on the fact that language is at the heart of the processes which inform and stratify social behaviour and would claim therefore that popular culture, expressed through the language of the popular press, must be considered as being fundamentally rhetorical in its practice.

Defining popular culture as a rhetorical process which takes place at a particular time in a specific historical context has much to recommend it if we are to assess the extent to which particular artefacts of printed popular culture have gone beyond simple commercial success and have become the articulation of aspects of the experience and aspirations of ordinary people who are outside the institutions which produce the popular press but included in the rhetoric of its textual appeals. More importantly it is essential to assess the complexity of the process which enables powerful media communicators in a society to claim the right to speak on behalf of the people and in their political interests. The popular press is a significant terrain for the securing of provisional consent for this process.

Morag Schiach claims: 'The analysis of popular culture is severely limited by the extent to which the rhetorical power of "the people" far outstrips its descriptive specificity' (1989: 9). The rhetorical power which many seek to draw upon is a power which, far from being subordinate to the specificity of a description of the people, gains because of its lack of definable characteristics which lends more plausibility to its persuasive pull for it is so difficult to contradict in any direct way.

Raymond Williams (1976b: 199), in defining 'popular' as 'work deliberately setting out to win favour', indicates the conscious efforts of cultural producers to find language which will appeal. Some commentators see this as where the popular turns into the populist (McGuigan, 1992: 1). Yet Brummett, writing of popular culture, points out how important that process of winning favour is to any culture wishing to be acclaimed by and consumed by the people and how important rhetoric is in achieving these goals:

> If culture means those objects and events that nurture, shape, and sustain people, then popular culture must be those artifacts that are most actively involved in winning the favor of the public and thus in shaping the public in particular ways. Popular culture is the cutting edge of culture's instruments that shape people into what they are. The work of popular culture is therefore inherently rhetorical ... (1991: xxi)

Thus any claim that popular culture simply reflects the people, which is a particularly frequent assertion from within popular media industries, is to be jettisoned in favour of the rhetorical perspective which insists on a processual approach. The latter is a more inquisitive approach politically, inquiring how the process of exchange occurs. Therefore any claim that an artefact belongs to or represents the people is immediately a rhetorical one, a persuasive act attempting to win the approval of the many and to claim to be speaking on their behalf, even in their voice. This rhetorical aspect to popular culture is a crucial complement to the strategies of hegemony as outlined by Gramsci.

Such debates as there are about popular culture and their political implications are not simply linguistic reflections of issues residing elsewhere in our society. They locate the creation of popular identities within the rhetoric of popular cultural forms. One of their most productive sites is the popular newspaper.

de Certeau's writing, though not designed to clarify specific points of definition, is helpful in indicating, often in a most poetic fashion, the rhetorical nature of the popular and its opposition to many of the discourses of powerful elites: '"Turns" (or "tropes") inscribe in ordinary language the ruses, displacements, ellipses, etc., that scientific reason has eliminated from operational discourses, in order to constitute "proper" meanings .... These tricks characterize a popular art of speaking' (1988: 24).

In many ways these 'tricks' can explain the attractiveness of the rhetoric of the popular press. It is interesting to note that de Certeau also sees the popular (as in what belongs to the people) as nostalgic. We may no longer believe in the pastoral fantasies of communal or folk culture but our language acts as if to construct those spaces rhetorically around a discourse of that idyll in popular culture:

> We no longer believe ... that, behind the doors of our cities, in the nearby distance of the countryside, there are vast poetic and 'pagan' pastures where we can still hear songs of 'what belongs to the people'. These voices can no longer be heard except within the interior of the scriptural systems where they recur. They move about, like dancers, passing lightly through the field of the other. (de Certeau, 1988: 131)

He describes the people as mythically located in the rural when they are in any tangible way a product of the forces which led to increasing urbanization, such as commodity capitalism, technologies of transport, communication, imperialism and the industrial revolution. Nevertheless, the popular is located within that 'scriptural system' known as capitalism and must accommodate itself to the demands of a market. de Certeau seems to acknowledge this yet insists that there is, because of the rhetorical formation of the popular, an uneasy element which is, in volatile fashion, always likely to escape and resist. It is one of his best-known conclusions that this power to resist and reappropriate for purposes other than those designed for the power elite is inscribed within the very nature of the popular. It is difficult to see how this functions materially within the popular press but the utopian appeal and success of these papers can be said to reside in their ability to replicate this potential to dissent if only rhetorically.

BAKHTIN: STRUGGLE AND DIALOGUE IN POPULAR LANGUAGE

Another writer whose work is often cited in analyses of popular culture is Mikhail Bakhtin (1984, 1996). Bakhtin is an essential contributor to debates on the popular press because his work includes a seminal and provocative study of the early practices of folk culture and in particular how this culture could be analysed in terms of linguistic exchanges. His work is particularly appropriate for this analysis because of the ways he interprets questions of power and culture much more than Gramsci in terms of the fabric of language. In Bakhtin the contesting of absolute power comes from voices from the margins and the observation that any utterance takes its place among many conflicting voices. There is an openness about Bakhtin's approach which reflects the power interests of specific historical moments in a text but which stresses, in the last instance, the ability of texts to be open to oppositional readings. The key terms which we will borrow from Bakhtin are 'carnivalesque' 'dialogue' and 'heteroglossia'. These terms will assist us in integrating rhetoric into a discussion of the textual strategies of the popular press and explain the continuity of appeal in this format.

Carnival was 'the suspension of all hierarchical rank, privileges, norms, and prohibitions' (Bakhtin, 1984: 10). Carnival represents the participation in the overturning of orders of hierarchy by the common people themselves. 'Carnival is not a spectacle seen by the people; they live in it, and everyone participates because its very idea embraces all the people' (Bakthin, 1984: 7).

Carnivalesque is an ambivalent term. It does not refer exclusively to the actual inversion of social hierarchies or utopian enactments of events which develop and play out *as if* they were taking place in such an inversion. It is once again the rhetorical dimension which is important. The popular becomes carnivalesque when it claims aspects of the carnival tradition. The popular pleasures in such an enactment also tell of the constraints and power relations at that time. Bakhtin is also keen to specify time and place. John Docker, in a study of popular culture which draws heavily on the work of Bakhtin in this area, sees a carnivalesque perspective on the world as having been 'part of popular culture for centuries' (1994: 150). Docker claims that the carnivalesque keeps alive alternative conceptions of life and power relations. Although not a panacea it is, as in other rhetorical strategies within popular culture, a continuity in positioning the popular vis à vis the power elite while being encompassed by its constraints – popular culture as breathing space we might say.

Popular print is able, at its most succesful, to blend the attractiveness of these features of the culture of the common people and their perceptions of a utopian alternative to their daily existence and represent them as part of its own activity. The strategic importance of the language of these transactions is hard to underestimate.

Dialogue, from Bakhtin's perspective, implies that all language transactions are open ended but within authoritarian systems there are attempts to close this down to an overriding perspective, a truth. One of the tasks of the popular newspaper is to close down the infinite heteroglossia into a unified editorial voice but one which may still appear to draw on the energies of the muliplicity of voices and attitudes of its heteroglossic original. All the newspaper's popular appeal lies in its successful reconciliation between these two dialogic poles.

For the popular newspaper, as daily commodity, its monologic truth emerging from within the political-economic structures of the news media needs to be constructed with a rhetorical appreciation of the formalities of dialogue. The popular newspaper is succesful in its ability to pander to a realization that the reader is positioned within an exchange of dialogue and this dialogue draws upon the multiple and shifting textualities of contemporary popular culture.

Bakhtin prefers an optimismtic account and it is one which must also to an extent hold true for the readers to be willing to identify with the rhetoric of the papers: 'Alongside the centipetal forces, the centrifugal forces of language carry on their uninterrupted work, alongside verbalideological centralization and unification, the uninterrupted processes of decentralization and disunification go forward' (1996: 270–1).

Heteroglossia is Bakhtin's conceptualization of the fact that all language transactions take place in the context of alternative expressions. They are structured between the centrifugal potential of the multiplicity of contesting voices of heteroglossia and the centripetal tendencies that allow language to retain a socially shared coherence. Heteroglossia contests the dominant social-linguistic norms. The notion foregrounds the linguistic nature of our experience of the world. It is a world which is narrated to us and through us, drawing on a vast array of voices and modes of communication, all vying in particular times and places for our attention. Official versus unofficial. It is assisted in the popular newspaper's exploitation of miscellany in hybrid form, reinforcing Bakhtin's claims that the stratifications of heteroglossia emerge from the 'extra-literary languages' (1996: 67).

POPULAR RESONANCE

A combination of these perspectives, Gramscian and Bakhtinian, begins to open up the question of how the most producerly of texts, the popular newspaper, is able to carry such a resonance of the popular for it to be successful with the people themselves.

The distinctiveness of popular culture lies in its ability to combine commercial success with its rhetorical power to claim to speak in the people's name and with their voice. Fiske's libertarian reading of the popular does not address this ventriloquism. However, although the commercial success which enables it to claim a widespread approval among a population is relatively straightforward, its rhetorical success is more complex. It is complex because, as we have seen, it is not a simple case of the producers inscribing a set of rhetorical devices which can be read off a text as belonging to the people. This rhetorical negotiation of popular culture must be deeply involved in the negotiating and evolving dynamism of hegemony and it is historically contingent.

The ability to credibly claim the voice of the people is formulated through rhetoric: 'The authority to speak for the people is not simply given by a set of formal political rules. It has to be established' (Street, 1997: 22). Street continues: '... the way "the people" are defined ... takes place within a wider context in which political interests and values shape popular culture, just as the political economy of popular culture determines the political possibilities of that culture' (1997: 22).

This indicates the dialogism in which the discourses of the popular and the people are constructed, never wholly authentically and never wholly exploitatively. It is also a movement which reaffirms the hybrid and overlapping nature of the popular. It may not be wholly authentic and its culture may not be hermetically sealed from the influences of antagonistic forces but the people's choice does stamp the possibilities of the range of expression of popular culture.

Popular culture may therefore be seen rather as a mutation of folk culture which has adapted to the mass markets of capitalist economy. Its appeal lies in the ways it manages to preserve its claims to authenticity with the ordinary people – those outside the power-elite. It does this, in part, by maintaining aspects of the real relationship between people and artefact. Consumers identify with the products, they are of the people and sold to the people. Of course this is a profoundly political manoeuvre, securing the inclusion of the people in the machinery of the political economy by articulating aspects of people's authentic experience and being able to deliver them in a way which has the power to convince them of their place in it. The channel for this persuasion is rhetoric.

This rhetoric in other's eyes has a profoundly political educational purpose: 'the cultural terrain of everyday life is not only a site of struggle and accommodation, but also one in which the production of subjectivity can be viewed as a pedagogical process whose structuring principles are deeply political' (Giroux and Simon, 1989: 10).

There are then two popular presses emerging from the complexities of popular culture. There is one which is politicized, suggesting alternatives and campaigning on behalf of radical social change. There is also the element of the popular which resists any engagement with the high culture of representative democracy, which prefers a strategy of ironic or playfully cynical resistance. As we will see these were rarely mutually exclusive and any articulation of the popular must contain elements of both entertainment and information: pleasure and propaganda, profit and altruism. Debates about citizenship and public knowledge are only one half of the popular story.

Colin Sparks (1988) has made the point that the whole history of print and in particular the newspaper is part of a negotiation with the evolution of a capitalist economy and its information deficit. Although a useful insight, he implies perhaps too neat a match and leaves open the question of how ruptures have occurred in this system. The popular press can tell us much about the tensions within the culture of capitalism as it represents the primary site of negotiation between those in powerful communicative positions and those in weak positions. This needs to be related to the debates over power, information and the rhetorical aspects of hegemony once again to explore the ambiguous political aspect of the popular press. Speaking for the people but in ways in which it shifts them from the fulcrum of activity.

The popular press can therefore be best envisaged as an aspect of popular culture expressed in a particular and persuasive rhetorical style appropriate to a particular epoch. There has been no decline from authenticity, merely the reformulation of a complex range of rhetorical devices claiming the support of a wide-ranging audience.

Curran and Sparks (1991) see the challenge lying within a compromise between Leavisite pessimism and relativist celebration. My approach will attempt to chart a more dialogic interpretation, drawing particularly on the work of Bakhtin to inquire at what points in the history of the popular process the struggle over the discourse of the popular and its claims to authenticity have been demonstrated in the language of the popular press.

Such an approach will need to develop a theory which can demonstrate how a rhetoric of appeal to the people and the legitimacy of that claim to representation has been woven into traditional genres chosen to most effectively incorporate the popular voice. It will also need to draw attention to the ambivalence of the relationship between the popular and politics in economic and political terms in order to question the extent to which the question of whether popular culture is broader or narrower than the political or whether it is older or more recent than the involvement of the people in politics.

The emphasis here on the location of the popular press within popular culture as a set of power relationships will help retain a lucidity concerning the dialogic elements of this form of journalism. As Yeo and Yeo have observed: 'If we see popular culture neither as exclusively of the people nor provided for the people but try to probe the relation between both elements in any cultural form, we are led into questions of relations of power' (1981: xi).

If we accept Bakhtin's thesis that the sign is always the site of struggle between competing and conflicting discourses, then, in the context of the popular press, the following chapters will endeavour to illustrate how, at different historical moments and in specific political locations, popular culture has been articulated as speaking for the people in a rhetoric which is able to claim an element of authenticity with the 'residual orality' (Ong, 1982) of folk culture. It is clear that this is a political process and one which enables the discourse of the popular to stabilize around practices compatible with the interests of the ruling elite. What will be of interest will be to see how particular voices in this heteroglossic exchange come to dominate.

2

THE POPULAR PRESS AS
POPULAR CULTURE

THE EMERGENCE OF POPULAR CULTURE

According to Peter Burke (1978), we can identify commercially reproduced printed matter as an important element in the formation of something which could properly be called popular culture as distinguished from common culture or folk culture. This folk culture had been organic, associated with distinct ways of life and dependent on long-standing traditions of communal behaviour, both economic and in terms of entertainment. It is characteristic of a pre-capitalist era.

It was the commercial imperatives of print culture to generalize formats and maximize profits that created the conditions in society, which saw the division between the elite and the populace and the erosion of a common culture. This is implicit in the argument of another writer on this evolution: '... with the rise of the middle classes and the spread of print, folk culture was simultaneously represented, appropriated, and marginalised' (Hayes, 1992: 3). It was therefore, most pertinently for our argument, with print capitalism that a taste formation, which could be called popular culture, emerged. This taste formation was commercially profitable, reflected traditions of popular belief and was consumed widely by ordinary people.

Popular culture developed in printed form to the extent that it could incorporate elements of the previous folk culture and versions of the 'great tradition' commercially altered for a wider readership. Before the rise of the newspaper, chap-book culture, newsheets, broadsides, printed ballads and the almanac provided the links from the older traditions to the modern capitalist culture of printed entertainment and information. It was the new popular culture's ability to blend elements of tradition into a new cultural setting which supported its claims to be representative of the people.

Another feature that supported the popular's claims to authenticity in Burke's analysis is that of local specificity. Emergent popular traditions

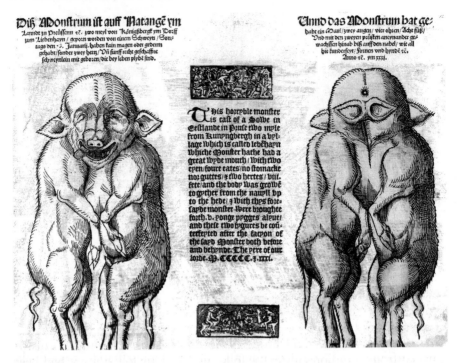

The Horrible Monster   Broadsheet, 1531 – Freaks of nature as sensational news

were often profoundly conservative in themselves while continuing to be representative of the beliefs of ordinary people. Burke expresses the continuity of this pattern from the folk to the popular in these terms:

> Popular culture was perceived as local culture. 'A cada terra el seu ús' as the Catalan proverb has it, 'to each land its own custom'. It was the region, or town, or even village which commanded loyalty; these units formed closed communities with hostile stereotypes of outsiders, reluctant to admit new people or new ways. (1978: 50)

The content of popular printed matter does not suggest any violent break in continuity to match the violence of the ruptures in the economic sphere of the early modern period. Genres, texts, audiences and performance elements were all familiar from previous ages.

> To a modern reader, the parallel between broadsides or chap-books and the 'mass culture' of the contemporary world is likely to be striking. He will notice the increasing standardisation of format, he will be sensitive to the devices for attracting buyers, like sensational titles or the (frequently false) claim that a narrative is 'full', 'faithful', 'true' or 'new'. The fact that executions or royal visits were sometimes described in print before they happened is reminiscent of our own 'pseudo-event'. (Burke, 1978: 254–5)

The significant economic shift from a folk culture was that these familiar features of popular culture were increasingly being sold back to the people as a commercial transaction. They were being incorporated as a new popular print culture into the traditions of an older oral folk culture.

Indeed one clear aspect of a residual culture often used to describe popular culture is its orality (Ong, 1982: 131). The new print culture consequently incorporated this into its formats and its language. Popular print depended on its generic consistency with oral tradition as well as on its ability to reproduce echoes of the spoken culture it was supplementing. Burke points out an important issue for the claims that popular culture contains many elements of continuity with its folk past when he writes: 'Cultural changes, in this case as in others, were not so much "substitutive" as "additive"' (1978: 256–7).

It has been claimed (Fletcher and Stephenson, 1985) that the breakdown of the 'common culture' meant a drift which cut off parts of the former peasantry and artisans from the bulk of the people, and, yet, as we will see in more detail in later chapters, there was a great deal of the new popular printed culture which was incorporated commercially into the vibrant new print culture which continued the traditions 'additively'.

The Anatomy of the Early Popular Press

As a development of that process, the popular press encapsulates many of the paradoxes and conflicts inherent in the representation of non-elite culture in general. Before the emergence of regular popular newspapers, print culture was a popularized culture in the ways it built upon oral culture and folk tradition to distribute a commercially successful blend of genre and vernacular in ways which prefigured the content of much of the later popular press in its various manifestations. Newsheets and pamphlets were more targeted at the commercial classes who could better afford the more expensive offerings and had a clearer vested economic interest in doing so. Chapbooks and printed ballad broadsheets were for the poor. With the advent of printing came two developments that were to shape popular culture. First, it provided a continuity between oral/folk culture and a written culture; second, it extended the patterns of hitherto oral formulae to a wider audience. The printed ballads and the broadsides which were sold on the streets and in the market squares of Western Europe from the fifteenth century onwards were made up from conventional themes and characters; piety, adultery, women in general, monsters, disasters, freaks of nature, great men and events, criminals and executions, morality. Within these there was great scope for stock descriptions and other mnemonic devices to lend a powerful normative and conventional force to the outpourings of popular culture. The most common popular form of unauthorized commentaries were the printed ballads whose content was intended to inform, entertain and provoke debate on matters of common, popular interest about matters of state. They were aimed predominantly at the lowest end of the social and economic spectrum.

The broadside ballad has been described as 'a kind of musical journalism, the forerunner of the modern prose newspapers, and a continuation of the folk tradition of minstrelsy' (Shepard, 1973: 21).

'The Invincible Armada', a ballad from 1588, supports this claim:

> This great Galleazzo, which was so huge and hye:
> That like a bulwarke on the sea, did seem to each mans eye.
> There was it taken, vnto our great reliefe:
> And diuers Nobles, in which traine Don *Pietro* was the chiefe.
> Stronge was she stuft, with Cannons great and small:
> And other instruments of warre, Which we obtained all.
> A certaine signe, of good successe we trust:
> That God will ouerthrow the rest, as he hath done the first. (Palmer, 1979: 10)

Printing was a relatively expensive business and a politically volatile undertaking in the fifteenth and sixteenth centuries and so printers were encouraged to spread the risk of their venture by reproducing well-known formats and conventional genre in their printed material and also to ensure that they managed the broadest possible appeal to cross over between the literate and the semi-literate. They produced printed material characterized by hybridity, a breadth of appeal to maximize their market.

Before the formal commercialization of popular newspapers and journals there had always existed a demand for printed matter which dealt with matters of common interest. This had been hawked around Europe and sold by peddlers at fairs, carnivals and other public gatherings. The markets and fairs of the German and Dutch states were important sites for the distribution of news and the circulation of scandal, sensation and gossip. These geo-political areas were important in the fifteenth and sixteenth centuries because of the diffuse nature of state control there and were influential in allowing a more liberal commercial attitude towards the reproduction of all kinds of information to percolate through Europe. The printers were increasingly eager to reach a wider market and strove to provide the best information, the latest gossip and the most exciting versions of events. Thus economics has always played a part in the appeal of popular printed matter from the start. There has never been a pure popular print culture. Commerce has always had to broker that relationship between the people and their print culture.

Entertaining and informing the people came closely juxtaposed, physically and textually. Throughout late medieval Europe, ballads and one-off pamphlets were easier to organize and distribute than formal and periodical news. It seems that both forms of printed material emerged simultaneously. Many of the political and social movements of three centuries were represented in the ballad and broadsheet forms. One example of this is when the facts of Emperor Maximillian I's death and funeral were printed they were sold with a choice of two melodies. Print, in the form of ballad and broadsheet, was quick to capitalize on the desire of a readership for material that mirrored the traditional aspects of folk culture, for instance discussion of unexplained events and the news of catastrophe and sensational crime (Shepard 1962; Rollins, 1969).

Perhaps the prime motivator for printed news was its oral ancestor, gossip, a social involvement in events outside and at the margins of our direct experience (Neubauer, 2000). Because of this, it retains a frisson of novelty and excitement, even a vicariousness, bringing the exotic or the elite within the discourse of the less exalted members of a community. The location of printed news distribution was also that traditionally privileged for the exchange of gossip. The street and the marketplace have always been important centres for the exchange of information; hawkers developed that, and the street literature and later newspaper sales on the streets indicate how important it remains as a location for news. Continuities between this gossip element of both printed news and the printed versions of current affairs distributed commercially as ballads and broadsides indicates a further broad aspect of popular culture – its ability to involve ordinary people as participants, not simply as observers.

VERNACULAR AND POPULAR

The emergent popular genres were expressed in the vernacular of the particular country or area in which they were published and as such specifically addressed the people in ways in which texts produced by medieval scribes in the ancient languages of Greek and Latin had never done. Print plays a dynamic role in determining the way in which theology and social protest combined at the time of the Peasants' War and the Reformation (Blickle, 1984). Heine, for example, compared the impact of Luther's Reformation hymn 'Ein Feste Burg' to that of the French Revolutionary anthem 'La Marseillaise'. One of the most spectacular early examples of the conjunction of politics and the popular came with the German reformation triggered by the posting of Martin Luther's theses on the door of Wittenberg cathedral and the translation of the Bible into German. It was Luther's insistence on the vernacular which was to play an essential role in the development of print as a medium of involvement for the people in general. Printing in the vernacular threatened to sweep away the close control over the reproduction of knowledge held in Western Europe by the clergy and the monarchy and to allow the general educated reader into this new public space of popular knowledge. From 1517, one could with justification consider the printed pamphlet indicating doctrinal battles and their social and political consequences as the shock troops of the Reformation.

It is hard to underestimate the effect of the Reformation on the relationship between print and most sections of German society. It triggered a flood of printed material aimed at an increasingly wide circle of mercantile, artisan and lower bourgeoisie. It has been calculated that Luther's teachings were being printed at a rate four times above the norm for newssheets as early as 1520 (Lindemann, 1969: 45–8). The inclusion of wider sections of society into discussion of religious affairs was accompanied by a wider distribution of printed matter, couched in a language which attracted this readership. A rhetorical call for real popular involvement in these political and religious debates took place in the language of the commoner; a powerful demonstration of the political potential of linking language and popular politics.

Of equal importance to their use of the vernacular was the style of their approach. There was less propaganda material printed by the Catholic establishment and its supporters and what there was lacked the popular tone of the Protestant propaganda sheets. The Catholic material tended towards a more bookish style in keeping with its more elitist patterns of control over information and debate.

> In order to make the German Bible accessible to a broad popular readership, however, Luther had to expand the chancery language by blending it with colloquial German, using words and idioms that would give expression to the imaginative and conceptual world of the common man. Explaining the theoretical principles of translation into German (*Treatise on Translation*, 1530), he wrote: 'We must consult the mother at home, the children on the street and the common man in the marketplace, looking to see what is on their lips, and then translate accordingly.' (Beutin *et al.*, 1993: 81–2)

There was also a commercial side to mass appeal even at this early stage. Tracts and pamphlets which sold in enormous quantities from 1520 were printed in a language which was accessible to readers and profitable to the printers. Its connection to oral-religious disourse is indicated in the following commentary:

> The striking agency has seemed to us not merely 'the press' but the ability of both writers and printers to collaborate in producing the cheap pamphlet, written in terms of mass-appeal ... The evidence shows clearly that the press did not displace the pulpit. Indeed it confirmed and extended the spoken word to regard the two as 'rival' forces is to divide the indivisible ... But printers can have made money out of Lutheran propaganda only in proportion to its acceptability among a large reading public. (Dickens, 1976: 215)

CONTROLING THE PEOPLE'S PRESS

Events in the German Reformation alone were indicative of the potential of printing to circulate ideas and news in the language of the ordinary people which could take on the weight of a material force for change. In England, the circulation of matter likely to express ideas and sentiments unapproved by authority was clearly of concern to central government. The fact that as authoritarian a figure as Henry VIII by 1531 felt compelled to distribute printed versions of controversial events in his proclamation, 'The determination of the universities of Italy and Fraunce, that it is so unlawfull for a man to marie his brothers wyfe, that the pope hath no power to dispence therewith', indicated that he acknowledged the need to counter rumour and distribute an officially sanctioned version of events to influential parties throughout the land.

The form of control which developed over this information in England and elsewhere in Western Europe was one which astutely attempted to locate an element of power in the hands of those with a vested interest in the profits and in a degree of political stability – the emerging commercial classes. In the Tudor period, growing mercantile affluence, an emergent sense of national identity among the bourgeoisie, particularly through the exploits of army, navy and the evidence of the benefits of colonial trade, all prompted a healthy measure of self-interested restraint among those responsible for the publication of licensed printed matter. A stable polity encouraged a healthy climate for the early capitalists to exploit and this included the printers.

Since the printers themselves were not members of the powerful elite, a way had to be found of incorporating their commercial interests with the interests of the state. The Stationers' Company was established in England in 1557 to help regulate the burgeoning quantity of printed matter and its distribution without the direct interference of the central power of the Crown. It was inevitably influenced by the commercial ambitions and political sensitivities of the printers who, in the main, made up its membership. Popular patterns of news and entertainment may have developed from traditions which preceded the invention of printing but this commercially successful combination did not include any direct appeal to the common people as a force for political change.

Early newsbooks were, in Herd's words, 'mostly a rough blend of fact, conjecture and transparent sensationalism' (1952: 14). Sensation, deriving from oral traditions of gossip and tale-telling, was from the start a driving force in the popular. Cranfield cites a newssheet report from 1601 which combined war, sensation, sexual abuse and murder involving Spanish troops – as a dash of xenophobia – in The Netherlands:

> James Messier being striken over his belly, so that his intrailles did issue forth, dyed a few dayes after. The wife of the said Messier was so sore beaten, that she can never be her owne woman again. Peter Riondet, killed as he came out of his bed, although he was seventy yeares olde, his wife is sore hurt, and is like hardly to recover it. Both her daughters defloured, and the one so hurt that the intrals came forth of her body, fifteene and eighteen years of age. (Cranfield, 1978: 3)

Nathaniel Butler, himself a freeman of the Stationers' Company, was prescient enough to print news of murders in Yorkshire, as an experiment in public taste in the new medium as early as 1605 (Herd, 1952: 13).

In Vienna an early broadside parodied the sensationalist material and presentational style of the newssheets, claiming: 'Oyez, Oyez, Latest News, The Devil has died' (A satire on the persistent search for novelty among the news writers) (Lindemann, 1969: 75).

The Radical Potential of the Popular

England's own convulsive period of growth in the content, variety and quantity of its printed press dates from the years of the English Civil War (1642–51). This was the first indication in England of the potential of the printed press to address political issues to the people at large. It constituted a shift from merely reproducing continuities with existing popular genres.

Gilbert Mabbott, exploiting his position as the official licenser, claiming to speak in the people's name from a Levellers' perspective, pronounced on 7 November 1648 in *The Moderate*:

> The law and Government of this land, being Tirannous, and Arbitrary, and destructive to the freedome of the people, may be lawfully taken away by the people ... and till that be done, the people of this nation are slaves, and not Free-men ... All Power and Authorities, either by King or parliament, acting ... against ... the people are void by the Laws of God, man and Nature: the people ... give these powers and Authorities, expecting they should not abuse their Trust in acting against the good of their Electees (their Lords and Masters), to whom they ought to give account, for breach of the Trust, because the servant cannot be above his master, nor the creature above his maker. (Cranfield, 1978: 14)

What is remarkable in this extract is the cumulative effect of the call to the people which serves to locate them in direct opposition to a series of oppressions. The antitheses of the people are expressed as tyrannical, arbitrary, slaves, and the proper flow of influence claimed to be from the people to those entrusted to run their affairs. The discourse of the people here is an emotive and structured call to a dynamic and interventionist role for the people, a rhetorical call to grasp an interpretation of the world which insists upon as the legitimation of a call to invert power relationships between the elite and the populace.

Newssheets and pamphlets, the more formal channels of political information, were not the only means of communicating with popular readerships. So widely distributed and disturbing for the political elite were the street ballads of this time that they were banned from 1647. The ban on their sale continued until the Restoration of 1660.

The inclusion of gossip and malicious newsmongering went hand in hand even at this early stage with the loftier ambitions of an appeal to sections of the people as political subjects. *Mercurius Aulicus*, for instance, from 1643 exploited a perennial interest in royal affairs. Edited by John Berkenhead, this staunchly Royalist weekly published human interest stories about the royal family and lewd, vicious but entertaining articles on the parliamentary faction. It claimed to be 'Communicating the Intelligence and affaires of the Court, to the rest of the Kingdome', and this is a useful indicator of the rhetorical claims of these newspapers, since to be speaking to the whole of the country – in the breadth of its appeal – is central to their claims to authenticity. Such a rhetorical claim, when allied to the popular appeal of the vernacular, was an added legitimating element of what performed as predominantly political news.

After the Restoration, the potential of printing to destabilize the government and incite the feelings of ordinary people by means of legitimate information or satirical propaganda had been well appreciated. It was to limit the effectiveness of such publications that from 1663 Sir Roger Lestrange was appointed the official Surveyor of the Press. His views of the relationship of the people to the press were an indicator of how the press had become able to present a plausible and interesting alternative version of the world to its readers. His views also articulate the economic tensions in the relationship between printers and politicians for the attention of the people. In *The Intelligencer* of 31 August 1663, he claimed:

> Supposing the Press in order, the people in their right wits, and news or no news to be the question, a Public Mercury should not have my Vote, because I think it makes the Multuitude too familiar with the actions and counsels of their superiors, too pragmatical and censorious, and gives them not only an inch but a kind of colourable right and license to be meddling with the government. (Cranfield, 1978: 21)

Lestrange expresses a scorn for the masses which is one of the continuities within the tradition of the popular press. It has continued to provide a suspicion among society's elite. This can be expressed as a disdain for the people themselves, as above, or their taste in the vulgar or the sensational, as in this description of the type of person likely to be involved in the pleasures of popular printed material: 'Henry Chettle, for example, wrote in 1592 of "idle youths" who, "loathing honest labour and dispising lawfull trades, betake themselves to a vagrant and vicious life, in every corner of cities and market townes in the realme singing and selling ballads"'. (Palmer, 1979: 6; taken from 'Kind Hart's Dreame', a blackletter tract).

Such negative reactions form part of the taste community that begins to define the bourgeoisie from the late Middle Ages onwards. The suspicion of popular taste goes right the way back to the start of print technology – almanacs, chap-books and printed ballads had been predominantly aimed at the lower end of the market – as soon, in fact, as print allows forms of expression which have escaped from the authorization, approval and sense of good taste of the elite classes to have large circulation. This suspicion becomes a defining characteristic of the narrow bourgeois rationalist public sphere. Habermas (1992) emphasizes that the public sphere was constructed from a particularly class-based perspective, the interests of the bourgeoisie, and as such it bore the hallmarks of their rationalist and commercial preferences that there is a world which is reducible to the exercise of reason and the conviction, in the public sphere, and that this is best exercised through the written communication of contemporary knowledge, forming a part of the modern suspicion of pleasure.

This perspective is emphasized by Golby and Purdue when they write: 'Religious reformers strove to make men more godly while the effect of the Enlightenment was to raise hopes that they might become more rational. Popular culture appeared neither godly nor rational' (1984: 10).

The common good of expanded and improved knowledge had been expressed as early as the seventeenth century by Hartlib, a sympathizer with the forerunner of liberal ideals of the printed word, John Milton: 'the art of printing wil so spread knowledge that the common people knowing their own rights and liberties will not be governed by way of oppression' (Harris and Lee, 1986: 23).

This hope that printing will serve solely the extension of the rational, public intellect is a contrast to the evidence of most popular early print.

All the evidence from this quarter would indicate that enjoyment was just as important as the informational content in the development of popular readerships. In England, a tradition was well developed by the middle of the seventeenth century for a combination of features in printed form to be successful with a wide audience. The features had begun to graft an increasing interest in politics onto longer conventions of the scurrilous and entertaining.

After the English Revolution, it has been observed by commentators that the vast potential of the popular markets was not being traded on, although the trade in almanacs averaging 400,000 copies a year by the 1660s indicated that this market did exist (Harris and Lee, 1986: 20).

The potential of this large market was generally ignored as the interests of the printers coincided with those of an elite that wished to preserve control over the involvement of large sections of the population in political discussion. The majority found their printed entertainment and information in the margins of the publishing trade in the circulation and hawking of cheap literature and broadsides and the ballad. The common people and their interests only became included permanently in the newspaper press as their economic status and political allegiances became financial concerns of the newspaper owners. This interest of a popular press with popular concerns has always been economically mediated.

MISCELLANY AND THE POPULAR IN THE ALMANAC

A major aspect of print culture that illustrates how popular print traditions were to culminate in the popular newspaper is that of the almanac. In fact, nothing demonstrated better the reciprocal influences of commerce, politics and entertainment at play within popular culture than the complex evolution of the English almanac of the seventeenth century. The first almanacs had been used in ancient China and Egypt. It was the development of printing in Western Europe that allowed them to step beyond the arena of specialized practice and to become a significant contribution to popular culture.

As with print and news in general, they first came to England from the Low Countries, translated from the Dutch or German. The English printers were quickly aware of their commercial potential and began to develop indigenous varieties. They came to prominence at the same time as the printed ballad and were sold in similar ways at fairs, from printers' premises and on the highways by peddlers and chap-men. The almanac was published in the last two or three months of the year and became popular for its blend of utilitarian information about tides, phases of the moon and the configuration of the stars and planets and their effect on the planting and harvesting of crops, the husbandry of animals and treatment of medical conditions.

AN EPHEMERIS

for the Year 1652. *646*

BEING

Leap-year, and a Year of Wonders.

Prognosticating

The Ruine of Monarchy through-out *Europe*; and a Change of the Law.

Manifested by Rational Predictions:

1. From the Eclipses of the Moon.
2. From that most terrible Eclipse of the Sun.
3. By Monethly Observations, as Seasonable Warnings given to the Kings of *Europe*, more especially to *France* and *Portugal*.

By NICH: CULPEPER, Gent. Student Astrol.

ACT. 2. 19, 20. *And I will shew wonders in the Heaven above, and signs in the Earth beneath, fire, and blood, and vapor of smoak.*
The Sun shall be turned into darkness, and the Moon into blood, BEFORE *that great and notable day of the Lord shall come.*
1651.

London, Printed for *T. Vere,* and *N. Brook*, and are to be sold in the *Old Bayly,* and at the *Angel* in *Cornhil. 1651.*

Culpper Ephemeris – Politics through prognostication in a seventeenth century ephemeris

At their peak in the 1660s they were selling almost half a million copies annually and the social extent of their readership can be gleaned from the fact that many included crude woodcut illustrations of the more spectacular aspect of their prophecies to appeal to the illiterate. Capp estimates that this meant that one family in three bought some kind of almanac in the middle years of the seventeenth century (1979: 23).

As with the newssheet and ballad, the almanac was given added vigour by the complexities and partisanships of the English Civil War. In their prognosticatory function, the almanacs were able to become a focus for the most contentious political and religious debates of the century, partly informing the development of the two-party parliamentary adversary system through the development of Tory astrologers and Whig astrologers and the partisan press that accompanied it. They were largely responsible for the dissemination of political awareness to increasing sections of the population throughout this volatile period of English history. The most popular almanacs managed to combine elements of political comment yet again interwoven with the lower forms of popular sensationalism and gossip.

Perhaps, not surprisingly, given the economic interests of the printers of the Stationers' Company, the almanacs were chiefly cautious in tone although they often dealt with predictions of great turmoil and involved themselves in no end of political controversy. In their popular appeal, they remained fundamentally conservative economically and also with regard to the populace, even decrying the baleful influence of the mob at the same time as depending on the ordinary people to buy their wares. Capp has described this state of affairs thus:

> ... many astrologers were equally swift to denounce the potential danger of lower-class discontent. Like many Tudor and Stuart writers, they displayed an uneasy mixture of benevolent paternalism towards the poor, and fear and hatred of the mob. Such phrases as 'perverse and giddy multitude', 'foul-mouthed multitude', 'rabble-rout of rural wretches', 'raving' and 'monster-headed multitude', 'rabble and giddy-headed multitude' were common currency especially in the decades after 1640, and were used by both Royalist and Parliamentarian... (1979: 111)

In all forms of commercially produced popular culture there is such an element of ambiguity. On the one hand, the people are necessary for the circulation and profit of the popular commodity. On the other hand, the commercial interests of the printers are not served by encouraging the populace to mass agitation: it is simply bad for business after a certain point. The Stationers' Company was concerned with maintaining the power relationships between government and printed press. It had a large financial incentive in regulating this market and in maximizing the profits. The fostering of this relationship was no doubt one of the reasons why the hugely profitable distribution of almanacs escaped the direct interference of the censors. Thus the equilibrium between profit and appeal to those excluded from direct power must be ever negotiated to retain the support of the people while maintaining the economic and political upper hand for those of the commercial elite. This is an early example of hegemonic negotiations within popular culture.

One of the key strategies for including the people in the political project of the ruling elite was to persuade them that they had common cause with others as part of a national project. The rhetorical power of nationalism has a mythical, almost messianic aspect to it and it is therefore no wonder that we find early examples of nation building based on a rhetorical division of the world into insiders and outsiders in the almanacs.

Justifying colonial activities could best be achieved by presenting the colonized as barbaric and a threat to the values of the civilized insider group. Thus Booker's *A Bloody Irish Almanac* of 1646 is one of the most striking examples of this process in action in early popular printed material. Capp has commented on this alignment in the popular: 'The combination of apocalyptic with astrological themes helps to explain the extravagant nationalism and xenophobia of the almanac-makers. Their jingoism reflected a belief in England as God's holy and elect nation, chosen to fulfil divine plans and execute divine vengeance on His enemies' (1979: 80).

In all their popular economic success the almanacs depended on an astute matching of rhetoric to readership, and in what Capp calls their use as 'printed pulpits' there is the same recourse to a ventriloquism of the masses which we can see throughout the history of the popular press, the attempt to write in a version of the spoken vernacular for its persuasive appeal and constituting 'the greatest triumph of journalism until modern times' (1979: 292).

The leap to a fully popular form of journalism came with the inclusion of these newly emerging social classes into questions of political power. These questions had mostly remained dormant within popular and folk expression or had become sublimated through carnivalistic practices, satire, gossip and sensation. In the early modern period, as political power struggles shifted towards the interests of the newly wealthy and influential commercial classes these political interests became increasingly explicit and found their expression in the printed material of the time. These new readerships needed a regularized flow of news and entertainment. The journals and newspapers which combined these elements were often most successful if they could combine elements of the entertainment of popular culture with appeals to the political ambitions of those same social orders. By claiming to represent those readers these newspapers took their claims to represent the people as emblematic of their inclusion in the political process. Although the people was at this point a restricted readership, part of the strength of its claim was based on the rhetoric of a wide inclusivity.

THE PRESS AND THE REVOLUTIONARY POPULAR

Increasingly, claims to popularity in printed form go beyond broad appeal and become linked to the combination of the popular and the political in the press. The debate becomes one about representation and the legitimacy of that representation. The evidence of that legitimation can be found in the success with which the press is able to claim the voice and the ear of the people through its rhetoric. Whether the press is able to articulate the voice of the people depends on its perfecting a form which is liked by the people and in a language and style which speaks to them in an authentic fashion. Whether it is 'for the people' or 'of the people' in its popularity is, of course, a political question and one which in its complexity indicates the subtlety of the struggle for the hegemonic definition of the people's interests. The popular revolutionary tradition which we will examine runs from Wilkes, Paine and the American and French Revolutions through to English dissent and the self-appointed people's champion William Cobbett.

Our first example of attempts to explicitly rouse the lowest orders of society in any concerted fashion occurred in England in the era of the Wilkes's agitation from 1763. This saw the emergence not only of the common people as a threat to the stability of the Whig–Tory duopoly but, most importantly for our purposes, the expression of concerns in a language which was designed to appeal to the interests and political concerns of those classes hitherto excluded from the bourgeois public sphere of the established commercial press.

Not only did Wilkes attack the King and his ministers but, in contrast to the later, more puritanical journalism of, for instance, Paine, he employed many of those tactics designed to appeal to the lowest common denominator which were to become the hallmarks of succeeding generations of popular journalism: gossip, personal abuse, scurrilous mischief-making and satire. Wilkes's abilities to express the sentiments of the people also exploited the potent attractions of gossip, in another continuous tradition of popular print culture, into journalism. He routinely involved himself in speculation on the rumoured affair between George III's minister, Bute, and the King's mother.

More specifically, the criticism focused often on the nationality of the Scottish Bute. Wilkes's attitude towards Bute is a further example of the parochialism and xenophobia so redolent of popular culture. Wilkes draws elements of the strength of his rhetoric through appeals to the limits and securities of the nation-state as an imagined community. There is a parochialism manifest even in his most famous dictum which links nationality with the rhetoric of liberty: 'The liberty of the press is the birthright of a BRITON, and is justly esteemed the firmest bulwark of the liberties of the press' (North Briton, 6 June 1762). Indeed the anti-Scottish bent of Wilkes's writing was, according to Linda Colley, a key element in understanding the appeal of Wilkes to certain quarters of the London labouring and artisan classes: 'He was a popularist who made his fortune by knowing how to tap mainstream opinions and prejudices' (1994: 106)

His popular appeal was grounded in a rhetoric which encompassed the more parochial, anarchic instincts of the common people. His ability to exploit these instincts justifies the claim that he was representing the people's views. For all its unappealing nature this was and remains the bedrock of a certain form of popular print journalism; Wilkes was its first English propagator. Others may have chosen to write in a more radical political vein or have sought to express the views of the people in a more democratically representative way, but Wilkes established a passionate rapport with the people through his writing and speeches. The rhetoric that roused sections of the ordinary urban workers and that claimed an empathy with them was attractive in its anarchic tendency, which echoed elements of 'the world-turned upside down' of the English Civil War. His own ambitions for power meant that he did not necessarily share the political ambitions of the mob he appealed to so effectively for support. Wilkes's rhetoric illustrates the point at stake in Gramsci's argument that the popular is a contested site and one which demands a closure around the question of authenticity, albeit a closure which is provisional and rooted in rhetoric. The rhetorical state of the popular, as Wilkes demonstrated, does not in any way lessen its real effects.

The newspaper-fuelled revolutions of America and France of the late eighteenth century saw the first truly effective mobilization of the masses through the printed medium. This would further establish the popular as a category of political inclusion on a non-elite basis. The American Revolution was intrinsically linked to the articulation of such popular power in the press and, just as in the French Revolution which was to follow hard on its heels, the American Revolution was revolutionary as much in terms of the writing and the opinions formed through the influence of printed material as in any change of political authority.

In the long build-up to the outbreak of hostilities in the American Revolution of 1775 the press played an early part in dissenting against the authority of the British Crown and employed the language of popular politics to support its cause. We can follow the progress of the Revolution through the writings of three journalists who came to represent the range of competing views in the flux of those years. These were James Rivington, John Dickinson and Samuel Adams; Tory, Whig and Radical respectively. What distinguished the latter were his conscious attempts, in writing for his chosen constituency, to mobilize the masses. In order to further his democratic-republican aims he sought to phrase his writing in terms that the common people could understand and sought to employ persuasive rhetoric in enlisting them to a shared cause.

Although there is a degree of scepticism about the influence of the role of the Revolutionary press in the United States among historians (Sloan and Williams, 1994: 211–17), one thing which seems to be clear is its role in the run in to the conflict itself. If minds were set enough to require only a constant diet of partisan propaganda once the conflict had started, then at least most concur that the winning of hearts and minds before the Revolution was due in large part to the writing of journalists as radical propagandists who were able to articulate a particular moment in the aspirations of the people to be involved in political affairs. Radical editor and journalist Samuel Adams was aware of the five main tasks to be achieved by his writing if the popular involvement was to bring about real political change:

They must justify the course they advocated. They must advertise the advantages of victory. They must arouse the masses – the real shock troops – by instilling hatred of enemies. They must neutralize any logical and reasonable arguments proposed by the opposition. And finally, they must phrase all the issues in black and white, so that the purposes might be clear even to the common laborer. Adams was able to do all this, and his principal tool was the colonial newspaper. (Emery and Emery, 1992: 46–7)

For all his political acumen, Adams could only achieve his objectives of broadening the involvement of the majority if he managed to weave a strand of writing which was able to combine two distinct trends of popular tradition: clarity and appeal to the masses.

Thomas Paine was also aware of the need to present political argument couched in a vernacular voice, which included a sentimental, emotive appeal to sacrifice in the cause of one's country built upon a language of antithesis, comparison and repetitive construction:

> These are the times that try men's souls. The summer soldier and the sunshine patriot will, in this crisis, shrink from the service of their country; but he that stands it now deserves the thanks of man and woman. Tyranny, like hell, is not easily conquered; yet we have this consolation with us, that the harder the conflict, the more glorious the triumph. What we obtain too cheap, we esteem too lightly; it is dearness only that gives everything its value. (Thomas Paine, *Pennsylvania Journal*, 19 December 1776)

The best illustration, in these years, of the combined influence of polemic and mass appeal was the impact of Thomas Paine's pamphlet 'Common Sense' which in 1776 is attributed with bringing the less radical patriots into the revolutionary movement. An instant bestseller, it sold 120,000 copies in three months. It gained widespread popularity and was written in an accessible style in the cause of a people's revolution against the ruling power thus fitting the triangular demands of a popular press. This was however the last time that mass readerships in America were to be attracted by genuinely radical political concerns not linked with the imperatives of economic massification.

Eras of great political turbulence brought change not only in society but in the organs which contributed to the representations of those societies: the press. The press was at the heart of the American Revolution as well, not only because it was reporting the changing landscape of power structures and the results of the bloody Revolutionary war, as the country shifted from colony to independent republic, but also because of the specific ways in which it called upon the people of that emergent nation. In this fashion, shifts in power were also implicated in a shift in political representation towards the ordinary people. To that extent the Revolutionary press of the American Revolution was a popular press.

Sloan and Williams survey the historical approaches to the emergence of the newspaper in the United States in these terms: 'According to the standard historical view, early newspapers were either the origin of modern American journalism or the automatic result of huge impersonal forces such as economics that were at work in the milieu of the time' (1994: 199).

Yet from the perspective of this book, what this conventional view neglects in connection to a press addressed to a popular democratic readership is the people themselves and their representation in the rhetoric of print culture, and furthermore the relationship of this rhetoric to traditional patterns of folk culture. Revolutionary newspapers were able to take their place within a traditional development of themes common to popular culture as it had emerged in the United States. In attempting to speak to the people, newspapers in America as elsewhere had always been, to some extent, involved in speaking for the people. Alfred Lee points out how this conforms to longer traditions of popular discourse within which the newspaper had to negotiate: '... they had continually to work out compromises with other dealers in popular sentiments and catchwords, the politicians, business executives, labor leaders, and clergymen' (1937: 409). The important point to stress here is that the popular had always constituted a contested space, competitively fought over, of the views of the people in print. The popular aspect of this press was always a complex construct.

Following the Revolution there followed a period when the partisan degenerated into the slanderous and the political into an interest in the merely commercial. Lee takes a second look at what first passed as popular newspapers in the last decade of the eighteenth century: 'The legal as well as the popular meaning of press freedom took form slowly. Lacking accepted definitions for the press's status in a "free land", the printers assumed a freedom close to and frequently equivalent to licentiousness' (1937: 409–10).

The ideology of popular involvement in political life became, once again, an ambivalent process, on the one hand through political information and commercial acumen and, on the other, through the more populist attractions of scandal and name-calling. The discourse of the popular had moved once more from a concentration on political calls to the people to a more hybrid exchange. This shift indicates that the freedom of the press needed to attain a significance at a popular level if it was to have any legitimacy at all.

The French Revolution was, as in the United States, a revolution of legal and political dimensions, not of the printing process itself. The technology and style of the journals and broadsides of the Revolution predated the emergence of steam-powered printing and its massive leap in efficiency and circulation. Therefore the massification of the newspaper press during the revolutionary period was not the masses of people reading a particular paper, but more the masses of publications available to the people. At this moment, a different form of popularity and mass circulation were having their effects. It can also be said with regard to the explosion of public writing aimed at capturing the authentic voice and interests of the common people that it was also a revolution in terms of journalism: '... it was unbound literature – almanacs and the posting of notices and placards – that ... increasingly connected the common people of the French towns with the world of public events' (Street, 1997: 12–13).

If the bourgeois public sphere was ushered in by the historical compromise between European aristocracies and the emergent power base of the merchant classes, then the modern era, in terms of journalism, replaced that dominant bourgeois sphere by the rhetorical addition of the common people into that process of negotiation. This took place only on a rhetorical level, the common people's actual inclusion into the political process lagging centuries behind the claims of revolutionaries and reform movements, yet it was a rhetoric able to gather great support from wide sections of society at particular historical moments. Once again this indicates the additive nature of popular culture as outlined by Burke. However, at no point did the popular press have anything other than a highly ambivalent nature, just like its folk and carnival predecessors: part political protest against the abuses of power, and the pretensions of the high and mighty, part low humour, scandal sheet and gossip monger; part acquiescence in the process of subjugation, part protest at the helplessness of the popular position. This moment in the modern construction of the popular depended for its authenticity on notions of a shared, communal 'folk' past forged together with the modern concept of the 'citoyen'. (Gough, 1988; Chiswick, 1991). This comes with the support of the rhetorical force of the 'people' in the French Revolution.

The aspect of political protest and agitation was evident in many journals and newspapers of the French Revolution, as in the American, and was driven by powerful individual players in the revolutionary environment. They succeeded in popularizing politics because they were able to encourage the people, identified as those excluded by the political elite and the aristocracy, to defend their emerging rights and their ideas. Indeed Jean Noel Jeannery has observed: 'The French Revolution is incomprehensible without the role played by newspapers' (1996: 51).

The journals, pamphlets and newspapers were often couched in a language whose passion shatters any illusion that the Revolutionary press's ambitions were to be part of that sedate and merely rational exchange of views among intellectual peers of a previous version of the bourgeois public sphere rehearsed particularly in England in the eighteenth century. They scream for attention and for a monopoly on right thinking. Marat, in the journal he edited, wrote and distributed, *L'Ami du Peuple* (The Friend of the People), wrote: 'What are a few drops of blood that the people have caused to be shed in this revolution in order to recover their liberty compared to the torrents that a Tiberius, a Nero or a Caligula have poured?' (*L'Ami du Peuple*, 10–11 November 1789).

Many of the leading political figures were journalists and pamphleteers, including Brissot, Marat and Robespierre. All professed to represent the people, the new standard of political value. It is reported that the Paris Commune accused Marat of directly inciting the people 'to elect a tribune and to arm it with public force' (Bellanger *et al.*, 1969: 431).

The popular political element of journalism, speaking to the people and exhorting them to action, was best articulated by the young editor of *Les Révolutions de Paris*, Elysée Loustallot, who considered journalism, according to Michelet, as 'comme une fonction publique, une sorte de magistrature, un apostolat' (like a public function, a sort of judicial authority, an evangelism) (Bellanger *et al.*, 1969: 320–30).

In the United States of course, this process of the popular press linking the traditions of the public forum to the people established during the years before the Revolution becomes reversed as their popular press from the 1830s becomes increasingly one which writes on behalf of the people rather than inciting them to act on their own behalf. This constitutes an important paradigm shift in the relationship between any popular press and its readers.

Another form of popular public writing, which came to the fore during the Revolutionary years, was exemplified by the vulgar, farcical and rather reactionary Père Duchesne. Robert Darnton (1996) has explored how the strategies of satire and sexual innuendo were employed in the run-up to the French Revolution as a means of satirizing the Ancien Régime and the hypocrisies of the clergy. These elements were to form part of the rhetoric of the popular press after 1789 but in a much more intense and widespread fashion. The work by Elyada (Chiswick, 1991: 281–93) adds an interesting perspective to this view through the assessment of the appeal of Le Père Duchesne – voicing the people's concerns in a language of vulgar familiarity and contempt but having as a consequence a growing fear to be among the masses on the streets. Hébert was an arch-ventriloquist of the common people whose main aim was a handsome profit.

The eponymous Père is interesting precisely because he offers in a novel form, during a revolutionary period, a link to the traditions of the fair and the carnival. He was a type, traditionally a stove merchant, who articulated unbridled and scatalogical criticism of abuses of power from the perspective of Everyman, the man on the market stall. He also projects in this persona the popular voice in much of the popular press from that period to the present day. The most lasting and famous version of this journal was that edited by Hébert. It was eight pages long, cost two sous and had as its motto, parodying the Revolutionary newspaper slogans of the time, the mock-propagandist 'Je suis le véritable Père Duchesne, foutre!' (I am the authentic Père Duchesne, fuck!).

Père Duchesne is a catholic and a patriot, confirming above all, once again, the parochial element within the popular and particularly within popular journalism. He hates the English and the Germans and styles himself as the bad-mouthing spokesman of the san sculottes. At this point of limited circulation the influence and popularity of Le Père Duchesne is best measured in terms of the number of imitators and copies of the paper all over France. It was also fashionable to read it among the bourgeoisie and aristocracy 'pour se sans-culottiser' (to turn oneself into a republican revolutionary) (Bellanger et al., 1969: 459).

> Comment, tonnere de dieu, nous ne mettrons pas à la raison les riches, ces égoistes infames, ces accapareuers, tous ces scélérats qui affament le peuple! C'est donc un parti pris de nous faire périr de froid et de faim. Il faut donc, foutre, que la République soit bien avantageuese aus sans-culottes, puisque les riches font tant d'efforts pour la détruire! (No. 289, 1793)

> (Why don't we, by God's wrath, put the rich to rights, these infamous egotists, these hoarders, these scoundrels who starve the people! They are committed to making us die of cold and hunger. The Republic, for fuck's sake, must give the advantage to the ordinary people since the rich are doing their utmost to destroy them.)

There was also a fear attached to the popular press and this was fear of the irrationalism of popular genres from an elite-taste culture, but, moreover, it was at this point a fear of the potential consequences of a popular readership beginning to go beyond the rhetoric of equality and translate it into direct political action. This was the consequence of a popular political agenda ousting the anarchic, escapist pleasures of the people, and attempting to substitute something more tangibly politicized. Economic developments were soon to enable the political popular to be incorporated once again within these post-Revolutionary societies.

3

THE AMERICAN POPULAR PRESS
FROM THE NINETEENTH CENTURY

COMMERCIALIZATION AND THE PENNY POPULAR

From the clarion call for the freedom of the press during the American Revolution a respectable press developed which became rather rapidly a functional branch of the commercial community, and the freedoms it had wrested from the British were exercised with a decorum suited to serving the needs not of the general public, let alone a radical popular audience, but rather the economic and political needs of a business elite. Having shaken off the restrictions imposed by a colonial power, America settled down to the serious business of developing itself as a powerful economic player on the world stage. What the popular newspapers of the nineteenth century were to achieve was a palatable and profitable combination of serious journalism and popular entertainment.

Nerone identifies popularization as key to understanding the development of the American press in these terms:

> The expansion of the press in the United States was a result of ideas and expectations popularized in the American Revolution. This change, beginning in the eighteenth century, was deeply affected by two grand developments in the nineteenth century: the rise of popular partisan politics and the appearance of a market economy. (1987: 377)

The era of the Jackson presidency has come to be seen as a blossoming of the self-confidence and egalitarian impulses on which the new American democracy was founded (Douglas, 1999: 1–9). The confidence of this era is expressed perfectly by the appearance of a style of newspaper explicity drawing on those democratic currents and commercially able to sell a sense of that involvement back to the people – the penny press.

The presence of a strand of vulgar populism was to become as important to the nineteenth-century popular press as it had been to the early colonists' broadsheets and ballads (Nordin, 1979). What this chapter will explore is how the new popular press in America developed the discourse of popular culture in a more extensive way and what rhetorical, graphic and strategic devices were employed to ensure a credible and economically viable representation of the people in this press.

One component in the development of a press which was both broadly popular and commercially successful was the identification of an appropriate strategy to reach a large urban readership. Sales needed to match any rhetoric of popular inclusion. In New York by the early 1830s the chief newspapers were sold on a subscription basis. This means of selling papers appealed to the sedentary and financially secure lifestyle of the city's professional classes to whom the newspapers were directed. On 3 September 1833 Benjamin H. Day's *New York Sun* made its first appearance with its emblematic motto, 'It Shines For ALL'. Its popularity was to be achieved by targeting a cross-section of readers from most social classes through a more accessible distribution system and a diet of news to match. This was the first paper to be able to claim availability by price and wide readership and to cross class-partisan lines which could claim to be popular according to Sparks's triadic. Its non-partisan nature was an important element in the construction of a particular perspective on the people's interests. The people were construed as involved, as informed and yet, above all, content with the socio-economic parameters of their country.

The success of this paper came in addressing the people in a familiar language. According to Whitby, 'the tone of the *Sun* was based on the language of the common man and reinforced its motto, "It Shines for All", with plain talk that was athletically lean and representative of realistic human conditions' (1982: 25).

If the style of writing more than the content marked this transition in newspapers, it also marked its continuity in terms of popular culture. Commentators tend to divide into two camps on questions of the relative novelty of this penny press: those like Hughes who claim that the new penny press simply indicated a continuity with the traditions of broadsheet ballad and older oral practices such as gossip (Hughes, 1940: 47), and those like Schudson who claims the penny press was the herald of a new shared universe where public and private were being redefined (Schudson, 1978: 30). To some extent both are true. The public and private realms were being redefined but in terms of established patterns of expectation which underpin the popular and its discourses.

Crouthamel (1989) has argued that the development of technology and technique at this juncture led to the emergence of newspapers aimed at a more general and larger audience at a lower price but this ignores the emergence of what Schudson has described as the 'democratic market society' (1978: 43). This distinctive social formation of the Jackson democracy was, as articulated in the press, the popular continuation of many of the ideals of the American Revolution. Technologies assisted in the success of the cheap and popular press but its readership was driven by a more ideological set of motivations. For all its primary location in the profit motive, the popular press of the 1830s answered the demands of an audience hungry for papers which were 'spokesmen for egalitarian ideals in politics, economic life and social life through their organization of sales, their solicitation of advertising, their emphasis on news, their catering to large audiences' (Schudson, 1978: 60).

Crouthamel tends to downplay the continuity from folk and earlier popular traditions, yet their continuity with a rhetoric of the voice of the ordinary people was one element which enabled the exploitation of new technologies and new markets to be so successful. Economics always has its cultural aspect and it was this cultural component of the mid-century popular American newspaper venture which connected the folk traditions of popular readerships with the popular expectations of the Revolutionary tradition. Thus the earliest popular penny papers were enacting a form of inclusive hegemony, binding their readers into the project of American democratic modernity – speaking their language.

The reduction of the cost of a range of daily newspapers to a cent from six cents brought the readership of these papers to a new social and economic class just as the early century industrialization of America was bringing about a breakdown of previous classifications of class and economic status. Axiomatically, this reduction in price could only have occurred if the technologies were available to reproduce quickly and cheaply the numbers of newspapers needed for this mass circulation. The revolution was one of the printing processes themselves but it nevertheless effected a shift in the widening of a shared notion of popular involvement. Located somewhere in between the folk cultures of previous generations and the increasingly massified and urbanized popular cultures of the industrializing and expanding cities, these newspapers were part of the industrial-economic growth and at the same time acted as formative agents of those new social groups. It has been observed in relation to Day's *New York Sun*: 'it was in 1833 that the first successful penny newspaper tapped a reservoir of readers collectively designated "the common people"' (Emery and Emery, 1992: 95).

The lower price also meant that increasingly sophisticated means of production and distribution could be developed which were able to respond to the transient nature of the daily market for news. Poorer sections of the growing population of the cities, migrants from other areas whose lives had been disrupted by the economic changes sweeping the country or immigrants new to the country could not have afforded the high-brow political-commercial press of the time, especially as it depended exclusively on long-term subscription. The new one-cent newspapers were sold on the day, by the day, by vendors who also had a financial interest in the sale of their wares on the streets. This aggressive marketing was called the 'London Plan' and divided the city up into grids. Print returned to the streets and returned to the tradition of the hawker and the balladeer in the person of the newspaper vendors. Based as they were on the fickleness of public attention, it seems clear that these new newspapers, if they were to be successful in the longer term, needed to both provide some riveting new story each day and also to build a perceivable bond with a community of readers who would identify themselves with its views.

The style of these penny newspapers was deliberately set at a level at which it could genuinely claim access to a general readership. From the first, Day's *Sun* was able to present clear, lively reports in a language which echoed the informal elements of the vernacular: colloquial and personalized. This in turn helped to forge the bond between newspaper and reader which was so important in their economic success. Another feature of the *New York Sun* which assisted this popular identification was its sale of small classified advertising space and the 'Help Wanted' section, which particularly appealed to the unemployed. However, it was a bond that needed to be negotiated each morning anew. Just as the early periodicals and newssheets in the coffee houses of London had represented the voice of an emergent social class – the bourgeoisie – these newspapers sought to consolidate the extension of that public sphere to the lower middle classes and employed the successful and persuasive strategy of the rhetoric of a popular voice to enact it.

This rhetoric could further claim to include the ordinary people in the popular heroism of the newspaper project: 'Already we can perceive a change in the mass of the people. They think, talk and act in concert. They understand their own interest, and feel they have the numbers and strength to pursue it with success' (*Sun* editorial, 28 June 1838, cited in Nerone, 1987: 379). What matters here is less whether Day's thesis is true or false but whether this call to the people was legitimated and representative of a popular level of support for these sentiments with their implications of a power shift in favour of the people. One is reminded of the words of Benedict Anderson (1986) in another context emphasizing that it is the style not the veracity of any claims to community which is decisive. The new penny press may not have heralded the open democratic exchange that they claimed but the style of their delivery was persuasive enough and resonant enough with its readers to draw them into that discourse of popular involvement.

Day's most famous journalistic coup was the moon hoax of 1835, which claimed scientific respectability for its account of life as observed through a telescope on the moon. While bringing criticism of other papers down upon itself, the *Sun* was able to turn the hoax around and claim confidently that it had been 'diverting the public mind, for a while, from that bitter apple of discord, the abolition of slavery' (Mott, 1961: 226). This indicated the rhetorical exploitation of strategic entertainment and illustrates the central role which these papers were to take in the entertaining of their readers as part of a popular service. It also illustrates the fact that this sort of sensationalism had, as always, an obverse political role in diverting public attention from larger political issues.

BENNETT'S POPULAR

Any competitor to the *Sun* for the popular market would clearly have to provide an even finer-tuned expression of the aspirations and lifestyle of the ordinary inhabitants of New York. Bennett, in his court-reporting days at the *Courier and Enquirer*, was already employing the rhetoric of popular enlightenment, insisting in terms reminiscent of the French Revolutionary press, 'The press is the *living jury* of the nation' (Crouthamel, 1989: 13). Bennett, in these formative months, was able to outline his view of the importance of writing targeted at the people. Indicating his belief in the centrality of the people, he claimed optimistically: 'An editor must always be with the people – think with them – feel with them – and he need fear nothing, he will always be right – always be strong – always popular – always free' (Mott, 1961: 232).

James Gordon Bennett launched a successful competitor to the *Sun* between May and June 1835. His New York *Morning Herald* developed its own version of a newspaper aimed at the new readership and combined business, news, crime and sport in a successful blend which indicated that, in terms of popularity, continuity was as important as novelty. Bennett, confirming the essential nature of a voice which could appeal directly to the lives of his readers, speaking in their words in his opening number – the weight of personal pronouns and adjectives building a picture of individual ownership of the newspaper as well as its whole project as a compelling popular contract: 'well I have got a paper of my own which will tell me all about what's doing in the world – I'm busy now – but I'll put it in my pocket and read it at my leisure' (Crouthamel, 1989: 22).

Above all, at this time, Bennett wrote in an idiom and with a content that aligned with the interests of the 'common people' as mediated through his newspaper. The advertising included the popular sport of racing and even took the racing seriously as something worth writing about, indicating another link between the strategic identification of an audience and matching it with reporting focused on its own interests and obsessions. Indeed the first full-time sports reporter for a daily newspaper was Henry Chadwick for the *New York Herald* (Oriard, 1993: 58).

An appeal to those outside the financial and social elite forms a link with traditional popular resentments at inequalities in wealth distribution, especially in a country such as post-Revolutionary America with its developing open-society ideology. In its emphasis on the single cent, Bennett and his rivals were again sending out a signal of solidarity with the lowest common economic denominator. Yet the discussion of economics or politics were relatively conservative and lacking in any analytical solution to the issues raised. It was a populist discourse which defused issues in a depoliticized manner.

Later, once his own paper the *Herald* had become established, in a confident self-advertisement he could boast of what he considered was the chief secret of his success: 'I have entered the hearts of the people – I have shown them their own sentiments – I have put down their own living feelings on paper – I have created a passion for reading the *Herald* among all classes' (Stevens, 1991: 38–9).

Part of the discourse of popular culture in the press was the involvement of the people in their own affairs. The penny press was able to incorporate into its approach an insistence that ordinary people had a right to know and to make up their own minds on what was exposed to them. Bennett set out with an overtly populist version of this, giving 'a correct picture of the world – in Wall Street – in the Exchange – in the Police office – at the Theatre – in the Opera – in short, wherever human nature and real life best display their freaks and vagaries' had been kept' (Crouthamel, 1989: 24).

News, once again conforming to older paradigms of popular interest, was predominantly of a local nature even if that localism was expressed in national terms. This helped to cement the specific loyalty of a community of readers rooted in place. Bennett, in his *New York Herald* was one of the most vehement contributors to this aspect of the emergent patterns of the popular press. Attempting to reflect and contribute to the debate around Manifest Destiny, his patriotic fervour bordered on chauvinism and sometimes stepped over into blatant xenophobia. Half a century before the eruption of jingoism in the press war between Hearst and Pulitzer in America and half a century before the *Daily Mail's* campaign against the Boers, Bennett could write stridently in the summer of 1843:

> The Anglo Saxon race is intended by an overruling Providence to carry the principles of liberty, the refinements of civilization, and the advantages of the mechanic arts through every land, even those now barbarous. The prostrate savage and the benighted heathen, shall yet be imbued with Anglo-Saxon intelligence and culture, and be blessed with the institutions, both civil and religious, which are now our inheritance. Mexico, too, must submit to the o'erpowering influence of the Anglo-Saxon. (Crouthamel, 1989: 57)

One of the key voices which Bennett perfected early on in his *Herald* was that of the age-old figure of the gossip as a vector of news within the community, 'in all ages and in all lands … the favorite form of conversation' (Bessie, 1938: 150). This was particularly noticeable at the time of the Robinson–Jewett case of 1836. This case involved the murder of a prostitute, Jewett, in New York and was a perfect opportunity to bundle many aspects of traditional popular culture into the format of the new penny press. The suspicion fell on a young and wealthy socialite, Robinson, but in taking the side of the murdered prostitute, Bennett was able to simultaneously appeal to the prurience of his readers, launch a campaign against the hypocrisies of New York's wealthier classes and launch into the differential treatment of the lower classes by the police. Bennett managed to extend his democratic concerns to his more intrusive personality-based news coverage and justify it explicitly in terms of social improvement:

> Instead of relating the recent awful tragedy of Ellen Jewett as a dull police report, we made it the starting point to open up a full view upon the morals of society – the hinge of a course of mental action calculated to benefit the age – the opening scene of a great domestic drama that will, if properly conducted, bring about a reformation – a revolution – a total revolution in the present diseased state of society and morals. (Crouthamel, 1989: 30)

In short he could speak to wide sections of society in a popular tone. In order to support his aims in this case he managed to include background, reports from friends and acquaintances, speculation on multiple theories – shifting the finger of blame – and central to all of this was his deployment of the interview technique, not for the first time in a newspaper but certainly with a skill never before matched nor so skilfully harnessed to the requirements of this sort of journalism. The crossover and interdependence of popular genre is illustrated by the fact that the Robinson–Jewett case spawned at least 11 chap-book accounts (Schiller, 1981: 57).

The report of the interview with Rosina Townsend, the brothel-keeper, from 17 April 1836 includes the following passage:

> Did you hear no other noise previous to the knocking of the young man to let you in?
> I think I heard a noise and said who's there, but received no answer.
> How did you know that the person you let in was Frank (the alias Robinson used at the house)?
> He gave his name.
> Did you see his face?
> No – his cloak was held up over his face. I saw nothing but his eyes as he passed me – he had on a hat and a coat.

From the start, the tone of the editorials in both the *Herald* and the *Sun* was fresh, ironic but always direct. This combination fitted the target audience well in their healthy scepticism of their political and economic masters. This scepticism and its expression in popular, entertaining form is a further continuity with the older traditions of broadsheet and ballad. However, such scepticism never undermined the assumption that capitalism was the natural way forward for the people of America. Embedded in the economics and technologies of capital as they were, the popular newspapers' rhetorical address to the people could clearly see where the boundaries of its own interests lay.

In addition, it added a further element into this popular discourse which illustrated continuity with older forms of folk culture – the imperative for entertainment. Tales of scandal and titillation survive from traditions which precede the bourgeois public sphere and are often considered lacking in political importance because they do not advance the political interests of an enlightened people; more, they reflect the playful and anarchic disempowerment of the mass of the people when faced with a world outside their jurisdiction and control. This seems a development at odds with Schudson's claim, and the paradox here must be explored further. Are these newspapers part of a democratic imperative embedded within folk and popular culture as its successor or are they escapist means of withdrawing from the real power relations of society into areas which are relatively safe to deal with? Either way these themes were to remain central to commercial popular newspapers in America and beyond.

Bennett's *Herald* became the first newspaper to develop the society reporting which was to become in time the forerunner of our celebrity-based news. Bennett's approach was novel in the way it fitted into a particular social setting. The genre itself was as old as communication – gossip about one's social betters. This represented a social awareness not in ways in which members of a relatively homogeneous public sphere converge to debate and discuss the changing face of society in a more enlightened post-absolutist fashion, as in the England of the *Tatler* and the *Spectator*, but more a flattened and curtailed critical perspective limited by the epistemology of wealth in a capitalist society.

In the increased reliance on scandal and gossip of a popular press which claims to catch the ear and eye of the masses with a vivid style of reporting, one is left to consider the role of such prurience in the overall agenda of these papers. Human interest became one of the chief modes of educating the readership into the new urban morality of the American city. In celebrity news and gossip the popular press was able to allow an increasingly pseudo-democratic access to the lives of the rich and the politically influential while at the same time reinforcing conservative agendas of what the responsibilities of success should be within a capitalist economy. There is much less of carnivalesque inversion here than of social and moral convergence around the cautionary tales of the great and good.

Perhaps hybridity best describes what the mid-century popular press was able to bring to the American reading public. It took elements of the traditional press such as coverage of political and economic issues, combined them with features of older traditions of public dissent and local gossip, couched the resulting product in a rhetoric of popular participation and vernacular debate, and claimed that they spoke for the people in terms of their own concerns and did so in a stylized version of their own voice. Thus the popular press emerges as a mixture of genres, a heteroglossia; some of which had already become established as features of journalism. This Bakhtinian concept allows us to appreciate furthermore that the popular is a complex variety of genre and form made up of competing and conflicting voices. Furthermore his formulation of the function of dialogue provides a dynamic solution to the potential contradictions between Gramsci and Foucault in allowing us to make connections between the responsiveness of hegemony, allowing strategies of popular resistance to gain provisional representation, and the bleaker conceptualization of the power constraints within the discursive formations at work in these varieties of popular culture. It is in the American penny press that economics first meets political rhetoric and expresses it in a vernacular form, confirming the accuracy of the comment that 'the *Herald* was remembered not so much for *what* it said as for *how* it said it' (Emery and Emery, 1992: 102).

THE AMERICAN NEW JOURNALISM

The foregoing account indicates the patterns and traditions to the emergence of the popular press in America in the middle of the nineteenth century. Social and economic developments meant that the end of the century saw the emergence of a form of journalism that developed distinctly on those patterns. It heralded itself as the 'New Journalism' and had a huge impact at home and was influential in the development of the popular press abroad particularly in Britain.

An important part of its appeal was directed once again towards the interests of the people. The sales strategies of the New Journalism coincided with the emergence of the ordinary people as a truly mass market that could be represented to great effect in order to make profit in the newspaper business. But in order to achieve this the New Journalism had to become even more closely identified, in its rhetoric and approach, with the interests of the ordinary working masses.

In part, it developed as the nature of popular culture and also the nature of popular participatory democracy shifted. If the 1830s were characterized by fragmentation and disruption of social structures, the last 20 years of the century in America saw the enforced cohesion of millions in rapid urbanization. This era saw the creation of newly extended communities and newspapers became adept at finding ways to reach these communities as they became economically and culturally interdependent.

New Journalism's popular culture consisted of four interlocking strategic elements: a rhetoric of the working people, a broad popular appeal, a high entertainment factor and, increasingly, the exploitation of chauvinism to reinforce popular sentiments of community.

PULITZER AND THE RHETORIC OF THE PEOPLE

Even in his early days in St Louis, Pulitzer had appreciated the rhetorical necessity of appealing to the people he claimed to serve. In the first edition he asserted: 'The *Post and Dispatch* will serve no party but the people' (Emery and Emery, 1992: 171). On moving to New York he bought the New York *World* in 1883, adapted it to his strategic articulation of the people and thus New Journalism was born. In his first edition Pulitzer claimed in suitable style that his paper was: 'not only large but truly democratic – dedicated to the cause of the people rather than to that of the purse potentates – devoted more to the news of the New World than the Old World – that will expose all fraud and sham, fight all public evils and abuses – that will battle for the people with earnest sincerity' (Mott, 1961: 434). This is in effect a remarkably concise and self-aware summary of the role of the popular press and its ability to make claims to authentic popular appeal.

The tone of his reporters, developing more subjective approaches to news, also matched the conversational patterns of his readers. Building on the tradition launched by Bennett, particularly with regard to news of celebrities or socialites, he defined news as that which was 'apt to be talked about'. As with all aspects of the New Journalism, in isolation, this was clearly nothing other than an astute development of more ancient patterns of gossip but, in combination with other variations on familiar themes and techniques, it became a radical force for change within the cultural industry of the newspaper.

All major commentators on the history of American journalism point to the lively style of writing and the willingness of the newspapers to scour the city for news which would be of interest to its readers as the foremost features of what became known as the New Journalism. This lively writing was, of course, not simply a stylistic or editorial preference but also a concerted attempt to match the content of the papers to the people in a way that could enable them to become identified as sharing the concerns and interests of their readers, and to reinforce this perception by presenting them in a language which sought to construct an echo of the rich vernacular of the urban masses.

CAMPAIGNING JOURNALISM – INCORPORATING THE PEOPLE'S INTERESTS

Campaigning journalism was one way in which the aims of the New Journalism and its successors were able to phrase their solidarity with the worldview of their readers. This was a combination of rhetoric and strategy.

Claiming to be the spokespiece of the people is an extremely volatile rhetorical strategy needing to harness and adapt to the ambiguities and tensions inherent in the popular and only works in print journalism when backed quantitatively with circulation. This aspect of the popular became a self-fulfilling prophecy in the laissez-faire economic climate of the turn-of-the-century American press industry. The mass circulation papers needed to build rhetorical bridges with their readership in order to legitimate and lubricate their claims. One way of doing this was on the back of self-promotions declaring common cause with the interest of the people.

Even before Pulitzer arrived in New York, his newspaper had conformed to certain patterns of the earlier campaigning of the popular press. To support the bond between people and paper he led local crusades in the St Louis Post Dispatch to clean and repair the city's streets, and others more designed to encourage financial hygiene such as those against gambling, tax-dodging and unofficial lotteries.

The New Journalism, because of the combination of factors which made it more widely read than previous American newspapers and because of its increasingly bold editorial style claimed a new kind of mass influence with its readers. This meant that its campaigns transcended the attempts of the earlier penny newspapers. Through his judicious blend of journalistic and economic techniques Pulitzer brought an influential campaigning agenda to a section of the urban population which could, for the first time, be referred to as the masses. Once again it is interesting to note that this involved nothing new in terms of style or content but reconfigured a range of hybrid forms and political claims for the press as an active element in the construction of a popular, or at least populist, public sphere. A key factor in all this was Pulitzer's ability to combine entertainment, identification and information in an acceptable balance.

The first edition of his paper urged ten measures designed to curry popular favour: taxing luxuries, inheritances, large incomes, monopolies, privileged corporations, levying a tariff for revenue, reforming the civil service, punishing corrupt office holders, vote buying and employers who coerce their employees in elections.

Pulitzer's campaign for a people's collection for the erection of the Statue of Liberty was argued in the pages of his own newspaper. He claimed that as the gift of the Statue came from the ordinary people of France not from their government, the money for the pedestal that would allow the monument to be erected should be collected from the ordinary people of New York: 'The *World* is the people's paper, and it now appeals to the people to come forward and raise this money' (New York *World*, 16 March 1885).

The appeal of these campaigns was often ambivalent. Stevens points out that Pulitzer's *World*, despite its campaigns against New York Central, the Standard Oil Company, the Bell telephone monopoly and the Pacific Railway, was primarily interested in the campaigns which supported liberal mercantile issues. Cheaper oil, telephones, taxes and transport were as much in the interests of the entrpreneur as they were of the common people (Stevens, 1991: 73).

Although Pulitzer claimed that he was aiming to 'rise above fear of partisanship and fear of popular prejudice' (Emery and Emery, 1992: 175), this did in fact indicate that he was not simply giving the people what they wanted, as in many populist claims before and since, but like all popular proprietors he was engaging in a much more subtle negotiation between his own campaigning and the projected conflation of this with the will of the people.

In addition to his direct calls to the people, Pulitzer's wealth allowed him to pioneer stunts, the best known of which was that of Nelly Bly and her successful bid to beat the record of the fictional Phileas Fogg in circumnavigating the globe. These stunts enabled him to set an entertaining aspect to his news agenda, which was in keeping with people's curiosity and desire for entertaiment and identify it closely with his paper. Less proactively, but equally in tune with popular taste, he exploited the most alluring of mid-century cults such as phrenology and spiritualism.

HEARST'S INTENSIFICATION OF THE NEW JOURNALISM

The career of Hearst in popular newspapers developed the notion, common enough to perspectives of popular culture, of popular journalism, as activity. Pulitzer's New Journalism, with his arrival on the New York scene in 1883, was intended to produce an active corps of reporters forever combing the city in active search for daily news. Hearst foregrounded this aspect even more in the rhetorical claims to the effectiveness of his newspaper, the New York *Journal*.

The New Journalism was able to merge the campaign with the rhetoric of activity in the people's interests. Building on the popular newspaper tradition of police reporting, the *Journal* went into the detective business, adding a new dimension to police reporting, involving the reader vicariously in the actual investigation. Its greatest success in this field was the solution of the 'Guldensuppe mystery'. *Journal* reporters, claimed Hearst, constituted '"a detective force at least as efficient as that maintained at public expense by this or any other city"' (New York *Journal*, 28 January 1899; quoted in Mott, 1961: 523–4).

The New Journalism insisted on the role of action and speed in its efforts to integrate itself with the speed of popular cultural developments transmitted by the press. On 7 July 1897 the *Journal* boasted competitively:

NEWS THAT IS NEWS

The *Journal*, as usual, ACTS While the Representatives of Ancient Journalism Sit Idly By and Wait for Something to Turn up. (Stevens, 1991: 93)

The real pace and action of news became part of the New Journalism's own rhetoric of self-legitimation.

Campaigns helped to forge a bond between the interests of the editor/owner of a newspaper and his readership and also contributed to the emergence of styles and genres which were to define the format of popular journalism. The contrasts between Bennett and Greely, and later between the combined campaigning styles of Pulitzer and Hearst, all, in different ways, showed the importance of public presentation in populist causes as a sine qua non of the popularity of the newspaper press. Writing in 1911, Will Irvin was convinced that: 'It was an axiom of old-time journalism that the newspaper must at least assume to stand for popular causes ...' (*The American Newspaper*, 4 February, 1911; quoted in Collier's, 1946: 20).

Sport incorporates many of the formulaic, heroic aspects so enshrined in popular practice and was exploited with great aplomb by the newspapers of Pulitzer and Hearst. In its coverage of newly popular, working men's sports such as professional baseball, fist fighting and horse racing, the New Journalism sided with the great masses of ordinary people who were becoming interested in these new sports of the masses. In fact, in its coverage of John Sullivan, in the ring and in his private life, the New Journalism created America's first sports personality.

Oriard quotes an extract from the reporting of the 1884 Yale–Princeton contest to illustrate how the rhetoric of popular involvement was employed by the popular press through traditional narratives of a popular history to integrate itself with the burgeoning popular passion it was in the main responsible for generating.

A long time ago, when George Washington's father was a boy learning his ABCs, the lads of Yale College used to play foot-ball. Long before the blue stars of the American flag were born the boys of Princeton played at the same game. While yet both colleges swore by good King George, there was born a spirit of rivalry between them. Each year that added itself to the century added its weight to this feeling. So the game of yesterday was not a mere exhibition of boyish sport between athletic young men of two rival colleges. It was the outcome of a century of feeling and of athletic training. It forms one link in a long chain of historic games. So the mad enthusiasm of the 5,000 people that blackened the grounds of Yale, howling themselves hoarse over the score of 6 to 5 that gave the chamonship to Princeton, was based on more than a mere triumph of one year's strength and skill. (Oriard, 1993: 86)

Oriard has traced the effect of popular newspapers in popularizing football in America and one inclusive strategy was to provide coverage of the same event for differentiated audiences, drawing them into the same heroic, all-American narrative of the game. For one element of the *World*'s coverage of the Yale–Princeton Thanksgiving Day game in 1892 there was 'Experience of the Man Who Paid a Dollar to See the Game' and, for another 'Many Well-Known Persons in the Stands and on the Coaches' (Oriard, 1993: 114).

This hegemonic strategy of inclusivity was the way in which the popular press could provide a veritable heteroglossia, a variety of perspectives from the well-heeled in the stands to the hustlers in the crowd to the man who bet a dollar, combined in the articulation of one particular event. This allowed the relative openness of a popular sporting occasion and drew readers into the position of choosing which perspective appealed to them, giving it a potential plurality of meaning.

Entertainment and Pedagogy as Part of the Popular

The emergence of New Journalism, in addition to growing urbanization and industrialization, took place against another set of cultural influences on the representation of the ordinary city worker. Adult education, free public lending libraries and the cheap publication and wide distribution of American and British popular fiction helped form a sympathetic environment for the new newspaper-reading public with a greater appetite but with less time than ever before to pursue their quest for wider access to a range of knowledge in forms which were readily available. Seen in this way, the rhetoric of the press of the New Journalism contributed to the opening of this democratic America but defined within an identification of the popular as market rather than radical involvement.

The confluence of illustrated magazines and the daily and Sunday press provided one of the most interesting strategic advances on the popular press of late nineteenth-century America, particularly within the commercial environment of the time. The formula of the new magazines *Munsey's*, *McClure's* and *Cosmopolitan*, all launched in 1893, was based on short fiction, general, often educational articles and, above all, improved illustrations. These elements had a crossover influence on the daily newspaper. Focusing much more on entertainment than on the dry sort of enlightenment of their forebears – the imported illustrated magazines from Britain – they indicated the particular way in which popular education was to grow in American society as part of a market economy of entertainment. Education, particularly in this form as entertainment, extended that consumer democracy which the large newspaper concerns with their advertising revenues were keen to progress. Because of the fact that this broad popular culture was also a profoundly consumerist culture, Pulitzer has been described as 'one of the creators of an American consumer culture' (Steele, 1990: 597).

YELLOW JOURNALISM

The competition between Hearst and Pulitzer, spurred on by competition from the magazines, was given added impetus by economic and cultural contingencies. From 1893 a depression which was to affect the economy until early in the new century set in and forced the owners of large circulation newspapers to reconsider how best to retain their readerships and replace those too poor to continue to buy them regularly. Militarily, America began to flex its muscles on an increasingly international stage as was to be seen in the Spanish-American war of 1898. The war was to provide an important economic boost to the popular press.

As the rivalry between the two newspapers (the New York *Journal* and *World*) grew, criticism of the practices and excess of the extension of the New Journalism into what became known as 'yellow journalism' drew criticism from contemporaries that highlighted the inflammatory nature of their role in leading public opinion towards not only support of but relish for confrontation. Godkin wrote in the *Evening Post* a few days after the *Maine* disaster which triggered the outbreak of hostilities '"Nothing so disgraceful as the behavior of two of these newspapers this week has been known in the history of American journalism. Gross misrepresentation of the facts, deliberate invention of tales calculated to excite the public ..."' (New York *Evening Post*, 19 February 1898; quoted in Mott, 1961: 532).

As well as the familiar theme of outrage from the respectable press at the perceived excess of the popular press there is also expressed here the traditional fear that the common reader is being seduced naively by the content of these newspapers. There is a continuity here of reference to the people as almost child-like, as easily led, characterizing many elite views of the content and effect of popular culture since the Middle Ages.

This intensified form of popular journalism is often tested against a series of benchmarks for the press in general, as in this example: 'Yellow journalism, at its worst, was the new journalism without a soul ... This turned the high drama of life into a cheap melodrama ... instead of giving effective leadership, yellow journalism offered a palliative of sin, sex, and violence' (Emery and Emery, 1992: 191).

Yet, as in other developments of popular print culture, yellow journalism as popular journalism evolved through a timely and well-received combination of new technologies and stylistic adaptations which, nevertheless, rather than departing from the norms of serious journalism, conformed to longer traditions of popular print particularly in its search for a sensationalized angle on stories, as Nordin has demonstrated: '... sensationalism in the early Boston press was so pervasive that it exceeded the levels of even the most sensationalized popular newspapers of the nineteenth century' (1979: 302–3).

Many of the new developments were visual, as this description makes clear.

> The distinguishing techniques of yellow journalism were: (1) scare-heads, in which excessively large type, printed in either black or red, screamed excitement, often about comparatively unimportant news, thus giving a shrill falsity to the entire make-up; (2) the lavish use of pictures, many of them without significance, inviting the abuses of picture-stealing and 'faked' pictures; (3) impostures and frauds of various kinds, such as 'faked' interviews and stories, misleading heads, pseudo-science, and parade of false learning; (4) the Sunday supplement, with colored comics and superficial articles. (Mott, 1961: 539)

The development of the 'yellow press' out of the New Journalism marked the point of transition where the function of popular education becomes lost in sensationalism and entertainment. Mott is keen to distinguish sensationalism, arguably a longer and more complex popular tradition in all forms of print, from yellow journalism, which was a particular manifestation of popular journalism that not only had an impact then but has continued to have an effect on the content and layout of popular journalism ever since. Our concern is to see how the more carnivalesque, more atavistic journalism of the 'yellow press' fitted into the patterns of popular culture and what continuities it represented within the specific genealogy of the American popular press. Along with practices such as the unscrupulous invention of facts, the exaggeration of accounts and staged photographs of reconstructions of events accumulated within the pages of the yellow press. There was also an explosion in the coverage of pseudo-scientific stories that eroded the credibility of these papers but on the other hand continued in the older tradition of wood-cut and popular sensation. Mott writes: 'The pseudo-science, which was often in the fields of archaeology, medicine, psychology, or psychic research, gave readers the satisfaction of feeling themselves being educated at the same time that they were being thrilled; but it aroused the active resentment of scientists against newspapers in general ...' (1961: 524–5).

Hearst's *Journal* had the following typical headlines in the autumn of 1896, when its circulation jumped by 125,000: '"Real American Monsters and Dragons" over a story of the discovery of fossil remains by an archaeological expedition. "A Marvellous New Way of Giving Medicine: Wonderful Results from Merely Holding Tubes of Drugs Near Entranced Patients" – a headline that horrified medical researchers' (Emery and Emery, 1992: 196).

Perhaps the most disturbing aspect of the development of this style of popular journalism was the way in which it could make xenophobia a popular and therefore profitable pursuit. There are continuities in this tradition from earlier in the century in the newspapers of Bennett, and there was nothing new in the linking of popular culture to nationalism nor indeed in the exploitation of the popular press for nationalist objectives; Bennett had illustrated that some 50 years before. What distinguished yellow journalism was the employment of the new technologies and layout techniques to bypass reasoned debate and appeal directly to the common people powerfully and emotively to partake vicariously and self-gratifyingly in the conduct of the war. In many ways this interrelationship between newspaper and jingoism was mirrored in the *Daily Mail*'s coverage in England of the build-up and conduct of the Boer War.

Mott claims that one of the distinguishing features of this type of journalism was its 'more or less ostentatious sympathy with the "underdog", with campaigns against abuses suffered by the common people ...' (1961: 539), but, clearly, the Spanish-American War delineated where sympathies ended, a construction of national empathy based on the rejection of human consideration for the outsider. This was developed by carefully employing the dramatic communicative strategies of the new style of journalism and its layout to draw a negative image of the enemy and was an early example of the employment of such effective and graphic propaganda within a democratic society.

Between 1896 and 1898 both the New York *Journal* and *World* carried jingoistic stories calling for active American involvement in the Cuban crisis. Mott goes as far as to put the responsibility for the decision to go to war directly down to the popular fervour created by these newspapers (1961: 527).

A genre of story, the atrocity story, familiar from early newssheets and broadsides, was exploited for the new reading public and drew in part for its appeal on chauvinism and fear of the outsider. The melodramatic villain was General Valeriano Weyler, the Captain-General of the Spanish forces in Cuba from early 1896, and stories including graphic accounts of murder, rape and torture were related to avid readers both in words and in line drawings. Both newspapers sought to extend the sensation with little regard for accuracy of representation. Their impact was enhanced by the introduction from 1897 of halftone photographs to illustrate the same matter.

Stories of Cuban atrocities, clearly predicated on the racialized assumption that such behaviour was a characteristic of the Hispanic people, were good for circulation and meant that the sales of the two newspapers kept above the million mark throughout the crisis. The Miss Cisneros story was a key moment in the preparation of public opinion in support of the war: '"The unspeakable fate to which Weyler has doomed an innocent girl whose only crime is that she has defended herself against a beast in uniform has sent a shiver of horror through the American people"' (Mott, 1961: 530, quoted from New York *Journal*, 19 August 1897).

ILLUSTRATION AND LAYOUT

The technologies which were able to be employed to create large and striking formats to inflame chauvinistic sentiments were also to be deployed to enhance the entertainment elements of the popular press, again in ways which were to permanently mark popular newspaper journalism.

Illustration was an important contribution to this and can be located in the popular tradition of the broadsides and the ballads as well as the penny press itself. Bennett's *Herald*, as the first penny paper to successfully monopolize a large market, was the first American newspaper to exploit the wood-cut tradition in a whole-page illustration on 25 June 1845. This was on the occasion of the funeral procession in memory of Andrew Jackson.

Illustration was not the only visual aspect of the new popular papers. They needed also to be able to catch the attention of casual passers-by through the use of improved type and better layout which clarified the make-up of the front page. From wood-cuts to photographs the popular press had always been quick to use the latest appropriate technology to enhance its visual appeal. As an immigrant, perhaps Pulitzer was appreciative of the role pictures could play in drawing new citizens into the daily ritual of urban community which was the popular press. Pulitzer was fulsome in his praise of the role of illustration from 1884: ' "We are proud of our pictures. We observe that the populace appreciates them and that there is always an extra demand for the *World* when it is illuminated, so to speak. A great many people in the world require to be educated through the eye" ' (Stevens, 1991: 77). Illustration reinforces the ways in which Benedict Anderson (1986) has described the role of newspapers in drawing an imagined community of readers into a wider imagined community of simultaneity.

As photographic expertise developed it could be used, as we have seen, for purposes of simply stimulating circulation or for genuinely drawing attention to the great social issues of the day. From another perspective, that of social comment, illustration was employed to draw attention to social inequalities in the New York *World* when Jacob A. Riis published 12 drawings from his photographs of the New York slums with an article headlined 'Flashes from the Slums' (Emery and Emery, 1992: 191).

The use of caricature and cartoon is a good indication of how the popular press, while adapting to new technologies, was able to exploit older methods in a search for resonance with a changed popular public. Ballads and broadsheets had benefited from crude illustration for centuries before commercial newspapers and their more sophisticated pictorial techniques became a regular feature of American daily life.

Cartoons became a prominent means of including a wider audience in political debate and satire in the new journalism era. The *World*'s use of political cartoon in 1884 was the first of its type. Walter McDougal and Valerian Gribayédoff were the illustrators of the first series to enliven the campaign against the Republican James Blaine. McDougal's 'Royal Feast of Belshazzar Blaine' is apochcryphally credited with Blaine's loss of the 1884 election. Within a few years Walter McDougal's cartoons had become a fixture in Pulitzer's Sunday edition.

There was also the more sensational exploration of type to enhance the appeal of crime stories. Typically this might include not only the bold capitalized headlines but a picture of the scene of a murder with the addition of a typed X to mark the spot where the body had been discovered.

The addition of comics and colour to the improvements in layout and headline construction made for a substantial shift in the visual appearance of the newspaper which saw it move in the general direction of the magazine. Competition for readers with the new magazines had consequences for the language and content of the popular press as they sought to maintain their market share and enhance their identity as representatives of the popular voice and taste.

Comics seemed to encapsulate much of the new emphasis in the American popular press of the late nineteenth century. They formed part of a European tradition characterized by the *Fliegende Blätter*, *Charivari* and *Punch,* and most noticeably in the work of German caricaturist Wilhelm Busch. But in tone they conformed to the more conservative elements in popular culture. As Gordon has pointed out with regard to one of the earliest comic books in the United States, the German-derived *Puck*: '*Puck* often took the side of the working man against big business but warned against extremism' (1998: 20).

Building on the development and success of colour in magazines from the 1870s, in 1889 the *Sunday World* introduced its comic section and first used colour. It was in fact from this section that the term 'yellow journalism' actually originates. Richard F. Outcault's 'Hogan's Alley' drew a humorous portrait of life in the New York tenements. The central figure in each drawing was a toothless kid in a smock with a permanent grin. When he appeared one week with a dab of yellow on the smock he was christened the 'Yellow Kid'.

Mott draws one set of metaphorical connections between this character and the phenomenon of the yellow press: 'The figure of the silly fellow, with his toothless, vacant grin and his flaring yellow dress, struck some of the critics of the new journalism represented by the *Journal* and the *World* as symbolic of that type of journalism' (1961: 526).

The observations of another comentator on the American popular press, James Gordon, indicate another set of links, this time between a more vaudeville, vernacular urban popular culture and the cartoon strip. He points out that the origin of Hogan's Alley was probably a song from the 1891 vaudeville theatre, 'When Hogan Pays the Rent'. A carnivalesque element was apparent in the fact that the Hogan of the title did not pay his rent and the entertainment in the neighbourhood arose when the collector came to attempt to extract his dues. This ambience was enhanced by Outcault's use of working-class, inner-city dialect in his cartoons (Gordon, 1998: 25–9).

SENSATION AND 'MUCKRAKING'

The practice around the turn of the century of what became known as 'muckraking' is one of the most notable trends in the history of popular print culture. Once again, it showed the influence of the content of magazines on that of daily newspapers. It was a form of morality tale but conducted at a higher pitch of intensity. These morality tales not only crossed over from one popular format to another when they moved from the magazine to the newspaper, they also had an educational effect in the tradition of popular genre which had developed as part of a continuity with earlier manifestations.

Hearst's success seems to have been linked to the popularity of presenting the world as spectacle and as morality play in very much the same way as certain English popular newspapers of the time were doing in different ways. This depended on a depoliticized view of the world as the site of melodrama. Nevertheless, even in its depoliticization, it had a political potential. To the extent that it acted as a disciplinary discourse, it illustrates what Foucault termed 'all the utopian potential of the gaze' in more ways than one. First, it enabled the reader to look at celebrities and their downfall. Second, it portrayed a world in similar fashion to the melodrama as devoid of rational causality, broken, as Brooks claims, into a Manichean struggle (1984). Third, it allowed a privileged space for the voyeur/reader, once again proving the essentially visual even panoptical attraction of the medium.

THE TABLOID POPULAR

For its next newspaper revolution, America was to look for its inspiration to the English and their exploitation of the format and style of what was to become tabloid journalism. It is widely acknowledged that: 'For better or for worse, America owes its tabloids to the cradle of English-language journalism, Great Britain' (Emery and Emery, 1992: 281).

An early nineteenth-century example of the influence of successful journalistic genres from England enlarging the market in the United States comes in the form of Charles Knight's *Penny Magazine* of the Society for the Diffusion of Useful Knowledge. Launched in 1832 as an improvement on the dour material of Hannah More, it combined a better balance of knowledge and improvement with carefully selected, wholesome entertainment. It was illustrated with wood-cuts of imperial commodity production and natural and popular history. Knight claimed that in its first year of publication its circulation had reached 200,000. In America its circulation reached 20,000.

The flow crossed the ocean in the other direction as well. Reporting from the criminal courts in the USA, with its dubious claims to reinvigorate the public good, had preceded that tradition in Britain, where it was taken up with relish by publications such as *Cleaves* from 1834. Such developments not only reinforce the observation of mutual influence between these two anglophone communities but also act as an illustration of how popular culture attaches itself to different social trends in different places as they emerge.

As early as 1900, Harmsworth had been invited by Pulitzer to design a tabloid version of the *World* and an experimental run of the paper appeared on 1 January 1900, heralded prophetically as the 'newspaper of the twentieth century'. It was also Harmsworth, as Lord Northcliffe after his knighthood, who during the First World War met Patterson and urged him to experiment with a tabloid newspaper in the USA as he had by this time in Britain with his *Daily Mirror*. With fellow newspaper manager McCormick, Patterson launched the *Illustrated Daily News* on 26 June 1919 in a tone which captured the populist, nationalist agenda of the tabloid format:

WHO WE ARE

The Illustrated Daily News is going to be your newspaper. Its interests will be your interests ... it is not an experiment, for the appeal of news pictures and brief, well-told stories will be as apparent to you as it has been to millions of readers in European cities ...
The policy of the Illustrated Daily News will be your policy. It will be aggressively for America and for the people of New York ... It will have no entangling alliance with any class whatsoever ... (Bessie, 1938: 85–6).

The tabloids came to be associated with 'reckless sensationalism, ruthless invasions of privacy, and picture faking' (Mott, 1961: 673), as well as their use of smaller page size, heavy emphasis on photography and a dense yet colloquial style of news writing 'alive with phrases that were spoken' (Bessie, 1938: 99).

In *Jazz Journalism*, his aptly named history of the New York tabloids, Simon M. Bessie echoes Frederick Lewis Allen, making connections with broader cultural patterns of popular culture of the period:

The tabloid was part of a pattern which included speakeasies, jazz, collegiate whoopee, bathing beauties, movie-star worship, big-time sports and many other gigantic exaggerations. And, as these characteristics of the Twenties were but the manifestations of deeper forces sweeping through American life, so the tabloid was a journalistic mirror of the era. (Bessie, 1938: 119)

The tabloid was interesting not simply in its development of journalistic techniques and its deployment of technology but in the ways that it meshed with the aspirations of ordinary people and the continuities of their world experience. Patterson was known as a 'self-conscious commoner, mixing with crowds and keeping in close touch with popular ideology and emotional reactions' (Mott, 1961: 669), and his newspaper managed to communicate this intent in order to 'dig deeper into the masses' (Bessie, 1938: 79). There were competitions, gossip and coupons offering uncarned success in a hugely competitive society: an escape from the humdrum world. The *Daily News* paid readers between $1 and $5 for submitting their captions, limericks, jingles, embarrassing moments, and bright sayings. As many as 20,000 a day responded.

Prize money of $10,000 was offered in 1922 for the best solution to a mystery story and, in an illustration of the crossover of popular genre, readers were asked to vote for their 'Movie King' and 'Queen'. The *Daily News* elevated ordinary citizens into the limelight through citations for heroism each month. From 1923, The newspaper claimed through a promotional campaign that it was aimed at Sweeney, the archetypal New York worker. There are elements of a carnivalesque interpretation of the world through the pages of these tabloids and the people who bought them made fortunes for their owners. The 'People's Voice' was the letters' page which claimed to represent the views of the ordinary readers of the newspaper, including many that commented favourably on the *Daily News* itself.

Patterson was keen to present his popular credentials as part of the rhetoric of the new wave of popular journalism beyond the Wall Street Crash of 1929 and into the 1930s. Even in implicitly denouncing the former practices of his newspaper, he was keen to emphasize the feel for the people in the street. Giving space to the serious news of a people in crisis, Patterson's *Daily News* even became a firm supporter of Roosevelt's New Deal.

In 1930 Captain Patterson is said to have told his staff, indicating how the successful popular press had to move in step and in tone with its readers:

> We're off on the wrong foot. The people's major interest is not in the playboy, Broadway, and divorces, but in how they're going to eat; and from this time forward, we'll pay attention to the struggle for existence that's just beginning. All signs point to the prospect of a great economic upheaval, and we'll pay attention to the news of things being done to assure the well-being of the average man and his family. (*Editor & Publisher*, 24 June 1939: 5; in Mott, 1961: 669)

This reinforces the claim made previously that popular newspapers are part of popular culture and debates on their content cannot divorce themselves from that fact. The very fact of their commercial success illustrate how enmeshed they had become in the discourses of everyday life.

Patterson proved that there was a market for this type of popular newspaper. Subsequently Hearst began his tabloid *Daily Mirror* on 24 June 1924 and close behind him was Bernarr Macfadden on 15 September 1924 with the *Evening Graphic*. He had learnt his trade on physical culture magazines and confession weeklies. He sought to apply to a daily newspaper the techniques he had developed with these. The result was a newspaper that stretched the boundaries of acceptable sexual titillation to new extremes.

The opening tirades of the two rivals to the *Daily News* give ample demonstration of the ventriloquism and style of address of these new popular tabloids:

> HOW DO YOU DO?
>
> DAILY MIRROR is pleased to meet you, hopes to know you for many a year and to deserve your friendship.
>
> This newspaper will endeavour to render service to its readers, faithfully representing their interest. DAILY MIRROR'S program will be 90 per cent entertainment, 10 per cent information – and the information without boring you.
>
> We ask readers to write and tell us what they DO NOT LIKE. DAILY MIRROR's motto will be 'short, quick, and make it snappy.'

The opening leading editorial of Macfadden's *Evening Graphic* was obviously pitching at the same reader:

WE ARE OF THE PEOPLE

We intend to interest you mightily. We intend to dramatize and sensationalize the news and some stories that are not new.

But we do not want a single dull line to appear in this newspaper. If you read it from first to last and find anything therein that does not interest you, we want you to write and tell us about it.

We want this newspaper to be human, first, last and all the time. We want it to throb with those life forces that fill life with joyous delight.

We want to show our readers how to live 100 per cent.

Don't be a dead one! Gird up your loins. Make ready to fight for the thing that you want in life and if you read the GRAPHIC with sufficient regularity you can be assured of worthwhile assistance.

Patterson was eager to develop a strand of popular journalism which would appeal to the immigrant and barely literate New Yorker and in this the technology of photography assisted the broadening of his catchment. Stevens quotes Philip Payne, who edited both the *Daily News* and the *Daily Mirror*, saying his goal was to illustrate every story in the paper with a photograph: 'the very essence of tabloidism.' Stevens claims that this forged an important link in the bond between medium and popular readership as photography 'conveyed a story in a flash and made the reader feel he was part of the event' (1991: 119–20).

Emery and Emery (1992) use the highly euphemistic expression 'interpretative reporting' to cover the identifying character of the tabloids. At its most extreme, this form of journalism simply embroidered its own version of events, as in the case of the Kip Rheinlander divorce trial in 1936 where a model was pictured in the *Daily Graphic* stripped to her waist as a prurient and fabricated illustration of events in the trial of the wife of a famous socialite who alleged that he was unaware of his wife's ethnic origin. The 'composograph' was again used to great effect in illustrating the Prince of Wales in his bath. It is interesting to recall that in narrative terms, the distinction in popular culture between fact and fiction had been one which had only relatively recently gained currency. (Schiller, 1981; Humphreys, 1990) The excesses of 'jazz journalism' seemed to develop this generic hybrid from a previous era when this distinction was less formally defined.

The war of the tabloids in the 1920s saw the confession-story technique adapted to the news, using first-person stories, by-lined by participants in news events that were actually written by reporters. In fact, story-telling was very much a part of Patterson's overall strategy. He took great interest in the selection of material to print in short story and serialized form. The love stories were the most frequent and the most popular, but he also reprinted novels such as F. Scott Fitzgerald's *This Side of Paradise* and *The Beautiful and the Damned*.

The use of techniques of parody and ventriloquism to entertain were reminiscent of Bennett's previous coverage of court cases. The entertainment value of such stories and the style of their presentation were clear.

The rise of the tabloids and their influence on popular print journalism in general indicates the ways in which rivalries in the struggle within a capitalist framework of liberal economics reinforce the patterns and techniques of popular print in ever-more conservative and conventional circles. Even the socialist press in the first two decades of the twentieth century provided an interesting example of how explicitly political newspapers saw fit to blend their politics with the more commercially acceptable genre of scandal. The Kansas-based *Appeal to Reason* (1901–22) was a blend of 20 per cent socialism and related activities, with the rest devoted to the protest muckraking of that era represented as social protest.

Bessie argues that the tabloids were part of the tradition of a specifically American popular culture: 'The tabloid's comics, columnists, games, contests and romantic stories were but a twentieth century citified transformation of hay-rides, quilting parties, cracker-barrel gossip, horse-shoe pitching and fireside yarn spinning' (1938: 239).

Popular journalism in the United States was driven by commercial considerations in the main, but manifested in its content and layout popular aspirations that public communication should address the people in terms of the traditions that had formed popular culture for centuries but that had only become part of the industrialized newspaper certainly since Bennett had begun to develop them in the 1830s.

4

THE ENGLISH POPULAR PRESS IN
THE EARLY NINETEENTH CENTURY

POLITICAL REPRESENTATION AND A POPULAR COMPROMISE

The press in England was galvanized, first, by the events of the American Revolution and then, with a more profound impact on indigenous political culture, the French Revolution. It entered a period, from the start of the nineteenth century, where the struggle over the rhetoric of the popular in the press becomes emblematic of a very real political debate of the age; the extent of the involvement of the people in their government. The popular press is the site where the rising political classes, the power elite and the continuities of folk traditions of those excluded from power all wrestle for hegemonic control, from the appearance of Cobbett's *Twopenny Trash* in 1816 to the foundation of the *Daily Mail* in 1896.

The politics of the popular press in England in the nineteenth century are distinct from their American counterpart. The American Revolution had come to mean that any political claim to popularity could be encompassed within the liberal claims of the free market as the guarantor of a society open to the aspirations of its people. This rapidly resulted in a commercialized popular press whose claims to represent the people found a legitimacy and a widespread empathy among the broad mass of readers.

In England, handicapped by its truncated seventeenth-century revolution, the question of the political representation of the people remained a much more contested issue, since the polity was still based on the negotiated settlement of the 'Glorious Revolution' of 1688, which had acted to shore up the relationship between the aristocracy and commercial elite. No press in England could claim any popularity unless it dealt head on with those unresolved questions of political power for the classes excluded from the political mandate. Indicating the historical and national specificity of popular culture, the narratives of the popular press in England focus in the first half of the century, much more than in America, on attempts to legitimate political representation for the people. Nevertheless, any success it achieved lay in its ability to articulate its claims in a language that connected to older traditions of popular involvement. Alongside real political struggle, it retained a rhetorical element.

The radical press of 1816–20 in England was part of the mass reform movement that Edward Thompson has called 'the heroic age of popular radicalism' (1979: 660). It was heroic in that it went beyond words and became the catalyst for political action which was to transform the lives and political aspirations of the working people of the country. Yet even at this most politicized juncture in the history of the British popular press, the traditional relationship of popular print to the entertainment elements of folk culture meant that the popular was always a more diverse category than one that could simply be closed around questions of political representation. This was ultimately to cause problems for the continuation of a purely radical press, especially when confronted with a liberalizing capitalist economy of leisure and entertainment in the middle years of the nineteenth century.

The ambiguities of this rhetoric of the popular were familiar features of debates over the content of popular print culture in general. So acute were they that Vincent points out that many of the problems encountered by officials attempting to suppress the radical press aimed at a wide and popular readership were caused by difficulties in tying down any definition that could encompass the language and the styles of a genre which was cheap, authoritative and constituted 'a formalized version of oral modes of transmitting and debating information prevalent amongst the uneducated' (Vincent, 1993: 242).

Patricia Hollis acknowledges the breadth of the popular as exceeding the purely political when she refers to the Unstamped, the radical political newspapers of the early nineteenth century, as a 'species' of popular journalism which included the penny magazine and crime reports (1970: vii).

This description as a species indicates there was not one particular or even a certain privileged type of popular press but a range of types from which each version composed its miscellany. This range stretches from direct political propaganda, to innuendo, sensation and broad popular entertainment. In fact, one of the complicating factors in discussing the popular press is that it often combined both politics and scandal in the same writing.

Perkin illustrates the breadth of concerns and the extent of the readership of the popular press in early nineteenth-century England:

In 1828, when newspapers were at 7d., Toby Tims, the barber, quoted in Blackwood's Magazine, got Bell's Weekly Messenger 'from a neighbour, who has it from his cousin in the borough, who, I believe, is the last reader of a club of fourteen ... a most entertaining paper, and beats all for news. In fact, it is full of everything, sir – every, every thing – accidents – charity sermons – markets – boxing – Bible societies – horse-racing – child murders – the theatres – foreign wars – Bow-street reports – and Day-and-Martin's blacking.' (1991: 53)

THE PEOPLE'S VOICE – FROM INDIVIDUAL TO COMMUNITY

Part of the formative process of the nineteenth-century popular press in England which enabled it to articulate the changing discourses of the popular was the way in which it managed to move from the textual reproduction of an individual voice to the textual reproduction of a communal voice. This was a shift from speaking on behalf of the people to building a communal form of address. This was an important part of a rhetoric able to combine the triangular demands of the popular in an era which looked to the press to articulate the realities of increasingly compacted urban communities in a community of readership. The radical journalism of the first half of the nineteenth century was the high point of the individual voice speaking on behalf of the people and their political and economic interests. The second half saw the incorporation of that voice into the political and economic interests of the printers/owners.

The first aspect of this textualized voice essential to its authenticity was its ability to speak with conviction. This conviction was a continuation of the delivery of the individual singer of a ballad or reader of a broadsheet from earlier forms of news/entertainment. The second important feature of the individual voice was the way it was employed as a means to focus the new audiences and readerships into broader, more self-aware industrialized and urbanized communities, or in the case of rural communities, the changing nature of the economy for country people. The individual voice in the press of, for instance, Cobbett was a strategy employed to enable the reader to be eased from dependence on oral modes of political transmission to literate modes. It was also employed in what Patricia Hollis refers to as the 'older rhetoric' (1970: xiii) of the radical writers.

COBBETT AND THE OLD RHETORIC

The 'older rhetoric' highlighted the corruption at the heart of the political system and essentially expressed the problems of society in terms of the inadequacies of the powerful and wealthy. The particular rhetoric of the 'old corruption' was one shared by both middle-class and working-class radicals of the time. It drew on folk memory and the oral tradition of the Free Born Englishman established in the wake of the seventeenth-century English revolution. Harrison indicates that after the impact of the French Revolution on popular political aspirations and in the maelstrom of industrialization it was no surprise that the first champion of popular rights should be articulated in such a 'yeomanly' figure as Cobbett, for it was precisely the values of the rural artisan and traditional culture in its broadest definition as a whole way of life that the new mercantile and political elite seemed to be threatening (1974: 43). Nor is it any surprise that the voice that articulated this 'older rhetoric' should do so in a way which called on established traditions of common identity.

A particularly striking example from Cobbett combines the syntactic solidarity of a direct address which includes the reader within the broader patriotic themes of his writing which also attempt to incorporate the reader into one of those wider communities of popular sentiment, the nation. It attempts to incite resentment that the wealth of a country, expressed in its common people, is sullied by the condescension of an elite to their true worth and contribution. It is an extract from *To The Journeymen and Labourers of England, Wales, Scotland, and Ireland* and was contained in the first version of his *Twopenny Trash* in 1816:

> Whatever the pride of rank, of riches, or of scholarship may have induced some men to believe, or to affect to believe, the real strength and all the resources of a country, ever have sprung, and ever must spring, from the labour of its people; and hence it is, that this nation, which is so small in numbers and so poor in climate and soil compared with many others, has for many ages, been the most powerful in the world ... And yet the insolent hirelings call you the *mob*, the *rabble*, the *scum*, the *swinish multitude*, and say that your voice is nothing ... Shall we never see the day when these men will change their tone? (Cobbett, 1816: 433–50)

In part, the power of this piece is explained by its connection to elements of an older tradition of resentment grafted onto a particularly novel social situation, the beginning of the impact of the Industrial Revolution. Interestingly enough, the incendiary element is fanned by a string of epithets critical of the people and which are part of a popular awareness of how the elite viewed the lower orders.

Another radical journalist, Richard Carlile, similarly rooted very much in the tradition of 'older corruption', linked this with the well-being of the nation: 'Every priest, every great landowner, every cut-throat or soldier, every pensioner, and every other vulture who has been gnawing the vitals of the nation – every sloth, every glutton and every aristocrat ... shall be made to restore the illgotten prey to the insulted, plundered owners – the industrious Many' (*Republican*, 2 July 1831; quoted in Hollis, 1970: 214).

Vincent has claimed that such rhetoric 'heightened the accessibility of the realm of the political' (1993: 244). Certainly, the language of colourful insult and simplified villain was a continuation of folk traditions of mockery and deflation and the role of the individual writer in exposing these to his readers in a voice of individualized outrage was part of the shape of the popular press of the early century.

Cobbett, however, not only identified himself with the great mass of the people and wrote in a language designed to be as accessible as possible to them, but also ensured that he developed a network and a system of financial inducement for this 'mass' to be more than a rhetorical device, meaning that he could claim a regular circulation for his cheap, radical and popular *Twopenny Trash* of 40,000.

> For my part, I have full confidence in our own talents. I am convinced, that we, of the '*lower orders*', have a *hundred thousand times* more talent the the '*higher orders*'. I think,

> that we possess this superiority in all the branches of knowledge conected with the
> well-governing of a nation ... I, as far as I am concerned, am quite willing to trust to
> the talent, the justice and the loyalty of the great mass of the people ... I am quite will-
> ing to make common cause with them, *to be one of them* and to fare as they fare.
> (Cobbett, 1819: 980)

Cobbett was able to widen his readership, not only because he employed
a vernacular which attempted to popularize politics so that the ordinary
people could make sense of the dramatic changes of early nineteenth-
century England, but also because he wrote in a variety of forms and always
used an idiom which drew clearly on the traditions and speech patterns of
popular culture. His was a rhetoric which attempted and succeeded in
bridging the traditional and the radical and sought to bring that new community together in a range of common interests.

He understood that the common people had become politically aware to
the extent that they could no longer simply be preached at, and that in
order to incorporate their support for resistance to the great tides of change
sweeping through English society he must find a voice with which they
could identify. He was emphatic in not talking down to this readership but,
on the contrary, in highlighting its accumulated knowledge gained in the
lived experience of the times. Writing of the Bishop of Landoff's claim
that Paine's *Age of Reason* constituted an act of blasphemy, Cobbett
opined:

> However, I am of the opinion that your Lordship is very much deceived in supposing
> the People, or the vulgar, as you please to call them, *to be incapable of comprehending
> argument* ... The People do not at all relish little simple tales. Neither do they delight
> in declamatory language, or in loose assertion; their minds have, within the last ten
> years, undergone a very great revolution. (Cobbett, 1820: 737–8)

Dyck has pulled Cobbett's popular journalism into the complexities of
popular literature in general, illustrating how it formed an oppositional
stance but one able to be incorporated into the 'old rhetoric' of critique and
partial acquiesence: 'Popular literature, including Cobbett's texts, should be
seen as a discourse that resisted the politics of the dominant culture while
embracing some of its values and moral priorities' (1992: 220).

Cobbett was a traditionalist as well as a populist. He was a patriot as well
as being deeply resentful of the appropriation of the discourse of patriotism
by forces with which he disagreed. He was a paternalist whose vision of
rural self-sufficiency sat ill at ease with the industrializing pressures of the
day. He was outspoken and radical to an extent but lacked the analytical
insight which would have enabled him to transcend the restrictions of the
'old rhetoric'. Yet this rhetoric is a component of the historical stand-off
between radical protest and social revolution, a stand off which we can
observe almost perpetually in the popular press. We have seen how the
reform programmes of the great American newspaper owners stopped
short of truly radical agendas while claiming that they supported the rights
of working men and women. Cobbett's rhetoric was vitriolic but shifted
its target and personalized too often to focus on the root causes of social
and political dislocation.

This tension, as we will see, illuminates the complex pattern of popular journalism to the present day. If the popular press can no longer maintain the equilibrium between these aspects of resistance to and incorporation into the dominant culture, while retaining a wide appeal, then it will go out of business by dent of losing its readership or its profit-hungry owners. This is central to the concept of hegemony in relation to popular culture in general. The only solution for such a discourse of the popular is to shift approach and address. In this way it does not become simply a repository for noble sentiments about social involvement and social change, but more a multiplication of views of the world, a heteroglossia composed in accordance with the experiences of the underdog, of those on the margins of real political involvement. In his popular journalism, Cobbett demonstrates a certain conservative continuity of popular culture and its tradition of protest even at the time of a radical shift in the place of the people on the political stage.

THE NEW RADICALS

The English popular press was to develop after Cobbett a rhetoric of protest which was to transcend an individual articulation of grievances and one which was to stress the patterning of social experience. The 'new rhetoric' of popular journalism was to become one which sought to move beyond traditional caricatures of personal abuse and corruption and into a more systemic approach to the place of the people and their relationship with the economic system of industrial capitalism. One way to achieve this was by employing a rhetoric which, by concentrating on a system rather than individuals, on an embryonic understanding of social class rather than the simple dichotomies of the virtuous and the wicked, appeared to refract much wider communities through its pages rather than simply aligning popular discontent through the prism of one outraged commentator. An early radical attempt to do this in terms of the more analytical 'new rhetoric' of the socialist journalists of the early middle nineteenth century was to be found in the writings of Bronterre O'Brien and Henry Hetherington. These writers represented the opening of a second front of popular journalism in the 1830s. The more established middle-class radicals were about to inherit the benefits of the Reform Act while the more recent working-class radicals looked even more to the press as an instrument to foment social organization and change in support of what was to become the Chartist movement.

Hetherington, a print worker, produced the most successful and much imitated *Poor Man's Guardian* from 1831–5 – 'A Weekly Newspaper for the People: Established Contrary to "Law", To Try The Power of "Might" Against "Right"'. One of Carlile's polemic moments rooted in the 'older rhetoric' drew criticism from Hetherington. Carlile had written:

> I charge upon the existence of kings and priests, and lords, those useless classes, the common property of the labouring classes of mankind. I charge upon them the common warfare and slaughter of mankind. I charge upon their wicked usurpations, their false pretensions, and their general and tyrannical dishonesty, all the social ills that afflict mankind. I make no exception. The royal family in England is as great an evil ... I cry out to all Europe, and more particularly to my own countrymen, DOWN WITH KINGS, PRIESTS, AND LORDS. (*The Prompter*, 16 June, 1831)

This was reprinted in *Poor Man's Guardian* (18 June 1831) with an addition that perfectly encapsulates the distinction between the old and the new popular rhetoric:

> We perfectly agree with Mr Carlile on the propriety of abolishing Kings, Priests, and Lords ... but he does not go far enough – he does not strike at the root of the evil which exists ... Were there no property, there would be no Kings, Priests, and Lords ... It is property which has made tyrants, and not tyrants property ... Down with property.

A colleague and supporter of Hetherington's political analysis, Bronterre O'Brien, popularizing the thought of contemporary economic analyst, Hodgskin, wrote in a passage typical of this new analytical style:

> 'Now, since all wealth is the produce of industry, and as the privileged fraction produce nothing themselves, it is plain that they must live on the labours of the rest. But how is this to be done, since every body thinks it enough to work for himself? It is done partly by fraud and partly by force. The "property" people having all the law-making to themselves, make and maintain fraudulent institutions, by which they contrive (under false pretences) to transfer the wealth of the producers to themselves.' (*Poor Man's Guardian*, 26 June 1834; quoted in Hollis, 1970: 223)

However, their radical intent needed to be understood in a broader context. They made money and provided the platform for the development of a popular press which had a role in terms of defining the printed manifestation of the interests of the working classes of Britain. It was, in fact, their commercial success which encouraged the development of a particular style of popular press from the Chartist movement onwards. James has observed of this incorporation of the popular into a commercial paradigm: 'The Radical press was ... forced out by the popularity of the very cheap literature it had helped to establish' (1976: 36). Within the logic of a liberal print economy, any popular press which restricted itself to a purely political role would lose out against a more commercially orientated popularity. The radical press, even as it became increasingly commercialized, lost its potential to rival the increasingly broad appeal of the Sunday and daily popular press. If a paper claimed to speak for the people this could only be legitimated if in fact it had a representative and wide circulation. Increasingly the newspapers able to do this developed broader approaches than the more narrowly, didactically popular-political. These approaches included sensation and serialization of novels. They returned in many ways to previous patterns of popular print culture which had already become established as having a wide appeal. They included a heteroglossic and hybrid range of content in attempting to represent a broad and varied

THE
POOR MAN'S GUARDIAN.
A Weekly Paper
FOR THE PEOPLE.

PUBLISHED, IN DEFIANCE OF "LAW," TO TRY THE POWER OF "MIGHT" AGAINST "RIGHT."

| No. 5. | Saturday, August 6, 1831. | Lent to Read, without deposit, for an unlimited period, CHARGE ONE PENNY. |

Friends, Brethren, and Fellow-Countrymen,

Is not a " *King*" a man? is " a King" any thing more than a man?—what is a " King?" is he a *God?* We were induced to ask ourselves these questions, as we walked down the Strand and Fleet Street on Monday last; every avenue leading to the Thames was crowded by anxious spectators; every house that overlooked the river was filled, " yea, to chimney tops;"—and all the road from St. James' Street to Somerset House was thronged with men, women, and children, all upon the " tiptoe of expectation;"—even the churches, whose steeples commanded distant views of the " scene of action," were occupied, at an early hour, by favoured and much envied parties; from the roofs of the newly-erected and lofty houses in the Strand were suspended, by ropes, the bodies of hazardous individuals, whose lives were thus placed in " *giddy danger*;"—all approach to the river itself was impossible, and we were hurried along, in a crowd, to the cathedral of St. Paul's, whose elevated and spacious galleries were also thronged—whose very roof—whose very ledge or projection, where a foot could rest, was secured by rash adventurers!!! For the purpose of witnessing the appearance of London, " with all her children pleasuring," on such a day of apparent gaiety and excitement, we, ourselves, paid the *increased* price of admission demanded, on the occasion, and—with difficulty forcing our way through crowds which blocked up the narrow staircase, wherever a small window or crevice allowed a partial view of the river—ascended to the large and middle gallery, further ascent being utterly impossible; and this gallery was positively crammed with persons as far round as it commands a southern aspect:—by dint of perseverance and height of person, we contrived to catch a glimpse of—what to us was the object of our visit—the broad surface of the noble Thames, covered with gay vessels crowded with persons " in their best attire"—its shores presenting one dense mass of life—its spacious bridges apparently groaning beneath their weight of visitors—the houses on either side of it—every window—every balcony—envied situations to thousands and hundreds of thousands of luckless creatures; the steeples, too, of " our many churches," alike " goals of envy and contention;" and last, not least, the most envied, most elevated, and most central crowd of which ourselves were part; *these* were the objects of *our* visit!—But *why* the crowds we look upon? Why have you climbed

" to walls and battlements,
To towers and windows, yea, to chimney tops,
Your infants in your arms, and there have sat
The live-long day in patient expectation:"

To see one William rowed along the Thames!

" And when you see his wherry* but appear,
Do you not make one universal shout,
That old Thames trembles underneath his banks,
To hear the replication of your sounds
Made in his concave shores?
And do you now put on your best attire?
And do you now cull out a holiday?
And do you now strew flowers in his way
That comes in triumph———"

Over what? How comes in triumph? by whose means?—what triumph? why, triumphing in idleness, extravagance, and uselessness, over the misery and oppression and slavery of you, the millions—who produce the wealth in which he riots, but in the midst of which ye starve—triumphing in the plunder of which *you* have been robbed—triumphing in his attempt to suppress knowledge and truth—and triumphing, with reason, in the *ignorance*, the stupidity, of

" You blocks, you stones, you worse than senseless things,"

who, though the wretched victims of his triumph—whose plunder, slavery, oppression, and starvation, are the effect of such triumph—though you " grace with captive bonds his chariot wheels"--still greet his every approach with shouts of joy! Why do *we* advocate your cause? why labour for your redemption? why work for your salvation?—you kiss your chains, and love your jailer! Yet, poor things! ye know no better; 'tis *ignorance* fastens on your manacles—and your ignorance is the brightest gem in your triumphant William's crown—the strongest guard by which his triumph is supported! at your ignorance, *then*, let us direct our guardian efforts;—and the first point on which we have to throw light, is your *bar-*

* It was not a man-of-war covered with gold—nor a Cleopatra's galley—nor even a city barge—but a positive *wherry*: many were sadly disappointed;—poor fools! they forget that *they* paid even for the *wherry!*

Poor Man's Guardian, 1831 – A paper for the people

community, although one which increasingly was subjugated to the one overarching profit motive.

Hetherington, was forced to change his approach in another of his ventures, the Destructive, which in June 1834 announced that it would 'henceforward be a repository of all the gems and treasures, and fun and frolic and 'news and occurrences' of the week. It shall abound in Police Intelligences, in Murders, Rapes, Suicides, Burnings, Maimings, Theatricals, Races, Pugilism, and all manner of moving 'accidents by flood

THE PENNY MAGAZINE

OF THE

Society for the Diffusion of Useful Knowledge.

38.]　　　　　PUBLISHED EVERY SATURDAY.　　　　[NOVEMBER 3, 1832.

THE BRITISH MUSEUM.—No. 7.

[Gallery of Athenian Antiquities in the British Museum.]

THE above wood-cut will furnish, much better than any description, an adequate idea of the new gallery of the Athenian, or Elgin, antiquities. This very handsome room, as will be perceived, is of oblong form, and is lighted from above. Upon the walls are arranged, in the order in which they occurred in the Parthenon itself, those splendid sculptures in high and low relief, which, perhaps even more than the single figures and detached groups, attest the extraordinary spirit and power of Grecian art. In the centre of the floor are the large statues which ornamented the pediments of the temple. Fragments, removed from the ruins of other public buildings at Athens, are disposed in various parts of the gallery.

To a mind uninstructed in the taste for appreciating the higher excellences of art, this wonderful collection may, at first sight, appear uninteresting. The greater number of the figures have been sadly mutilated; some are so worn by time that little more than the general outline of the head or the body can be traced; others present only a disfigured trunk; and the surface of all is so corroded that the scrupulous care with which they were undoubtedly finished, although raised high above the heads of the spectators, can no longer afford delight. But quite enough remains to show the extraordinary genius by which these great works were created, and to present examples for imitation which will produce the most powerful effect upon modern taste. Let the spectator who has a growing feeling for what is grand in art, but who is unable to divest himself of the painful associations connected with the dilapidated condition of these sculptures, visit the gallery again and again till the real character of these immortal works has taken possession of his mind. He cannot look upon them many times without acknowledging how vigorous and infinitely varied are the figures of the frieze;—how bold and expressive are the larger sculptures in relief, called the Metopes;—and how simple and majestic are the colossal statues, such as the Theseus and Ilissus. That we may assist the diffusion of this taste, we shall give in future numbers some representations of the more remarkable of these remains, with brief observations on their peculiar merits.

VOL. I.

STATISTICAL NOTES—(Continued).

(26.)—THE development of manufacturing power that has taken place in Great Britain during the last century is, unquestionably, the most remarkable in the history of the world. Our exemption from foreign aggression and internal commotion, our deliverance from the feudal system, our practical enjoyment of free institutions, and the natural energy of our people, have tended to stimulate our manufacturing industry to a very extraordinary degree, and have placed it for the present, at least, beyond the competition, if not beyond the rivalry, of foreign nations. During the first half of the last century, and previously, woollen goods formed the principal article of our native produce exported, and next to it were hardware and cutlery, leather, linen, copper and brass manufactures, &c. After the year 1770, the cotton manufacture began to extend itself, and it is now of so great importance, that the annual exports of cotton stuffs and yarn, amount, at this moment, to about a half of the entire exports of British produce and manufactures. Next to it in magnitude are the exports of woollens, linens, iron, steel, brass and copper manufactures, refined sugar, hardware and cutlery, silk, tin wares, &c. The average value of produce and manufactures of the united kingdom exported from Great Britain in three years ending the 5th of January, 1830, was £52,925,440, *official value*, and £35,920,670, *real or declared value*. What is called official value, is a valuation according to fixed rates established in 1696, and is now the representative of quantity only. After this general statement of the importance of our manufactures, it will be useful to notice more particularly some of the principal branches of them, recommending those who desire more detailed information, to refer, among other works, to Mr. Mac Culloch's valuable Dictionary of Commerce, lately published.

(27.)—The cotton manufacture is supposed to have been introduced into England in the early part of the

2 R

and field.' In short it will be stuffed with every sort of devilment that will make it sell.'
(Vincent, 1993: 246)

Hetherington, and more successfully, Cleave, in his *Weekly Police Gazette* (1834), were able to bring together the radical opinion of the Unstamped and their profitability in formats and at a price which would challenge the supremacy, on the one hand, of the street literature and peddled broadsides and, on the other, the comfortable superiority of the middle-class papers and the class they represented. To an extent, the new popular papers were able to claim a growing political legitimacy, despite their sometimes ambivalent intentions, simply on the strength of their widespread reader-ship which took them beyond the reach of a social minority. As soon as the popular press was able to find this formula, it would appear that its democratic alibi was perfected.

Hollis concludes that ultimately these new radicals failed to replace the older rhetoric with the new (1970: vii). In this failure are many indications of how the political imperatives of this new discourse of the popular failed to appreciate certain continuities within popular tradition. It relied too much on the older strategy of the individual didacticism of the voice to be a long-term presence on the popular market, particularly one that was always linked economically to the success of the capitalist system. The last-ing shift within the popular press was to the articulation of an audience and its identification with a newspaper in a more holistic way. This holism, however, was one which acknowledged what neither the patronizing didac-ticism of Charles Knight or Hannah More nor the radical politics of Hetherington could and that was the attractiveness of orchestrated variety. The emerging working class could not be reduced to one function or one aspiration. Its popular press had to allow for a more dialogic interplay between the genres of information and entertainment and the economic system pushed for such a resolution to be found.

James argues that it was to a large extent radical journalism which cemented the disparate experiences and practices of the working classes into a sense of class solidarity while acknowledging that there was, even within this formation, a divide between those who wanted to read for entertain-ment and those who wanted to read as a political activity (James, 1976: 22). Clearly anything which was able to cross between these modes of appeal could begin to maximize this far from inconsiderable reading public.

THE LIBERAL POPULAR

Curran has argued that it was the convergence of commercial and popular interests which formed a distinct model of a free press in Britain (1978: 67–70). Mercantile interest, encouraged by explicit government inter-vention, led to a particular form of popular press and a particular form of political involvement for the people through the popular press, predominantly as consumers of news, entertainment, and most importantly, advertising. It is a press marked as an agency of social control (Curran, 1977). Certainly, just as the liberty of the press had always been articulated through the discourse of liberalism, its nineteenth-century popularized incarnation emerged similarly as a liberal discourse.

The repressed 'other' of the puritanical and bourgeois public sphere can also be identified in the continuity between the chap-book peddler culture and the melodramatic narratives in the popular newspaper of the nineteenth century. Although there had been a shift, this was principally in the distribution, moving away from the liminal character of the peddler and to the more rooted publisher/editor of the mid-century. This once again is a move consistent with the shift of popular journalism to a more lucrative position within a capital market and the recognition of its ability to accrue profits enough on a regular basis to reward further capital investment. If this intense commercialization represents a rupture with the past of popular literature and its distribution, the content at least of the popular press is a form of continuity.

This was not entirely the consequence of a new breed of commercially oriented owners and editors who recognized the financial appeal of a broader, popular readership. It had also to do with the ways in which the government selectively used various devices to control the direction of change. These included seditious libel laws, a penny stamp continuing so late in the day until the 1850s, a refusal to engage with any form of formal worker organization which would have provided the radical press with some form of parallel public forum for debate. This concern about the effectiveness of illegal newspapers because of their economic marginality was alluded to in government correspondence from 1833:

> ... the illicit cheap publications, in which the doctrines of the right of the labouring people, who say they are the only producers, to all that is produced, is very generally preached. The alarming nature of this you will understand when I inform you that these publications are superseding the Sunday newspapers, and every other channel through which the people might get better information. I am sure it is not good policy to give the power of teaching the people exclusively to persons violating the law, and of such desperate circumstances and character that neither the legal nor the moral sanction has sufficient hold upon them. The only effectual remedy is to remove the tax which gives them this deplorable power. (Mill to Brougham, 1832, quoted in Cranfield, 1978: 141)

Mill's sentiments drive the liberal agenda of a mass-selling popular press. The logic is one which delivers what the people want to buy without acknowledging the economical and social a priori which structures the demand. It is the elided logic of the popular press from the mid-nineteenth century in all of its Western variants and derives in the main from the fact that this popular tradition was an integral part of the development of capitalism. The fate of the radical Unstamped was also bound up with this development.

Hetherington and O'Brien both insisted that, in terms of the newspaper, wealth and representation were intrinsically linked and that this reflected the main political divide in society, which was simultaneously economic and political (Hollis, 1970: 299). Newspapers which could bridge that divide had to combine political with commercial imperatives and find a discourse in which to communicate; that discourse was articulated by first the Sunday papers and later the truly popular daily press of the late nineteenth and early twentieth century.

Hollis points out the limitations of the strategy and rhetoric of the socialist writers: 'There was no hint of dialectic in the London pauper press' (1970: 300). The radical press of these years tended towards reductionism and were didactic with little space for the reader other than as a function of the radical persuasion of the authors and their monologic appeals.

It was the cheap commercial press which first proved that the division could best be narrowed by acting simultaneously in the fields of politics and economics and in a rhetorical engagement with the lifestyle and world-view of the broadest range of their readers. It was a supremely liberal solution but one which served the ends of normative integration in a time of great social instability.

A.J. Lee has observed:

> ... it was in Victorian England, where the press had a distinctly integrative role to play ... As political sea-changes brought nearer the nationalisation of politics, and the replacement of earlier and more local forms of politics and political discussion by ones based on broad bands of class stratification, the press proved suitably adaptable. (1976: 18–19)

One of the most important areas for normative integration was in the national arena. Cobbett himself, even in his radical phase, remained essentially a patriot. Despite the fact that he embodied the early century paradigm of the popular journalist as an opinionated, authoritative voice of the people, he nevertheless expressed a force for cohesion in British society based around the concept of a readership of printed matter as a national community with interests in common. Newspapers had an important role in creating a sense of imaginary continuity across space better understood as a national community (Anderson, 1986). This narrative of nation (Bhabha, 1990) assisted social stability at home and pride in the achievements of the imperial effort abroad, which could also have a calming and integrative effect on the population. Growing awareness of national specificity had not been monopolized by Left nor Right, nor by working-class radicalism nor middle-class variants. The third version of Hetherington's *Poor Man's Guardian* addressed itself in patriotic terms to 'fellow countrymen' (No. 3, 23 July 1831) to resist the tyranny of oppression from those who sought to curtail their natural rights.

And if, as Linda Colley (1994) claims, class and national identity are but two sides of the same coin, then the role of the popular press in articulating an invigorated sense of national identity cannot be divorced from the growth of a working-class identity structured as it increasingly was around issues of patriotism. The popular press, from the time of the English revolution, through Wilkes's anti-Scottishness and through

An Elegy to the Memory of Queen Caroline, 1821 – The perennial popular attraction of royal news

Cobbett, had always functioned as one prime location for the conflation of class and nation and one where the interests of the ordinary people and the interests of the political nation became increasingly bound into the rhetoric of a single community.

THE *NORTHERN STAR* – ORGANIZING POPULAR POLITICS

The Chartist movement's *Northern Star* was to display a uniformity of appeal which ultimately made it vulnerable to printed material able to articulate a wider community of interest and approach. Epstein has commented that in fusing the functions of 'the powers of the press with those of the platform' (1976: 51) in his newspaper, Fergus O'Connor, the self-styled 'People's Champion', was continuing the tradition of William Cobbett. The tone of this organ was a written version of the political platform of the open meeting. It was a didacticism of political leadership aimed at bridging the gap between an oral and a written political culture which clearly aimed to lead the people through the complexities of contemporary politics – universal suffrage and anti-Poor Law campaigns to name but two – with a rhetoric that claimed to emanate from the people themselves, but was of course that of their champion O'Connor.

This aim was encapsulated in its editor's word from 1842: '"I set myself, therefore, to see the people in possession of an organ which, trumpet-tongued, might speak their will, and utter their complaint"' (Epstein, 1976: 63, citing *Northern Star*, 19 November 1842: 2). Epstein observes that the language of the paper was 'stridently class-conscious ... the razor-sharp rhetoric of class war' (1976: 71).

The *Star* could also claim the essential popular element of wide appeal and profitability, albeit within a particular social class, claiming almost half a million readers by the end of the 1830s. However, its profits were ploughed back into agitation and the support of political causes supported by the newspaper and involving the struggles of working people.

Certain techniques of the popular cheap press were adopted such as wood-cuts and steel-engraved portraits of heroes of the Chartist movement and key moments in its history. O'Connor himself was featured on a commemorative medal minted in November 1841 to celebrate his release from York Castle. In addition to the visual and circulation strategies, O'Connor also adapted to popular tastes by the anecdotal style, emotional and occasionally wistful tone of his weekly letters which he wrote with the keen ear for oral delivery of a skilled public orator practised in addressing popular audiences in public places.

O'Connor retained what E.P. Thompson has called the Wilkesite tradition of gentlemanly leadership to which the democratic movement still deferred (1979: 682) which would leave his paper open to criticism of speaking down to its readership. This also links up to the monologic tradition also identified by Thompson as 'intractable individualism' (1979: 688), which could be traced from Wilkes through Cobbett and Carlile to O'Connor, which tended to personalize politics from the perspective of the author and his unerring viewpoint. Such a restrictive voice would eventually drive readerships to a more commercially produced heteroglossia. Vincent points out this process when he writes that the *Northern Star* was '... too dependent on the position of its proprietor to escape the negative aspects of the personalisation of address which had been so characteristic of the working-class political papers. O'Connor's "My Dear Friends" ... had become "My Dear Children" by the time of the Third Petition in 1848.' (1993: 251).

It was the combination of all the heteroglossia of popular culture expressed in printed form and directed towards the general multiple experience of life of its readers which was to become the commercialized voice of the people.

COMMERCIALIZING POPULAR POLITICS

One of the reasons that forced the rupture of a politics, such as Chartism, which sought to include ordinary people actively in a representative democracy, and popular journalism is the fact that the lived experience of the mass of the people, particularly in their leisure activities, was much more varied than such a monologic voice or such a narrow view of the political experience of the working classes could encompass. A version of popular journalism predicated on leisure rather than active political involvement also shifted the focus of the popular towards a consumerist attitude to news and its relationship to entertainment. The popular had always contained a much more problematic variety of influences and expectations that could be encompassed within any one political philosophy. Popular culture was a broader category than its overtly politicized variant. This was particularly true of the increasingly affluent readerships of the mid-century. Vincent argues that the popular press played a large part in developing a commercial genre which 'in translating the discrimination of news into a completely new category of popular leisure coincided with the virtual disappearance of working-class politics' (1993: 252).

The first successful mass newspapers in England were the Sunday newspapers. They were popular in reach and in their ability to articulate aspects of authentic popular experience of everyday life and to express it in a language identifiable as belonging to its audience. The emergence of the popular Sundays in Britain is much closer chronologically and generically with the emergence of the penny press in the United States. It is as if, loosed from the restrictions of the taxes on knowledge and bound into an expanding capital market, the popular newspaper could only have moved in one direction. The same seems to be true of the development of the popular press at about this time in France (Palmer, 1983).

These Sunday newspapers were *Lloyd's Weekly News*, *Reynold's News*, the *Weekly Dispatch* and the *Weekly Times*. They all managed a skilful combination of radical rhetoric and the elements of popular cultural continuity: 'all radical, or at least Liberal, all catering for sensation, all containing stories and illustrations' (Lee, 1976: 71). Their most spectacular combination of the sensational, the radical and the nationalistic came in their coverage of the Crimean War.

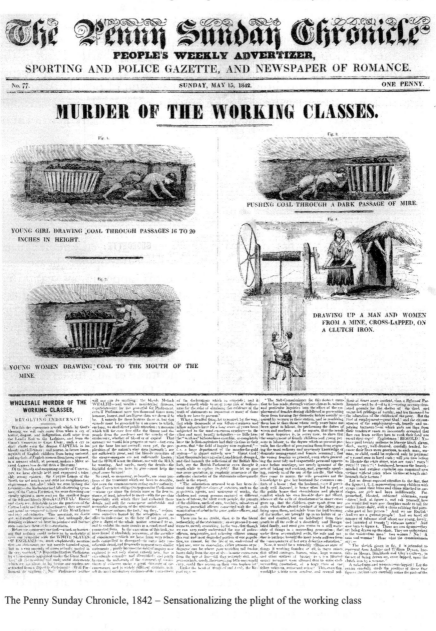

The Penny Sunday Chronicle, 1842 – Sensationalizing the plight of the working class

The ability of these newspapers to provide such a heteroglossic mixture highlights the point that these papers were not only a popular venture, incorporating the views of the general public, but also a commercial triumph. In this triumph they were carrying on the established tradition and style of the broadsheet, almanac and ballad form which had previously acted as profit makers for the printers and publishers before all else. The newspapers which were to become the most widely read learnt how to combine these elements in a manner which left them open to a readership eager to learn about the world and to be entertained but in ways which did not demand too much direct reflection on the political concerns of the readers as working people as such, although *Reynold's* was at first committed to support the six points of the People's Charter. Perhaps the disappearance of working-class political comment was more of an incorporation of working-class politics into an older version of popular participation, albeit in a style that favoured the emerging bourgeois consensus, not in the hurly burly of political debate but rather in a radically new form of consumer–spectator society.

THE POPULAR AS MELODRAMA

Victoria Berridge has noted that these papers employed the language already familiar to readers as part of the traditions of popular theatre and fiction, and not only exploited this commercially, appealing as it did to a ready-made popular mass audience, but furthermore that this consumer spectacle reformulated older connections between the political and the popular. She argues that the rhetoric of the popular in these papers helped to consolidate a form of class solidarity for their readers (1978: 217).

Humphreys take a slightly different perspective in arguing that Berridge claims too much importance for the economic motives and underplays the role of the narrative dominant of these papers. One is led to concur with her assessment in that any attempt to stress the economic pragmatism of the papers tends to deflect attention from the cultural expectations which lead to the pragmatic strategy in the first place.

Discussions emanating from Peter Brooks's (1984) work on melodrama suggest that the format of the melodrama constituted an attempt to provide a new form of narration to ensure that the politically disturbing contradictions of capital and community could be neutralized. In claiming that politics is narrated as a melodrama, Humphreys underlines that 'Melodrama ... helps invent the popular political thought that precedes the text' (1990: 42). Humphreys is arguing that the polarities of Good and Bad, of the 'old rhetoric' which inform the melodrama, already contain a subtle political perspective. This was not an analytical model but one which attempted a form of benign closure while exposing the wickedness of individuals and leaving the sociological bases for the behaviour underexplored.

The Sunday popular genre ensured a hegemonic closure of popular journalism around the commercial interests of the mercantile entrepreneurs but was couched in a language that allowed for continuities of older, possibly safer traditions of popular genre. Melodramatic narratives and tales of scandal and sensation were entertaining but reinforced a pedagogy which drew the politics of the ordinary people away from political analysis and activity and towards a perspective of consumption and observation.

Berridge highlights the essential ambivalence of the popular newspaper at the time in terms of its relationship with both politics and culture:

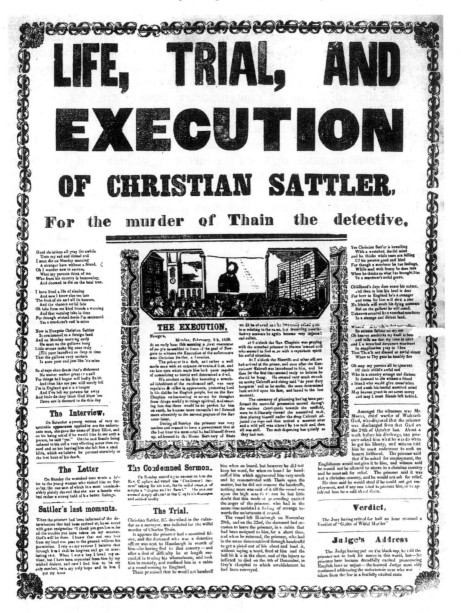

A broadside from 1858 – Continuities in popular layout

Reynold's itself fulfilled a dual function in terms of popular culture. It purveyed, in news, editorial, and advertising content, a social reality which acted as a form of social control – conveying the notion of individual betterment, nonpolitical leisure activities, and an archaic world view, both domestic and foreign. But this form of social reality also reflected the cultural attitudes of its readership, and the paper could not have flourished in this period without doing so. (1978: 218)

Although I would argue that to claim that *Reynold's* in some way 'reflected' its readership is too simple a transaction (the rhetorical transaction located in language seems more appropriate to the explanation of this relationship, a more problematic dialogic one), Berridge's insight does indicate, as I have claimed above, that to understand the role of the popular press we have to look beyond binary models to ones which incorporate elements of dialogue where the terrain is always contested, not simply synchronically in terms of contemporary power struggles but also diachronically in relation to longer traditions of folk and people's cultural experience and the modes and styles of their articulation.

The evolution of the popular Sunday newspapers into forms of consumer entertainment, matched the increasing affluence of the readerships it was aimed at. The pages dealing with the traditionally middle-class leisure activities such as literature and the theatre, catered for since the emergence of the early eighteenth-century journals such as the *Tatler* and the *Spectator*, were augmented with articles on the newly popular participatory activities such as sport and gardening. With the inclusion of considerable numbers of letters from correspondents and responses to them, they constituted an enlarged version of the bourgeois public sphere of the early eighteenth century. This extended audience may have increasingly consumed their newspapers in private but these newspapers were at greater pains to teach a sense of a popular public as a community based on profit.

The broadly educational aspect of these mid-century papers is worthy of further comment because there was a shift of emphasis from the collective to the individual, at the same time as the rhetoric shifted from the individual 'voice' of the newspaper to the collective voice of the community of readership through the normative morality and political consensus. This shift may allow us to better understand the imaginary relationship of individual reader to a hypothetical bourgeois community, and shed light on the rhetorical dimension of that process and the ways it engendered a normative closure around Victorian capitalism and allowed popular expression through entertainment which fed into this rather than into a politics of opposition to it. Other forms of writing and printed matter had provided broad-based class educational intent, such as the Corresponding Societies and the Mechanics Institutes, but the mid-century Sunday press contained a mixture of information and entertainment with an ethos of individual betterment in a competitive society. Victoria Berridge has claimed: 'The popular radical tradition had always contained within it an emphasis on self-education and co-operation through friendly societies and similar organisations; but seen more as collective means of resistance to class domination rather than as societies for personal advancement' (1978: 210).

The relative affluence of the expanded readers of the Sunday press and their disposable incomes were also linked to the emergence of advertising in these popular papers, and the content of the advertisements themselves can be seen as part of the symbolic interaction between the papers and their audiences, partially as individual consumers.

Humphreys argues that it was in the language of the new popular press that an articulation was sought of a new narrative able to close the contradictions of capital and community most acutely felt in the area of the press.

Daily Express, 1933 – Christiansen's revolutionary layout

This analysis illustrates how the rhetoric of the new popular press of the mid-century fitted well with the rhetoric of the old corruption which had been best personified by Cobbett and Carlile in their different ways and had also become the norm in the American popular press. The rationale for its adoption was easy enough. It was a form of analysis which allowed a modicum of public outrage against the foibles of the privileged and the abuses of the powerful without doing anything to either analyse a system which produced such abuse or to scrutinize economic and institutional structures that enabled newspapers to make money by offering such stories for public popular consumption.

Sensationalism and its reflection in the columns of questions and answers, corresponding to a plausible construction of everyday concerns and debates at a populist, if not popular, level, illustrate the role of pleasure in the popular. Furthermore, these newspapers' ability to articulate this through the variety of forms already familiar from other popular melodramatic forms provided a suitably heteroglossic appeal to the new readership. Edward Lloyd and G.W.M. Reynolds are the forerunners of the English mass media because their newspapers were able to place themselves within traditions of popular culture and adapt them to the very specific juncture of the Victorian period in England. The way they managed this was in the miscellany of their content and appeal, broadening the category of the popular press from a concentration of particular political issues and aligning themselves to an inclusive appeal to a community of nation and relative economic stability. The developing popular culture of the Sunday press, however, much as it lacked an earlier authenticity, retained enough of the rhetoric which appealed to popular audiences to legitimate its claims to be representative of the ordinary people, and the keys to this were the mode of address and the structure of its narratives.

The emergence of a focused, explicitly political press in the first half of the nineteenth century, often in the hands of the people themselves, in England constitutes an anomaly in the history of popular print journalism, as the newspapers and journals of the early bourgeois public sphere of one hundred years earlier had indicated a temporary lapse in a more continuous popular participation in printed culture in general. Perhaps it is to the detriment of the popular press and its traditions that it is often judged on how it conforms to or deviates from that bourgeois public sphere. The Sunday press clearly included many elements of the carnivalesque and sensational narratives which had been the staple of popular culture for centuries. There is a suspicion of reading for pleasure as opposed to reading for enlightenment which has a tradition as long as print culture itself. This is rooted in the ballad and broadsheet tradition which expressed worldviews not easy to bring within the disciplinary devices of the bourgeois rationalist public sphere. It was in the continuing triumph of the popular press that they managed to incorporate such apparent pleasure and radicalism within the framework of a successful business enterprise that managed to stifle most popular alternatives.

5

COMMERCIALIZING THE POPULAR
IN BRITAIN

LATE VICTORIAN DEVELOPMENTS

This chapter will explore the ways in which popular newspapers developed towards the end of the nineteenth century in Britain. This late Victorian era saw the emergence of the first newspapers which were able to combine on a daily basis the commercial acumen and the cultural mixture within the newspaper format which were to carry aspects of traditional popular genres to a mass audience into the twentieth century. This mutation of popular culture and its manifestation within the commercial press constitutes a highly specific configuration within time and place.

In the particular context of the late Victorian popular press in metropolitan Britain, one of the essential components for the development of such a popular press was its continuing evolution within a liberal capitalist framework. This necessitated a greater guaranteed market and a more predictable, less volatile readership. Capital developments necessary to maintain the production of a regular paper aimed at a mass market – such as investment in sophisticated machinery and a dependence on advertising revenue to support the outlay – meant that the balance in defining a popular readership and the extent to which that popularity could be based on the interests of the working people had been heavily biased against them and depended rather on maximizing the audience. The economic factor may have determined the type of popular which emerged but this had to find a place within the cultural traditions of the people. An ability to frame the economic imperatives within a realigned rhetoric of the popular was essential.

The continuities which lead from the mid-century to the appearance of the *Daily Mail* highlight the traditional elements of popular print culture amidst the innovations of the new newspapers as part and parcel of their legitimacy and therefore their success. We need once again to foreground the question of rhetoric in this appeal. How did the newspapers develop modes of address which reflected changing popular perceptions of the lives and culture of the ordinary people? Many have highlighted the economic acumen of Harmsworth, but the success of the new mass circulation newspapers was more to do, I will argue here, with their sensitivity to the refraction of readers' experience of their world through a language and representational style that built upon familiar frameworks and patterns. Popular culture had often been historically defined by its exclusion from the dominant economic interests of the day. The developments in newspaper readership from this period show how this trend came to be reversed and how the popular was drawn with increasing efficiency into the economic patterns of capitalism. This meant that the popular could no longer be defined without consideration of its place within capitalist economic structures or as something resistant to them.

Raymond Williams, for instance, had claimed an older, almost ur-Popular had existed which was radically connected to the interests of the people themselves and that mid-nineteenth century developments forced a divergence from this into first a transitional phase of compromise between hitherto popular genres and populist political attitudes, and then into a purely market definition of the popular (1970: 49). Yet this ignores the possibility that for the latter stage to succeed in attracting the people in such profitable numbers there must have been at least a residual modulation of popular appeal which could be interpreted by the people as genuinely articulating their interests.

THE POPULAR SUNDAY PAPERS ON THE EVE OF THE NEW JOURNALISM

The two obvious contenders in terms of continuity from Williams's second 'intermediate' sense of the popular which link the mid-century to late Victorian popular journalism were the weekly publications *Reynold's* and *Lloyd's*. They had evolved based on a combination of chap-book tradition and radical politics which proved highly marketable. They were the undisputed market leaders on the eve of the arrival of the 'New Journalism'. *Reynold's* had a sale into the 1880s of 300,000 copies and this was bettered by *Lloyd's* which, at the launch of the *Daily Mail* in 1896, was the first journal with a regular sale of over a million (Berridge, 1978: 249).

Two contrasting views of the popular are expressed in the banner slogans accompanying each of these popular miscellanies in 1886: *Reynold's* has 'Government Of the People, For the People, By the People', whilst *Lloyd's* has 'The World's Greatest Circulation'. *Lloyd's* provided a mildly radical blend of news and fiction and political comment with a preference for sympathetic but philanthropic views of the working class. *Reynold's* was more strident in its radicalism and more prone to propagating an increasingly tired version of the 'old corruption'. For these reasons it was less courted by advertisers who were becoming more prominent in the success of newspapers even by the 1880s. In their content and in their reliance on advertisers the papers had become 'the effective means of social control which the establishment had always hoped the popular press might be' (Berridge, 1978: 256).

The 'ideological incorporation' (Curran, 1978: 67) of the working class which Curran identifies in the second half of the nineteenth century could not be explained simply by the way in which men of property took over the increasingly capital intensive industry after the scrapping of duty and tax in the 1850s: nor could it be explained by the increasing involvement of advertisers and their preference for newspapers and magazines which supported either conservative or liberal positions, based within an understanding and acceptance of the economic status quo; they could only have become such a pervasive form of social control through the deployment of genres and rhetoric which gave their readers a sense of their place in the continuity of popular culture while refashioning that culture to fit radically different economic circumstances. Sensationalism and melodrama, whether intoned in social or political stories, had become part of a popular way of understanding and accepting the relatively helpless position of ordinary people; entertainment and consumerism offered a temporary and vicarious way out. It was in addition an individualized escape route despite the massification of society, which perhaps explains the strength of its appeal, and one which paid little attention to a sense of political community in terms other than capitalism and nationalism. What was lacking, because the economic cards were so stacked against it, was a genuinely radical representative voice of the people. The reason for the success of the 'ideological incorporation' was that it offered a pleasurable way into the emerging society – a normative rite of passage.

Popular cultural entertainment had been excluded from the radical press of the early century because it could all too easily become incorporated into middle-class, commercial ideology. The popular journalism of Cobbett and Hetherington did not provide a critique of class division that could explain how popular representations of their culture were being employed as ways to contain and control their more radical traditions, which would have had presented problems for capitalist norms of aspiration. Cobbett, for example, was a great believer in the transformative role of reading and in a very individualistic way his *Political Register* sought to do just that. The radical journalists of this era suspected that including popular cultural elements of entertainment would distract from analysis. The vestigial radicalism of *Lloyd's* and *Reynold's* leaves no room for optimism, no ground to recover, for it had not kept pace with the trajectory of industrial capitalism. It remains rooted in a moment whose time has gone. What it does retain is the ability to gather the people as audience for entertainment and to use the rhetoric of abuse and corruption to that end. The new journalism of populism and sensation was to perfect this for a new era.

Reynold's continuing as the more radical of the two, was still including a regular feature called: 'THE DEMOCRATIC SHOW; OR, THE WORLD WE LIVE IN.' It was a mixture of verse, commentary and general radical, political advice to readers. On 18 April 1886 it included a characteristic quotation from Rousseau: '"Each person offers for the common good his services and sagacity, under the supreme direction of the general will; each member to be received into the commonwealth as an indivisible part of the whole." – Rousseau's "Social Contract"'.

This is stirring stuff in terms of abstract political philosophy and a feature of its format which would be recognizably reassuring to its readership, yet in practical terms, by 1886 the old style of radical analysis could often imagine no other strategy than an inevitablist political philosophy of letting matters take their course. This is illustrated in a contemporary letter published prominently:

REYNOLDS'S NEWSPAPER

January 10

TRADE UNDER THE TORIES

To the editor of Reynolds's newspaper

SIR, – ... The capital which the working classes create, if stored up, and remaining unspent, would make the masses rich. Instead, however, of this being the case, it is drained from them by squire and lord, by the voluptuous and rapacious caste who look upon no social sin and no scandal as disgraceful so long as they can plunder the people and live without work. Such a social system cannot last forever. Sooner or later it must die.

There were still the sensationalist headlines from coroner's court inquests, indicating the continuities with the police weeklies and their broadsheet predecessors:

DETERMINED SUICIDE AT FARRINGTON STREET STATION

EXTRAORDINARY DEATH FROM FRIGHT BY A CAT

FATAL TERMINATION TO A CHRISTMAS PARTY – A LADY BURNT TO DEATH

SAD DEATH OF A BROKEN-DOWN CHEMIST

The social conditions of the poor were often relayed in a sensationalist and melodramatic way, and the framing of such stories by a politics of resignation and bluster betrayed a tradition which was trading on tired formulaic approaches to the radical politics of mid-century:

April 18

DEPLORABLE DESTITUTION

John Pilkington, a scaffolder, was charged before Mr Partridge, at Westminster on Friday, with stealing a 4lb. loaf of fancy bread, value ninepence ... He told the constable on the way to the station that his wife and children had been without food for two days. He was perfectly sober at the time ... Mr Partridge: I must remand your husband for a week. Are your children in distress?

The woman (crying): They are indeed, sir. Two days we had nothing to eat.

The resignation to an organic process of political change indicates a compliance with the status quo, and a belief that all could turn out for the best by the melodramatic intervention of fate is confirmed by a reference to parliament as the true representative of the working classes:

LABOUR'S BLOOD TOLL

[letter to editor from 'Northumbrian'] In protest at the high mortality and accident rate in the mining industry.

... Sooner or later the people will protest against this injustice ... With a few more working men in parliament we shall change all this. (April 25)

In an illustration of how such stories play their part in the general construction of the paper and their juxtaposition in the miscellany of sensationalism, on the same page we can read of:

A GIRL DEVOURED BY AN ALLIGATOR

ALLEGED WIFE MURDER

A MAD-BULL IN NORTH LONDON

The old radical rhetoric of privileged corruption as the ultimate explanation of inequalities in society is encapsulated by a tirade against those very classes, presented not within a framework of analysis but of vitriolic description. Consider the cumulative weight of the adjectives!

THE QUEEN'S JUBILEE AND THE 'DANGEROUS CLASSES'

We are about to witness a grand rally of all the dangerous classes of the community on the occasion of the Queen's Jubilee. Robber landlords, ravenous capitalists, knavish lawyers, slimy parsons, unprincipled journalists, title-hunting mayors, and working-men 'leaders' (December 26)

This style of popular critique is dependent on emotional force and lacking in any rational analysis. The people and their latent abilities to change or affect their lives had long since vanished from this form of popular culture.

In contrast to *Reynold's*, *Lloyd's* continued to evolve a more liberal line, economically and politically, as befitted a journal with a larger proportion of advertising revenue and a broader reading public to cater for. It included its fair share of sensation and serialized fiction and incorporated a sympathetic view of working people, although decreasingly as a class and more as a section of society suitable for the attractions of patronage and philanthropic instincts.

Lloyd's had maintained its dependence on police court news and continued to play, where appropriate, on the salacious implications of such stories when such a perspective was available:

January 3

THE CHARGES AGAINST A SURGEON AND ACCOUCHEUSE

'... AN ALLEGED ILLEGAL OPERATION ...'

It also had its blend of the tragedy of other people's lives as spectacle and chastisement:

February 7

TRIALS AT THE ASSISES

ROASTING AN INFANT. – At Nottingham, Elizabeth Harris, wife of a collier at Kirkby-in-Ashfield, was ordered by justice Manisty to be detained during her Majesty's pleasure, she being insane and unfit to plead to an indictment charging her with the wilful murder of her infant, whom she place before the fire and slowly roasted to death.

There was nothing, however, to compare with the potential of a long and complex murder trial, especially one with a bizarre, labyrinthine plot and a set of characters to do it justice. In the reporting of the Pimlico Mystery we have column after column of minutely observed court proceedings. In its detail and regularity *Lloyd's* is easily a match for its traditionally more sensationalist rival *Reynold's*. The widow, Mrs Bartlett, is accused, with her lodger, of murdering her husband with whom she had a complex marriage that involved elements of voyeurism and a hint of bigamy:

February 14

... Mr Bartlett was a man with one or two strange ideas. Among them was this, that a man should have two wives, one for love, and the other, as he expressed it, for use ... This rule was faithfully observed for about six years of the married life, and then was broken at her earnest entreaty, the result being that one child was born, which died at its birth ... He liked to surround her with male acquaintances and enjoyed their attentions to her.

She is described, every inch the model of Victorian pathos, in a story which was successful because it was a real court report, popular in any case, combined with all the elements of sensationalist and melodramatic fiction, also a staple of the popular weekly:

April 18

... Mrs Bartlett's eyes were drooping, and she stood motionless with arms straight down the sides – a small figure, without hat or bonnet, shawl or mantle, but wearing a well-fitting black silk dress, relieved by something white at the neck, and she was conspicuous by the great shock of short black hair which surmounted a somewhat broad and sallow face.

Later in the year we read a story indicative not only in terms of content but also in its prefiguring of the layout of the formula of popular success. The story of a rich couple's divorce allows a reflection on the lives and vices of the wealthy, a prurient glimpse of the sexual activities of a more leisured class and all the sensation of the courtroom drama unfolding. It has headlines of a style which precede the New Journalism's experimentation and perfection of such devices by only a few years:

CRAWFORD DIVORCE SUIT

MRS CRAWFORD A WITNESS

ASTOUNDING REVELATIONS

(July 25)

In the last edition before Christmas that year we have a good example of the discreet replies as a service to readers that its own 'Answers' column provides. This is one characteristic Victorian innovation in forging a bond between reader and newspaper and one increasingly attractive to a range of publishers including Harmsworth, who started his own version, exclusively concentrating on this piece of diversion in 1888 as *Answers to Correspondents on Every Subject under the Sun*.

December 19

ANSWERS TO CORRESPONDENTS

VIOLET. – The marriage is legal.
K.Q. – Yes; the money must be paid.
ELIZABETH TURNER. – No: you have been incorrectly informed.
SPICKR. – Being a married woman you cannot be sued.
J.O. – 'Pride, the never failing vice of fools.' – Pope's Essay on Criticism.

Its popularity as a newspaper incorporated a philanthropic, if patronizing view of the poor and destitute of the city and was, in its refusal to engage analytically with the issues, dismissive of any attempt at radical change to alleviate these situations:

November 7

THE POOR OF LONDON

... The more fortunate part of the population, with their usual liberality and large-heartedness, will not be slow in providing the pecuniary aid necessary to give effect to really useful and benevolent proposals.

In response to a series of proposals from the philanthropically inclined respectable classes of London, it railed against suggestions for more systematic assistance and understanding of the basic economic causes of urban poverty:

November 21

THE CRY FOR WORK

These and other points are already under consideration of the committee appointed by the new Lord Mayor, which held its first sitting on Friday, and which is likely to do more for the really deserving poor than all the Trafalgar square orators put together.

NEW JOURNALISM

The New Journalism embraced content and style, layout and industrial/commercial organization. Joel Wiener sees this period between 1880 and 1915 as a 'historic shift ... from a press limited by its own traditions and the modest demands of readers to one whose capacity for change was seemingly without end' (1988: xii).

Wiener has chronicled how the influence of a more advanced commercial press in the United States had a decisive impact on the newspaper in Britain, but the cultural roots of the success of the project shed more light on the processes at work within popular print culture. It was popular periodical journalism that provided the bridge between the mid-century popular press and the evolution of the recognizable mass circulation daily newspapers of the twentieth century. This journalism enabled the traditional aspects of popular literature to be moulded into a form that would be able to produce a rhetoric of popular involvement in a mass-commercial format. In doing so, it illustrated a change in the relationship between the popular newspaper and its increasingly massified readership. On the one hand, this relationship was encapsulated in reformulated style and rhetoric, while, on the other, it relied on the efficient deployment of technological advances and a commercial sophistication with regard to the relationship between the readers of the newspaper and its advertising.

The term New Journalism, which became commonplace in Britain in the 1880s, is reputed to have been coined in an uncomplimentary article by Matthew Arnold: 'We have had opportunities of observing a new journalism which a clever and energetic man has lately invented. It has much to recommend it; it is full of ability, novelty, variety, sensation, sympathy, generous instincts; its one great fault is that it is feather-brained' (1887: 638–9).

We have seen how the traditions of popular print had remained relatively stable, particularly in the Sunday press, but the real impact of changes in journalism was to come with the incorporation of these traditions into the daily newspaper. The daily newspapers had previously had no inclination to follow the Sunday populars into a more commercial and popular market. For over one hundred years their appearance and layout had changed very little. It was assumed that the daily reader wanted an informative digest of political and economic news unbroken by the intrusion of lighter information. The newspapers also assumed that the daily press was exclusively read by men.

In 1881 George Newnes launched his miscellany whose name proclaimed its content exactly: *Titbits from all the interesting Books, Periodicals, and Newspapers of the World.* To those who see the 1870/71 Foster Education Acts as the catalysts for the growth of the reading public, Newnes's intervention was evidence of a declining public literary sensitivity. Ensor writes:

> Newnes became aware that the new schooling was creating a new class of potential readers – people who had been taught to decipher print without learning much else, and for whom the existing newspapers, with their long articles, long paragraphs, and all-round demands on the intelligence and imagination, were quite unsuited. To give them what he felt they wanted, he started *Tit-Bits.* (1968: 311)

Healthy sales of weekly periodicals demonstrated that these readers already existed and had done so since at least the middle of the nineteenth century. They simply had never constituted a daily market before. Ensor's words are an example of the fear of the masses of which Williams writes so perceptively: 'Yet, masses was a new word for the mob, and the traditional characteristics of the mob were retained in its significance: gullibility, fickleness, herd-prejudice, lowness of taste and habit' (1961: 288).

In terms of its content the New Journalism was marked by a definitive shift towards entertainment, a deliberate policy of appealing to the masses as part of a cultural and commercial proposition rather than as the more sedate organ of enlightenment and instruction. In truth, the press had been moving in this direction since the development of cheap daily and Sunday papers in the wake of the abolition of duties and taxes on the press in the middle of the century. What occurred in the 1880s onwards was a paradigm shift to a popular readership on a daily basis, encouraged and made possible by other trends towards the massification of culture – urbanization, technology and advertising as part of the post-depression (1875) economic restructuring of the newspaper industry which necessitated a more economically integrated approach. Yet, as we will see, the shift was as much in the changing aspirations of the people as readers, as in the papers and their organization alone. From having a set of 'modest demands' the readers developed a broader and more intense set of expectations of what they wanted from a daily newspaper. From the perspective of the new popular press, it displayed a new confidence in the tastes of the many as they ushered in the first popularization of mass culture. In this process the people wanted their newspapers as companions. It was, in fact, the crucial distinction between the early New Journalism and the *Daily Mail* that the latter chose to follow the inclinations of the masses and with enormous success.

Pointing out that this revolution may have been located in its regularity and in its mass readership, but not in its popular appeal, Cranfield insists in his review of the history of the British press that it was 'simply reviving an old journalistic tradition stressing interest and entertainment as against instruction, but applying it now to a daily newspaper' (1978: 221). This echoes comments on the evolution of the penny press in the United States where the recombination of popular genre and journalistic features had been the secret of its success; an applied novelty of combination rather than a novelty pure and simple. The new application is what counted in that it was a novel formation of the popular tradition. Yet the most significant aspect of these developments was how the involvement of the readers was mobilized in order to ensure the new papers had their mass appeal. It was not an involvement with radical popular ambitions, but more the beginnings of a consumption of politics as part of a broader lifestyle. Boyce has put it in these terms which are reminiscent of Habermas's thesis on the refeudalization of society through its mass media: 'With the mass newspaper was born the politics of the image – the need to perform before democracy rather than argue with it' (1978: 168–9).

Neither style, technology nor economy were to achieve anything completely original but in combination, at a particular historical point, they were to prove decisive for the future of the British popular press. In terms of style their success was embedded in their ability to write for a wider section of the community and in a way which matched a readership to a new product, the popular daily newspaper.

Perkin has described the techniques of New Journalism in the following terms: 'A knack of clever writing, great enterprise in bringing together the kind of information which amuses or interests the public, tact in catching and following the first symptoms of changes of opinion, a skilful pandering to popular prejudice ...' (1991: 51).

The need to appeal to the people in a recognizable style, the emphasis on entertainment and the shadowing of popular opinion may not have been new but the public that they were targeting was. This readership which had previously read Sunday populars such as *Lloyd's* and *Reynold's* and cheap serialized fiction was created as a popular daily readership by a combination of factors all drawing on continuities within previous genres of popular culture. To do this on a daily basis and at a profit to publisher and advertiser alike was to call into being a community of great potential. Nevertheless, it was not designed to act on behalf of a radical populace: it already recognized its place and function in the framework.

Popular culture was becoming increasingly commercialized, and the commercial viability of popular newspapers was enhanced later by the integration of advertising as Harmsworth's contribution to the New Journalism in order to provide the revenue to enable mass circulation of such a variety of material at such regular intervals and to provide the communications network to support it. Williams points out that popular journalism had its roots in Britain in the Sunday newspapers of the 1830s and perhaps earlier (1976a: 25) but indicates that the content and appeal to the popular needed something more tangible for it to become a form of true mass, truly popular communication. This was its rhetorical dimension.

Bakhtin would insist that style cannot stand in splendid isolation and the New Journalism is a very good example of that, depending as it did upon the confluence of other features such as technology, market economics and the politics of the popular and participatory democracy. All this becomes encompassed by a rhetorical coherence. The dialogue between readers and popular newspapers, whether literal, as in the letters pages, or part of the textualization of the readership in the layout, language and advertising of the newspaper, became a critical and a dynamic component in the legitimation of its popular appeal and thereby its market success.

W.T. STEAD AND THE NEW JOURNALISM

As the assistant editor of the *Pall Mall Gazette* from 1880 and as sole editor from 1883, W.T. Stead managed to bring scoops, a flair for self-publicity, which drew attention to his newspaper, the development of investigative, campaigning journalism in the pursuit of socially progressive causes and the use of emotive and colourful writing. W.T. Stead, to whose journalism Arnold was referring, was keen for his writing to act as a pressure on government to bring about change in society based on the agenda of engaged, campaigning journalists. Campaigning, as in the New Journalism of Pulitzer and later Hearst, formed an integral element of his desire to form part of popular momentum for change by leading the people. This is in marked contrast with the later popular journalism of the *Daily Mail* and *Daily Express* and their preference for a more measured and reflexive approach. In an original interpretation of the old populist adage, 'vox populi vox dei', Stead claimed in an article setting out, appropriately, his journalistic credo that he wanted journalism 'to reproduce in a paper the ideal of God'.

All of this found a synthesis in the 'Maiden Tribute of Modern Babylon' stories in 1885. When he learnt that the Criminal Law Amendment Bill which sought to raise the age of sexual consent was certain to be rejected by parliament he himself founded his 'Secret Commission' and purchased a girl for £5 to enable him full access to observe the corrupt practices of child prostitution in London. He actually spent three months in Holloway Gaol because, in the course of his investigations, he was adjudged to have actually abducted the young girl with whom he intended to expose the corruption.

His forthright style combined well with his zeal to change society through his writing. His mode of address was to involve the reader, to appeal to the sentiments of the growing middle classes. He saw a way in which the older traditions of popular involvement which grew out of a commitment to social change could be harnessed to extend democratic involvement, but continued to draw upon a version of the 'older corruption': 'The future belongs to the combined forces of Democracy and Socialism, which when united are irresistible. Divided on many points they will combine in protesting against the continued immolation of the daughters of the people as a sacrifice to the vices of the rich' (*Pall Mall Gazette*, 6 July 1885).

His opening salvo on 6 July may have been framed by reference to ancient mythology but left outraged and concerned readers in no doubt as to its damning topicality:

> This very night in London, and every night, year in and year out, not seven maids only, but many times seven, selected almost as much by chance as those who in the Atheneian market place drew lots as to which should be flung into the Cretan labyrinth, will be offered up as the Maiden Tribute of Modern Babylon. (*Pall Mall Gazette*, 6 July 1885)

With the coining of the term 'New Journalism', the techniques and texts of this genre were being contextualized in terms of a battle between the new and the traditional. But this tradition connected with contemporary trends. Among other things, it involved the confluence of a tradition of prurience and the techniques of sensationalist undercover investigative journalism put at the service of a broadly socialist campaign against the abuses of the 'old corruption'. In time-honoured populist fashion, Stead had coined not only a striking theme, that of the 'Maiden Tribute', but also a slogan emphasizing the newspaper's position which, to its credit, did break rather with the tradition of foregrounding vice and playing down the systemic issues at stake: 'Liberty for Vice, Repression for Crime' (*Pall Mall Gazette*, 6 July 1885).

Because of the content and the style of the reports, combined with the self-promotion of their place in history which he claimed had 'an effect unparalleled in the history of journalism', Stead was accused of exploiting the story to produce scandalous material in order to profit from the new-found notoriety of the newspaper. In a letter to the paper, a Mr Charles R. Warren captures these concerns:

> as a private individual I hasten to tender you my congratulations upon the magnificent success of your latest venture. It is almost unique in the annals of journalism ... your

articles are the common conversation of every class; and your publisher's books must testify to the splendid pecuniary success of your enterprise ... juveniles have been seen eagerly perusing the columns of your paper ... In these days of advance we have witnessed strange sights; but none have equalled the spectacle presented of small boys travelling on their errands intent on a paper they never perused before, delaying their master's business, and informing their own undeveloped minds by striving to spell through column after column of what old-fashioned folk might foolishly term the vilest of vile brothel literature. (*Pall Mall Gazette*, 9 July 1885)

Stead was a skilled self-publicist, aligning his newspaper with its own editorially selected and directed chorus of support:

PUBLIC FEELING ON THE SUBJECT
Extracts from Correspondence (*Pall Mall Gazette*, 9 July 1885)

It reported itself on the developing crisis as the offices of the newspaper were besieged and it skilfully alternated opponents' voices with notices of support in order to claim the high ground of moral reason. In support of his position Stead was able to include letters from other radical papers, such as *Reynold's*, echoing his own view of the matter: 'The Pall Mall Gazette has done one of the most courageous and noblest works of our time. It has exposed the traffic by the rich in the daughters of the poor.'

The establishment was outraged: the newsagents W.H. Smith suppressed sales, the Prince of Wales cancelled his order of the paper. To counter this, Stead strategically moved to the people. He travelled the country talking at public meetings in defence of the paper and its campaign in the tradition of Feargus O'Connor and Cobbett – the journalist literally speaking to the public. The tradition of the platform was resurrected and bound to the activities of the newspaper. Calling it 'The New Crusade' he writes of the 'great popular meetings' – moving among the people, recognizing their outraged concerns and identifying quantity as being of the utmost importance in such a democratic crusade:

In the fourteen days ending last Friday, he [Stead] travelled 2,200 miles, addressed fifteen meetings, each of which was crowded to the utmost capacity of the standing room of the largest halls available for assemblage. He has addressed from 40,000 to 50,000 persons ... The real secret of this movement is the fact that 'The Maiden Tribute of Babylon' has aroused the Christian and humane sentiment of the United Kingdom to an earnest anxiety to remedy wrongs hitherto regarded as inevitable and to solve problems hitherto looked upon as insoluble ... It is no small boon to England that on the eve of a general election the masses should be so deeply stirred in favour of an appeal to protect the weak and helpless and to seek and save those which are lost. (*Pall Mall Gazette*, 19 October 1885)

This series of public meetings and demonstrations is described as a 'great popular uprising':

Today in St. James' Hall, to-morrow in Hyde Park, the great popular movement which took its rise in the publication of the 'Maiden Tribute of Modern Babylon' will be brought to an appropriate climax ... To-morrow in Hyde Park, multitudinous London will send forth its thousands to unite in solemn protest against hideous wrong and to demonstrate its generous aspiration after a purer and nobler future. (*Pall Mall Gazette*, 21 August 1885)

Stead combined many journalistic strategies of the New Journalism with skilful campaigning, lively impassioned writing and a missionary enthusiasm in his attempt to win over readers to his cause. This is exemplified in his proposed poll of the clergy on their views of the campaign:

> Let us know by all means what good men think before we listen to the clamour of the bad. The names of the place of worship and of the minister, and a line saying whether he approved, disapproved, or said nothing will, if this request is generally complied with, enable us to see how far organized Christianity is alive to the impulses of humanity and mercy which have throbbed so intensely in the streets of London. We will publish the result in our Monday's issue. (*Pall Mall Gazette*, 11 July 1885)

THE *STAR* AND POPULAR CULTURE

For all his campaigning zeal and his desire to use the *Pall Mall Gazette* to effect social change and to foster a greater sense of a community of readership through his journal, Stead did not direct his paper to the masses. It was aimed at the influential middle classes, the decision-makers in Victorian society. It was T.P. O'Connor who was to combine the techniques of the New Journalism with the mass appeal of a daily newspaper in an attempt to foster radical social change.

On its opening day the *Star* proclaimed in a 'Confession of Faith' on 17 January 1888:

> The STAR will be a Radical journal. It will judge all policy – domestic, foreign, social – from the Radical standpoint. This, in other words, means that a policy will be esteemed by us good or bad as it influences for good or evil the lot of the masses of the people ... In our view, then, the effect of every policy must first be regarded from the standpoint of the workers of the nation, and of the poorest and most helpless among them. The charwoman that lives in St Giles, the seamstress that is sweated in Whitechapel, the labourer that stands begging for work outside the dockyard gate ...

Here was at least a structural perspective promising to report from a particular viewpoint with the aim of estimating the effects of policy on a specific class of reader – the workers. The *Daily Star* provides the break in the uniform monotony of the daily press. Yet it still took seven years of *Titbits* before T.P. O'Connor was sufficiently convinced of the potential of this type of readership, one attracted by short and lively pieces of information and a variety of news and gossip, to launch the *Daily Star*. And yet the *Daily Star* was different in another way. It was also genuinely a radical daily, of a kind never seen before.

Radical in its approach to popular journalism as it was, it also combined this with a writing style which stressed brevity and human interest. Its first edition also claimed that it would 'do away with the hackneyed style of obsolete journalism'. To reinforce the connections between self-promotion, circulation and claiming the popular as a constituency, on its second day it announced after the competitive fashion of the press:

January 18 1888:

OUR FIRST DAY

AN EPOCH IN JOURNALISM

THE WORLD'S RECORD BEATEN

142,600 COPIES SOLD

Williams indicates the importance of the place of presentation and layout in the continuing and evolving rhetoric of the popular and the ability of the successful popular newspaper in publicizing it and drawing attention to itself when he writes: 'The essential novelty of the Star is that the new distribution of interest which the second half of the nineteenth century had brought about was now typographically confirmed. From now on the "New Journalism" began to look what it was' (Williams, 1961: 221).

Goodbody describes the new paper thus:

> Headlines often went across two columns, cross-heads were used extensively to break up solid type and leading articles were often intentionally restricted to half a column ... Later the *Star* used lower case for both secondary headlines and cross-heads, neither of which had been seen in British newspaper typography although they had been widespread in the United States. They also varied the position of broken lines in sub-heads, whereas previously they had been centred. This technique allowed lengthy second headlines which summarized the substance rather than pointed to the importance of the article. (Goodbody, 1985: 22)

The *Daily Star* was the first daily newspaper of the New Journalism that aimed at a mass readership but preceded the market popularization of the daily press which was brought about by Harmsworth's astute commercialization of his *Daily Mail*, in particular his ability to exploit advertising. At its height, between 1888 and 1891, political journalism in the *Daily Star* could be pursued without undue fear of loss of commercial appeal. It enlisted Fabians onto its editorial staff and the paper encouraged support for strikes by matchgirls and gasworkers and they opened a strike fund for the dockers. It could still report in much the same radical mode as some of the popular radical tradition from throughout the century. One feature which passed from the popular press with the eclipsing of the *Daily Star* was the ability of a mass-market newspaper to engage with the daily grind of popular politics, politics which involved the people on their own terms. With the arrival of Harmsworth's mass daily and its direct competitors, maximizing readers for advertisers and the necessity to keep the circulation up in order to keep the cover price down meant that, having identified a readership, the popular papers were more prepared to shadow their opinion than to radically challenge it or their advertisers.

Nevertheless, the *Daily Star* continued the tradition of mixing its radical policy with entertainment features such as 'Mainly About People' – a gossip column particularly theatrical and musical, a regular sports section and the first 'Stop Press'; and of course the paper enjoyed its greatest success, not as with the *Pall Mall Gazette* in the wake of some political campaign for social justice, but with the reporting of the gruesome Jack the Ripper murders of 1888–9, when its circulation peaked at a daily 360,598.

THE *DAILY MAIL* AND THE POPULAR

The late nineteenth century in Britain was an age of curiosity. It was no coincidence that the forerunners of the popular daily papers had been 'Question and Answer' magazines such as Newnes's *Tidbits* and Harmsworth's *Answers to Corresponents' Questions*. During this period the popular mind was expanding as the railways and telegraph brought quicker information from further afield than ever before and the Empire was becoming fully integrated into the public mind as a source of pride and vicarious achievement (MacKenzie, 1986). The popular press was instrumental in driving that new thirst for information on a daily basis.

Having learnt from the profitable publishing experience of Newnes (Harmsworth worked in the early days as a freelance contributor to *Titbits*) and his advances in popular psychology, defined as what the people wanted, through his own experiments with *Answers* and further spin-offs directed at similar markets, Harmsworth launched his own daily, the *Daily Mail*, in 1896.

It was an immediate commercial success, backed by the fortune Harmsworth had amassed and the appreciation of the importance of the link between advertising, capital investment and circulation. It had also learnt from the ways in which the *Daily Star* was able to appeal by its concentration on the lighter aspects of life, but had jettisoned its radical politics. Popular appeal was to be articulated as commercial momentum, not as the platform for radical reform. Although by contemporary standards a conservatively presented paper and certainly lacking any radical edge or concentration on scandal, the *Daily Mail* was to become a popular paper without being sensationalist. By 1900 its circulation had almost reached the million mark and the era of the mass circulation daily newspaper had arrived in Britain. The mass reading public now had a daily newspaper which was directed at them as consumers and as readers for the first time.

On 4 May 1896 the *Daily Mail* was brought out as a compact, reader-friendly morning paper aimed at a class of readers not yet attracted by the daily press. It was priced at a halfpenny and aimed at the lower-middle classes, shopworkers, secretarial staff, office workers, clerks and, as its greatest novelty, at women readers. Designed to be lively but respectable, it was targeted at a readership which Harmsworth had intuited from his previous publishing experience was conservative but rather excluded from the style of general contemporary daily journalism. The captions allowed the gist of an article to be taken in at a glance. The brevity of the pieces added to the overall impression of space in composition and variety in content. Even its advertising slogan in the early days was a call to an ambition for cut-price self-improvement characteristic of the epoch and the class of his readers:

THE PENNY PAPER FOR A HALFPENNY

THE BUSY MAN'S DAILY JOURNAL

Its first leader encapsulates the appeal of this combination of technology, value for money and a well-identified readership:

> ... the note of the Daily Mail is not so much economy of price as conciseness and compactness. It is essentially the busy man's paper ... It is no secret that remarkable new inventions have just come to the help of the Press. Our type is set by machinery, we can produce 200,000 pages per hour, cut, folded and, if necessary, with the pages pasted together! Our stereotyping arrangements, engines, and machines are of the latest English and American construction, and it is the use of these inventions on a scale unprecedented in any English newspaper office that enables the *Daily Mail* to effect a saving of from 30 to 50 per cent, and to be sold for half the price of its competitors. (4 May 1896)

Hindsight was to prove that this was not the usual first-edition self-promotion, soon to be compromised by the realities of the newspaper market. The *Daily Mail* had revolutionized the daily press in Britain and the capital intensity of its investment necessary to produce such volume at low cost was to change the structure of the popular press and dictate the contours of the popular for the rest of the next century.

Harmsworth was able to realign the popular market so as to create a popular journalism which was uninterested in political and social stories other than as a means to increase circulation, while eschewing any of the previous radical popular press's desire to provide an alternative view of the social order.

The newspaper was presented as being not cheap but a bargain well worth the small outlay. The short articles, clearly laid out, were written in order to have a breadth of appeal – a commercial as well as a textual achievement and one that became a hallmark of the construction of this type of popularity. Fashions, the personalities behind the news, in particular those of the politicians, and a more conversationally based style of news were all features of Harmsworth's appropriation of the style and content of the New Journalism. The *Daily Mail* also became the first newspaper to properly exploit the mass distribution of its product through improved rail links and trains to improve distribution in the north and the west of Britain and the exploitation of a dedicated print production plant in Manchester.

Harmsworth may not have had an interest in educating his readers other than in ways which would increase his commercial hold over them as consumers but he is rightly considered a hugely influential pedagogue of popular public taste and opinion. Spender has written of him that: '... he and his imitators influenced the common mind more than all the Education Ministers put together' (quoted in Herd, 1952: 249).

Conservative in its politics and layout with advertisements on the front page, it differed from competitors in not containing long, unbroken reports of political speeches and opinion, and was characterized by a light and lively writing style. It attempted to provide a miscellany in a newspaper to attract people from the full spectrum of society. One aspect of increasing the breadth of appeal was the increasing concentration on women as readers. This was achieved by including more material which imitated the print culture which had been demonstrably popular with women readers since the early nineteenth century – the weekly magazine. The magazine influence on the content and approach of the popular newspaper is corroborated by the fact that both Harmsworth and later the owner of the *Daily Express*, C. Arthur Pearson, were both men who had made their fortune in magazine publication and were well prepared for their launch into the popular daily market by an appreciation of popular reading tastes. The popular dailies were successful to the extent that they were able to integrate the tone and content of the magazines into their own pages, while maintaining a distinctiveness from the magazines themselves in their news coverage and political opinions. Its daily magazine which included a specific women's column soon expanded to a whole page. 'Woman's World' on Saturday 22 February, 1896 included: 'When Love Begins to Wane'; 'Sponge Cake'; 'What Do Your Eyes Say?'; 'Fortune Telling Teacups'; 'The Jewel For Each Month'; 'Your Character From Handwriting.'

Both the inclusion of increased matter directed at an idealized woman reader and the breakdown of the text to a more digestible, browsable format as time was at a premium enabled the paper to broaden the traditional market. These trends, in form and content, had first appeared in the Sundays when the majority of people had some leisure time to read and then in the daily newspaper for the commuter, and indicated the development of a layout and editorial policy better suited to the lifestyles of a new mass readership that included women.

The *Daily Mail* was a triumph in inclusive popularity. It had a cross-class appeal, attracted women readers by its increasing magazine content and specific women's pages and was determinedly lacking in anything which smacked of the sensationalist or the sordid. Yet it managed to combine, in Engel's words, 'triumphalism ... xenophobia ... and, of course, crime ... in about equal proportions' (1996: 60).

It placed itself at the centre of popular enthusiasms and events such as exhibitions, the relief of Mafeking in the Boer War of 1899–1902, flying and royal events. The Queen's Diamond Jubilee was celebrated on 23 June 1897 and was feted in no more effusively patriotic terms than in the *Daily Mail's* eulogy: 'We ought to be a proud nation today, proud of our fathers who founded this empire, proud of ourselves who have kept and increased it, proud of our sons, whom we can trust to keep what we hand down and increase it for their sons.'

Harmsworth was first to conceive the idea of a mass-circulation daily 'to bring the proud and vital spirit of empire to the breakfast tables of the queen's fiercely loyal, lower-middle-class subjects' (Hughes, 1986: 200). The commonsensical, low-key populism of the new newspaper is encapsulated in the conversational intimacy of a report on a meeting with a man recently back from the Cape province. On 21 February it ran under the following heading:

Is Kruger Toppling?
A Chat with an Englishman just returned from Johannesburg

The penetration of popular culture into the pages of the *Daily Mail* was reciprocated by its emergence in other popular forms, such as musical comedy:

I'm a lady, don't forget
All I say
Is in the Daily Mail next day.
Dances, music halls and plays,
Drawing rooms and smart soirèes.
Henley, Goodwood and Paree
Owe their great success to me.
(From Paul Rubens's musical comedy, *Floradora*, 1899; quoted in Engel, 1996: 64)

On 25 February 1896, in a long tradition of tales of execution and confession characteristic of popular print culture, we have an example of a hanging, reported and conducted with due, almost classical, deference for the order of formalities:

CHIPPERFIELD HANGED

For the Murder of his Wife in a Cab at Islington

HIS LAST MOMENTS

WILLING TO DIE

CHIPPERFIELD'S LAST LETTER

In true popular fashion the *Daily Mail* peaked in circulation when it reached almost one and a half million on 23 January 1901 after the death of Queen Victoria was announced.

The popular papers experimented with layout and typography and the use of illustration, cartoons and photography – all in a bid to widen circulation and to brighten the appeal of their paper. In terms of the writing, more emotive strategies were employed to include the reader in the story, to appeal directly to the feelings of the reader – a journalistic subjectivity, which was a feature of the New Journalism, fully found its commercial outlet in the popular newspapers of the early century.

Discussions of the role of illustration in the popular press have often been restricted to their part in educating a partially literate public and by attracting that public to a fuller participation in public affairs. These discussions often emanate from the editors and owners of the newspapers themselves, keen to stress the popular pedagogy of their commercial enterprise. In addition, illustrations also glamorize. They allow the illustration of certain genres of story to become even more romanticized or sensationalized.

The subjects of the illustrations are also interesting in the way they are integrated with the popular project. Often they are of popular characters, support celebrity gossip or represent the accused in court cases, or, in an illustration of the interweaving of popular sentiments of patriotism with the creation of a cult of heroism around imperial heroes, we have a large picture of Dr Jameson:

THE MAN OF THE MOMENT on 22 February

Following this, on we can read:

26 February

DR JIM

(popular hero of South African campaign in court) Special Descriptive Reports of the
Opening proceedings in the Great Trial
Dr Jim has sunk into the hearts of the people ...

The national narrative which was being constructed in the popular
press of the *Daily Mail* was confined to a version based on building pride
in community through the achievements and implied superiority of the
British. It was a persuasive strategy and expressed with all the rhetorical
confidence the late Victorian era could muster for the genealogy of
national greatness.

The front page of the *Daily Mail* included regular, light items such as
'GOSSIP OF THE DAY', 'OUR SHORT STORY', 'SOME INTEREST-
ING ITEMS' and 'LAST LOOK ROUND', and was traditional to the
extent that it did not focus heavily on news. The reports from the London
courts on page 3 entitled 'ON THE SEAMY SIDE' are a direct continuation of the tradition of *Cleave's* and other Sunday papers.

An interesting early indicator of the importance of directing news to
the reader as consumer as a populist strategy in its front page story on
24 February: 'COAL TRADE TRICKS: Various Little Devices Through
which the Poor Consumer Suffers.' This was an important part of incorporating the popular within the same economic orbit as the advertisers
whose interests they were encouraged to share while buying the newspaper.
The measure of a popular newspaper's commercial success would increasingly be interpreted by advertisers through its ability to match its popular
rhetoric with a sensitivity for the economic perspective of the financial
status quo.

Its version of 'SOME INTERESTING TALES' includes trivia reminiscent of the popular Newnes and earlier Harmsworth vehicles which
showed that this remained close to the heart of the curious lower-middle
class readership which the newspaper was directed at:

A FISH THAT ANGLES

HOW CHAMPAGNE BEGAN

There is, in the run-up to the outbreak of the Boer War which was to
become linked with the name of the *Daily Mail* to jingoism and the patriotic pride of the English middle classes, a telling interrelation of popular
performance and lively reporting, an intertextual miscellany. A man had
been put into a trance at the Westminster Royal Aquarium on 21 January
by a Mr Fricker. It was one of a number of highly popular public displays
of scientific and psychological innovation common to the age and was
endorsed by the coverage of popular science in the popular press. He was
due to be woken from his trance at 10.30 on the evening of 20 February
1896. Linking this event to the newspaper's perception that Chamberlain,

the Prime Minister, was 'asleep' to the possibility of a military strike by South Africa's Kruger, we can read on the front page of that day's *Daily Mail* a cartoon of Chamberlain lying in his own trance in front of an assembled cast of onlookers. The caption reads 'MR CHAMBERLAIN'S TRANCE', and continues under the line drawing: 'The Westminster Aquarium trance man wakes up tonight at 10.30; but when will the other Westminster trance man wake up to tackle Kruger?' The popular loop is reinforced the following day when the newspaper covers the story as a literal news item:

THE HYPNOTISED AWAKENED

To Find Himself the Centre of a Noisy Scene

A few days later, and this vocabulary is once again employed to draw the readers' attention back to the popular chain of signification in an article headlined:

February 24

WAKE UP, CHAMBERLAIN

The 'Standard' this Morning Urges Him to Vigorous Action

An unusually strong article appears in this morning's Standard dealing with our backdown in the Transvaal, and the buttering of Kruger generally. It concludes as follows: 'What our fellow-subjects in South Africa want to know is, to what extent, and in what manner, England intends to uphold its interests, and its dignity, in that part of the world.'

The newspaper is keen to stress the longevity of the British Empire and its claims to be a civilizing influence, as part of a strategy of praising the ordinary people who have created these traditions:

March 5

OUR BIRTHDAY

Four hundred years ago today the foundation stone of the British Empire was laid. On March 5 1496, Henry VII granted the petition of John Cabot and his three sons, of Bristol, and on the same day the Privy Seal was attached to a charter granting these four bold mariners liberty to hoist the English flag on shores hitherto unknown to Christian people, and to acquire the sovereignty of them for England ... Today that flag flutters in the eye of the sun at every hour of his endless march from day to day, and bounds have been set to the British Empire by the limitations of terrestrial space ... That England has done so well in the race for empire, and has secured the pick of colonial locations all over the world is due to the fact that we started early and worked manfully before Europe had grown too big for its peoples, and for this our race may thank the hardy pioneers whose charter we commemorate today.

This is not surprising in tone in a newspaper that in a banner headline a few days earlier had indulged in a similar semantic tradition:

March 3

OUR FLEET SHALL REPRESENT THE SELF-RELIANCE OF THE NATION

SPEED AS A RHETORICAL DEVICE

In addition to the other identifying features which, in combination, created the new popular press style, their greater capital intensification, their employment of the latest technology and their identification of a broader readership Lee has observed that the Victorians were most impressed by the sheer pace of it all (1976: 59). There was nothing quite like the popular daily newspaper for matching their perception of life as a continuous cycle of change and discovery, and of course their vicarious sense of involvement in the rapid progress or even perfection of society for this was an age deeply imbued with belief in the perfectibility of man and his cultural achievements.

Lee has pointed to the combined impact of both press and railway in the public mind: 'Perhaps only the steam railway rivalled the newspaper press in the Victorian estimation of the progress of civilisation' (1976: 21). In the *Daily Mail* we have the perfect complementarity in its distribution through this mode of transport – papers and trains, the miracles of the age. This juxtaposition enhanced the credibility of the new popular press as being genuinely informed by the enthusiasms of the people who flocked to buy the newspapers. They were authentically in tune with their era. Goodbody has gone as far as to suggest that in terms of targeting their popular readership, Harmsworth '... did not lead or follow the public mood, he accompanied it' (1985: 24).

Catherine Hughes has argued that it was this speed which began to unravel the more sedate cultural patterns, following and leading popular impulses and reactions in turn and threading new patterns around narratives of empire and the place of the people in that project as refracted in the popular press. It was this press which for the first time on a daily basis was incorporating the people as readers into the imperial project:

> The dawn of a new technological age involving more rapid transport, the telegraph, and the growth of organizations such as Reuters meant that the urbane literary style that had characterized the established news publications of a leisured age was inevitably subject to change ... the newly affluent lower middle classes ... their enthusiasm for empire and the implicit, if vicarious, sense of superiority it bestowed. (1986: 187)

The rapidity of social and technological change allowed the new popular daily newspapers to articulate the late nineteenth-century awareness of a shrinking world; shrinking because of the speed of travel and the consequent acceleration in the pace and quantity of information which enabled this world to function and develop and at the same time draw more and more participants into an awareness of this stage of globalization (Featherstone, 1993). The late Victorian era was characterized by a widespread popular grasp of this shrinking effect as people developed perspectives of the Empire as an institution that they participated in on a daily basis. The daily popular press was an important factor in this closing down of the world and in the imperialistic and nationalistic discourses in which it was conducted. Part of the appeal of the popular was being connected vicariously to this sense of global triumph. Bennett, and after him Pulitzer and Hearst, had demonstrated the popular appeal of Manifest Destiny in America and the popular commercial press of the turn of the century in Britain was to be as effective in constructing a popular imaginary of empire and the place of Britain in it.

Why though does it seem inevitable that this technological and commercial shift should necessarily be accompanied by a stylistic one, a shift from one form of popular newspaper style to another, new enough to be hailed as the 'New Journalism' on both sides of the Atlantic? This is true not only in terms of its practices but also in terms of its rhetoric about itself and the world it covered and reported. Any observation of the combination of rhetoric and technology should also stress the difference between the institutional conservatism of the press and its rhetorical and technical insistence that it is forever innovating and moving at a great speed.

THE *DAILY EXPRESS*

The *Daily Express* was started in 1900 and introduced the American novelty of news on the first page for the first time successfully in a British daily newspaper in 1901. If the great popular newspapers have always been in tune with their times, then the contribution of the *Daily Express* to that zeitgeist was in its unbounded enthusiasm and confidence. It maintained this stance through its glory years up to the Second World War.

The *Daily Express* was launched as a popular, commercial newspaper in 1900, and, to contrast with the individualistic bent of the *Daily Mail*, which appealed to the reader as individual and was increasingly a conduit for the voice of a single powerful owner, it claimed on 24 April 1900:

MATTERS OF MOMENT

Good News.

This paper is produced with the intention of supplying its readers with news.

That is the excuse for its existence. It will not be the organ of any political party, nor the instrument of any social clique. It will not provide a parade-ground for marshalling the fads of any individual ...

In the same editorial it continues by pointing to the overwhelming desire for a newspaper with entertainment as its focus to pander to the established tastes of a large commercial public.

...The daily chronicle of the world's doings must include accident and disaster, the crime that is expiated at the scaffold, the paltry misdoing that is dealt with at the police-court. But we have no scent for blood, no appetite for horrible detail. For choice, we will tell you of the comedy of life, putting its minor tragedies in the background. We will try to bring a smile to your breakfast table for every morning in the year.

As an early example of the breakfast-table smile, from the editorial page of 26 April 1900 we have:

GOOD MORNING

The new dogs' cemetery in Paris is in the Ile des Ravageurs. This is indeed giving a dog a bad name and burying him. When we in England start a dogs' cemetery we shall be more polite to our departed friends, for of course our cemetery will be opened in the Isle of Dogs.

Among its innovations, and one which supported its emphasis on being 'the chronicle of the world's doings', was the introduction of news on the front page in a break with a tradition which was as old as the newspaper in Britain.

In an era where world records acted as an index of constant human and technological progress it announced that it had achieved:

1,500,000 COPIES

World's Record By The '*Daily Express*'

The style of illustration supporting this claim matches the enthusiasm of the time for speed and distance, both affected by the new dynamism of the daily press, and is an excellent example of the popular entertainment format associated with the self-publicity of this popular journalism whose brash self-promotion was an echo of the successful exploitation of the formula in the United States:

The 'DAILY EXPRESS' yesterday broke the world's record in daily journalism. It is very gratifying to have issued more first copies than any other daily paper has done since newspapers have existed ... A gigantic idea is more easily grasped by the method of comparison.

Placed end to end, the papers comprising the first issue would cover the enormous distance of 1,704 miles, or about ten times the distance between London and Manchester. To travel along this 'Express' road at express speed would take about 43 hours or nearly two days and nights.

From the courts we have reports laced with all the melodramatic tradition of the genre:

Friday May 18 1900

TERRIBLE STORY

WIFE GUARDS HUSBAND IN HIS SUICIDAL AGONY

SHAME AND DEATH

A remarkable story of man's wrong-doing and his wife's Spartan devotion in holding the door against the police while he saved himself by suicide was told at an Edmonton inquest yesterday ...

From within came sounds as of a man in fearful agony, groans, shrieks, and the rattling of his heels against the door in the torture of death ...

Turning defiantly on the detective ... the widow said: – 'my Tom, you are safe from your enemies now.'

From the start there were magazine-style features about exotic places overseas, often tinged with a vicarious frisson of danger and even a cultural voyeurism. On the 26 April editorial page a series continues on Haiti:

WHERE BLACK

RULES WHITE

A Visit to the Almost Unknown Republic of Hayti

III VAUDOUX WORSHIP AND HUMAN SACRIFICE

These sensational reports continued in the hybrid tradition of Knightley's sensational-educational pieces from the early nineteenth century which attempted to draw a popular audience to more uplifting reading matter than radical pamphlets. Now they were bolstered by a more confident, effusive patriotism and pride in empire.

This sensationalism was used to contextualize contemporary events. The synthesis of daily news and the exoticism of far-flung places were woven into a vicarious experience of the supremacy of the British and the relative savagery of those the British came across on their travels. The Boxer Rebellion was reported in this popular miscellany form:

Boxer rebellion June 21

HOW THEY PUNISH THE BOXERS IN CHINA

... Ling-Chee, for example, the way capital convicts are executed in China need only to have been suggested to have caused the Boxer to hesitate and think twice before entering upon his present wild frolic ... Execution is a fine art in China. First, the criminal is

BOUND TO A CROSS

and, as the wretch with bulging eyeballs looks upon the scene with horror, the gentlemen upon whom devolves the principal work advances with drawn sword. Possibly the offence was a light one, or it may be that the wretch has obtained partial remission, in which case he will have the felicity of being killed with eight strokes instead of twenty-four – or possibly seventy-two. At the first stroke, the executioner nimbly whisks off one of the eyebrows – so neatly as to scarcely draw blood. Hey, Presto! off comes the other ... After that all that remains is to decapitate the lifeless and maybe still quivering body, and the execution is complete.

Foreignness is an excellent complement to the sensationalist and entertainment news agenda. It creates the Otherness required for one aspect of news value and it binds the popular audience within a broader discourse of popular entertainment into the representation of the Boxer Rebellion in other parts of the news and editorial opinion. It also has illustrations that further compound the connections to the educational project of the popular newspaper as part of the Empire. They seem to confirm the intrinsic superiority and civilized status of the British in much the same way as the Cuban atrocity stories aimed to persuade an American popular readership of their own value.

So much for the sensationalist and entertainment features of this new popular press. But what had become of the people, the ordinary workers, their culture and their political interests? The framing of labour disputes takes place in a less than positive light and in the context of the Boer War we have a clear indication that the strikers are malevolently anti-patriotic, built up in a variety of editorial strategies:

June 13

DOCKERS DEMANDS

EQUALITY AND AN EXTRA PENNY PER HOUR

'But why strike now?' Mr Ben Tillet's assistant was asked.
'Because we have a fair excuse and the time is opportune,' was the frank reply. 'Labour is scarce, and the freights are high. We think the dock labourer ought to share in the general riverside prosperity.'

This approach is reinforced by a confessional, subjectively styled feature based on an interview that exposes the alleged real-life experiences of a former docker.

June 18

THE DOCKER

A FEW FACTS ABOUT HIM BY AN EX-DOCKER

One must work, eat, drink, and sleep with a dock labourer many months before one can understand the man and his devious ways...
Ninety per cent of the genus docker are the merest dregs of bibulous humanity, who, when not working in the docks, spend their time in loafing around the street corners and public houses. These are hard words, but, unfortunately, absolutely correct ... Give the average dock labourer the chance of a permanent position at £1 per week, and the chances are ten to one that he does not avail himself of the opportunity to shake himself clear of the docks ... Candidly, the docker does not like to work.

The *Daily Express* is keen to be seen as belonging to the company of the established American popular newspapers of the day as champions of the people, and reports with satisfaction the victory of the *Journal* over a large corporation:

June 22 1900

A NEWSPAPER DAVID

HOW AN ICE-TRUST GOLIATH WAS SLAIN

The power of a great newspaper as a champion of the people has never been more significantly illustrated than in the crushing defeat of the Ice Trust in New York by the 'Journal', which is owned and edited by Mr W.R. Hearst, an absolutely fearless young man, who has all the power of practically unlimited wealth unhampered by any selfish consideration of class.
   In this fight, as in many others, Mr Hearst sought to secure the greatest good of the greatest number...
   The panting folk sleep on the roofs, on fire escapes in the streets – anywhere to get air. Ice is a necessity and as grateful to them as the oasis to a desert traveller.

As we have seen, the late Victorian epoch's was a popular press that wanted to deflect attention from the legitimacy of working people to organize their own agenda. Concentrating on the achievements of the owners of the papers that sought to articulate the views of the people was to become an integral part of this strategy. Its rhetoric was paternalist and consumerist.

CONCLUDING DEBATE

Debates around the impact of the Foster Education Acts of 1870–1 (Vincent, 1989: 1993) indicate that there had been readers able and willing to spend a part of their income on published material for decades. They were not new readers – they were a new readership for a new sort of popular publication. The break from the New Journalism into the first mass daily newspapers in Britain was above all else a commercial triumph, yet it depended on the particular cultural and generic mix of the newspapers than simply an appreciation of the economics of mass markets. This combination of industrial and cultural forces in the form of the popular press was to trigger the first signs of mass culture.

The evaluation of the popular press of the nineteenth century in Britain needs to address three main issues. First, it had shifted from a radical and a people's culture to a cultural expression whose parameters were set by increasingly market-orientated interests. Second, despite its more commercialized tone, it had been able to retain an ability to address the ordinary people in terms that highlighted subjectivity, entertainment and broad traditions of popular miscellany. The production of these new popular newspapers was slicker, their layout made them more accessible, their distribution more regular and they were more atuned to the needs of their advertisers, but in all their novelty they still traded upon the longer traditions of popular print culture which had already proved their commercial viability. Third, they managed to incorporate the people, their political aspirations and their cultural traditions but in a different way to the earlier radical press. They chose a more effective, dialogic method, articulated in terms of reinforcing the political-economic interests of their owners within a set of formulae able to appeal to broad sections of the population. Increasingly this readership was appellated in terms of its commercial potential and its aspirations to middle-class values.

6

THE NEW JOURNALISM: THE
LONG VERSION

PERFECTING A PATTERN

This chapter will propose that the developments of the 1930s can be categorized as part of the continuum that was the New Journalism. The 1930s was the defining decade for the direction of popular daily newspapers in Britain. It was the period of greatest expansion in terms of sales and readers and of the commercialization of the popular newspaper markets. All the daily popular newspapers of the 1930s became enmeshed in the intensifying quest for circulation and depended on an expanding popular miscellany for it. Sensationalism, offers, campaigns, layout and aspects of writing style all followed the American pattern. These developments took place, as in the United States, in a celebratory process of modernizing. This pattern was not all one-way traffic however. The popular daily press of this period also successfully assimilated two traditional English newspaper formats – the illustrated newspaper and the popular Sunday paper (Williams, 1961: 231).

The story of the popular newspaper in Britain in the period up to the outbreak of the Second World War is a fascinating manifestation of the way in which a popular rhetoric developed through the competing efforts of four daily newspapers to attract and keep an increasing share of readers and to inspire them with their particular version of popular reality.

Circulation had become the key to popularity in the wake of the Northcliffe revolution and in the image of the American model of the popular press. There was no longer any public demand for a daily newspaper which was not well and truly enmeshed with the commercial status quo. The interests of the working people were assumed by the proprietors and the journalists to be aspirational to middle-class values and incorporated into the commercialized world of the popular press. Gimmicks and offers became essential to maintaining those indices of popularity. Offers of free insurance to regular subscribers from 1914 had become increasingly a prerequisite for any newspaper that wanted to remain a viable popular proposition. This trend extended through the 1920s, and then came free gifts, culminating in free collected works of Charles Dickens and entire encyclopaedias.

Popular newspapers increasingly included other popular cultural content, and in doing so became a significant part of broader popular culture. This included popular literature, popular educational aspirations, quizzes, competitions and prizes for readers, as well as reviews of the increasingly popular new media of cinema and radio. As popular culture became increasingly commercialized and the lives of the people themselves increasingly penetrated by commercial concerns, so too the popular newspapers played a more significant role in acting as cultural go-betweens. An example of the way in which the newspapers built up their popular credibility comes in newspaper sponsorship of popular summer holiday events:

25,000 PEOPLE SING

(from Southend-on-Sea) August 7 1933:
People love to sing, and the way the audience entered into the community spirit at the Cliff Bandstand here last night paid a remarkable tribute to the popularity of the 'Daily Express' outdoor concerts.

THE *DAILY EXPRESS* – LAYING OUT THE POPULAR

The summer of 1933 marked a significant breakthrough in popular newspapers in Britain with Christiansen's revolutionary matching of layout to the broader popular agenda in the *Daily Express*. He produced a paper with cleaner print, better spacing, more and bigger headlines and cross-headings to break up the page into more accessible sections. This was the turning point – accessibility. The new typography and layout constituted as important a part of popular rhetoric as the content of the newspaper or the language in which it was couched.

Christiansen also introduced two characters who were to epitomize the idealized reader of his paper – The Man on the Rhyl Promenade and The People in the Backstreets of Derby, a less class-conscious version of O'Connor's charwoman, seamstress and labourer – to be echoed in a later era with The Man in a White Van of the contemporary *Sun*. These everymen and everywomen were the carriers of populist sentiment. From a national perspective it was also significant that they were located far from the metropolitan heartlands of the proprietor or his journalists.

On August 7 the new layout was heralded in these terms in the paper:

A Triumph Of Type
The New 'Daily Express'
TODAY a new 'Daily Express' greets you
A better-than-ever 'Daily Express'
Of course, it is the same 'Daily Express' in
spirit, in outlook and in effort

But it comes out today in new and modern
'dress'.
All the type throughout the paper has been
changed (except headlines).
The new type introduced today is the last
word in the typographer's art.
You will agree it is clear and concise and,
above all, easy to read.
You will also agree it ideally expresses the
motive force of the 'Daily Express,' the newspaper with the world's record net sale of
2,054,348 copies a day. – August 7

There are forms encouraging new subscribers to take out the newspaper's insurance scheme. The *Daily Express* also puffs the scheme and ties it in with the holiday season:

Sign To-day And You Will Have A Care-free Holiday

August 7

The *Daily Express* was also involved in astutely targeted self-promotional campaigns. One is reminded of Cudlipp's (1953: 225) comment on the efficacy of campaigning journalism in appropriate seasons in the following:

'DROWNED' BOY RESTORED

'DAILY EXPRESS' LIFEGUARD RESCUE

... This example is quoted to show the timeliness of the 'Daily Express' campaign for volunteer lifeguards.

All along the coast the 'Daily Express' campaign has crystallised opinion on the need for every bathing resort to have a marked enclosure set aside from bathing where there is no actual bathing pond....

Competition between lifeguards to be included among candidates for the 'Daily Express' V.C. is very keen....

Details of any rescue should be ... marked 'Daily Express' Award for Heroism. – August 8

Direct feedback from its readers was woven into a further explanation of the perceived benefits of the new layout in its entirety, including the following which seems to combine popular education in the advantages of the new typography together with an academic endorsement:

Thank You! Readers Hail 'Daily Express' New Type

CONGRATULATIONS!

That was the message that reached the
'Daily Express' by telephone yesterday from
countless readers.
They were enthusiastic over the new and
modern type in which the whole of the paper

(except headlines) is printed.
Clear, concise, tasteful – and especially easy
to read. Those were the virtues with which
readers credited our new type.
One of the warmest and most discerning
tributes was paid by Dr. A. Compton-Rickett,
the University of London lecturer in English
literature and history, who from his studies and
research has a wide knowledge of English type-
faces. 'It's a wonderful improvement,' he said.
The new type is extraordinarily clear.
'I usually read my "Daily Express" in bed
every morning. Reading in bed, with its accompanying risk of eye-strain, is a real test of type.'
'But this morning, as my eyes flitted over
the columns of the "Daily Express," and I noted
the change in the type, I felt really pleased at its
clearness. The improvement has certainly been
justified.' – August 8

There is much to appeal directly to an idealized woman reader. This
includes articles of a directly educational nature, teaching women who
were becoming increasingly aware of the commodification of beauty and
clothes:

What Every Woman Wants to Know
HANDS, ARMS and ELBOWS can be BEAUTIFUL – says Jean Cleland – August 23

One of its daily cartoon strips is 'OFFICE HOURS', with clerical
characters including the much put-upon Herbert who acts as a comical
figure of identification for the readers, many of whom would have been in
similar working situations if they were indeed fortunate enough to have
kept their job during this era of high unemployment. His catchphrase
at the end of one strip sums up another aspect of the buoyant outlook of
the *Daily Express*: 'I'd rather be a miserable millionaire than a miserable
office boy.'

The catalogue of popular disaster and crime which had remained a
staple of popular print culture is well represented here but in a much more
attractive layout, inviting the eye to peruse the headlines and catch more of
the story at a glance.

HUSBAND FINDS WIFE STRANGLED

Girl 'Duellist' On Stiletto Death
BOY SHOWN TRICK OF STABBING
SHE OFFERS HER BLOOD FOR HIM – TOO LATE – August 22

Falling Bough Kills Two Sisters
TREE THAT LOOKED HEALTHY

KILLED BY LEAPFROG
TRAGEDY AT A FAMILY PARTY
August 11

Unemployment makes its way into the paper on August 22. The front page announces that this will be a series of articles looking at the issue from the inside.

What Do The Unemployed Think? – 1
A WORKLESS MAN LAYS BARE HIS SOUL

This is a sentimental account relying on the New Journalism's subjective interview techniques to bring the issue of unemployment to the fore in a moving way. It steers clear of radical solutions and displays in the person of the unemployed man a scepticism of those in power. Ultimately it is a philanthropic and rather defeatist attitude which lingers in the mind. The issue is raised but the causes of mass unemployment and the political solutions to the problem take second place to the rather maudlin, sensationalized representation of the 'workless man'.

This version of popular print culture was able to fashion an escapist version of reality to counter much of the gloom of the period. At the same time as mass unemployment, the *Daily Express* was relying on coverage of the glamour and sensation of high society. William Hickey is already writing his celebrity and showbusiness gossip column: **'These Names Make NEWS'.**

The improved deployment of photographs meant that there were pictures adorning all main front-page news stories, including on 11 August:

Life Drama of Drugged Hungarian Beauty
ROMANCE THAT DIED AT 28
THE FOUR LAST DAYS OF LUCY DE POLNAY
RICHES AND RUIN

There is also a fairly routine smattering of stories with a didactic tone that might have come from some of the educational pamphlets of the early nineteenth century. One in particular seems to summarize popular misgivings about the perceived loosening of moral norms during the years of depression:

CHEAP KISSES Make OLD MAIDS
Why Thousands of Girls Will Never Be Wives – August 11

The *Daily Express* was rapidly becoming the perfect vehicle for portraying the news of the day and a great deal else besides in a language and format accessible to the common reader. The world of the economic depression in Europe was not closely scrutinized. The gaze of the reader was distracted elsewhere into the miscellany of popular escapism. The status quo was fine by the *Daily Express* and its readers enjoyed the escapist aspect to its presentation of the world and appeared to go along with the notion that the world was in the safe hands of trusted politicians and businessmen. It also had little truck with radical solutions and presented the ordinary reader with a trusting view of the aspirations of the common people.

DAILY MAIL AUGUST 1933 – RESPONDING TO COMPETITION

The *Daily Mail* did not want to be left out in the race to improve its visual attractiveness to the expanding reading public. It too considered that the new potential of typographic developments and illustration needed to be harnessed to the continuing tradition of the newspaper's appeal. Its revitalized new look was trumpeted in terms which make clear the evolving rhetoric of the paper:

'EXCELSIOR'

'Daily Mail'

New Type on Monday

... The object is to render its columns not only more attractive in appearance but also more easily readable.

In the modern world the first aim of salesmanship is to make an article both the best procurable and highly attractive to the eye.

This result the *Daily Mail* will achieve by its new type, which will enable the eye to assimilate the news without strain and the mind to appreciate it without conscious effort.

In less time and with less effort the reader becomes 'well informed'...

This new type has been named 'EXCELSIOR,' and it will bring much nearer the realisation of the old saying that 'he who runs may read.' – August 5

The relationship between the popular press and its commercial ambitions is made abundantly clear here with the explicit mention of 'salesmanship'. The salvo also makes plain the desirability for popular papers to become an automatic accessory of everybody's daily life and points out how an easier typeface and layout will facilitate this. In another celebratory passage on the success of the new type launch, it echoes the aspirational objectives of the paper first launched by Harmsworth in 1896 in its stress on the well-informed reader:

Every well-informed man and woman in Great Britain today reads the 'Daily Mail.' He or she has to 'make time' if necessary to do so – August 7.

There were many aspects of the paper which, despite its new livery, were rooted in its traditional set of values and the characteristic tone of appeal to its particular mass readership. Its slogan is still 'For King and Empire', betraying its profoundly loyalist and imperial perspectives. The paper still promotes itself as the 'world's greatest advertising medium' and, as if to reinforce that claim, still contains predominantly advertising on its first page. The sections 'Looking at Life' and 'Court and Society' are aspirational in tone. In addition we have a familiar example of the pseudo-science the paper had done much to popularize with a mass daily audience, which on 22 August on page 7 the spread headline appeared:

DOCTORS WILL NOT BLAME THE MOON FOR SLEEPLESSNESS

Despite its more reserved tone, the *Daily Mail* had become as adept as its rivals in linking itself with contemporary developments in other areas of commercial popular culture. One example is the combination of Hollywood stardom and the craze of the decade, cycling, combined in the picture and interview with Mary Pickford on 16 August.

We might also compare stories such as these, which on a daily basis acted as a bridge between the glamorous world of the stars and the more routine desires of the ordinary reader for an escapist popular fantasy:

MISS SYLVIA SIDNEY INDIGNANT
TREATED LIKE A NOBODY – August 5

£28,800 FOR GRACIE FIELDS
BIGGEST BRITISH FILM SALARY – August 2

Miss Fanny Holtzmann
WOMAN WHO UNRAVELS HOLLYWOOD TANGLES
WHY MARRIAGES FAIL – August 2

In stark contrast to the coverage and gossip of the lives of the economically privileged, the struggles of the working classes to improve their condition or even to retain an element of dignity in the dark years of the Depression get short shrift. The main headline is still demoted to the inside pages of the paper as an adjunct to the important business of advertising and its approach to strikers is politically distinctive from coverage in the pro-union *Daily Herald*:

MINERS NOT TO GET STRIKE PAY

REDS STIR UP TROUBLE

... It is significant that Russia is a strong competitor with South Wales for our anthracite trade with Canada, and evidence has been given to me by the moderates among the men's leaders that Bolshevist agitators have recently been busy fanning small, local difficulties into the semblance of a major issue. – August 16

As a further contrast to the *Daily Herald*, for instance, which celebrated the victories and struggles of the ordinary working men and women both nationally and abroad, the heroes here are the Territorial Army:

True patriots

Hats off to the thousands of men in the Territorial Army who are now in camp for their annual training! We owe them a great debt of gratitude for their splendid services.

They are sacrificing their leisure and their holiday to a national duty, for the performance of which they receive small thanks from the State. – Editorial August 8

In the competitive environment of the free works of, Dickens, the *Daily Mail* was at pains to indicate the links between its readers and its own continuing promotion of self-education, as an individualist pursuit in line with the newspaper's belief in the role of self-improvement in social progress.

DICKENS HIS INSPIRATION

84-YEARS OLD MAN'S 'DAILY MAIL' BOOKS

As a child he claims:
'... How much they improved my limited education is beyond belief.' – August 2

Its appeal to women was as strong as before and was based on the successful and popular formula of questions and answers on dress, cookery, children and the nursery, beauty and housewifery in a daily feature entitled "*Daily Mail*" Women's Bureau'.

On 1 August it indicated the response to its latest offer of discounted dictionaries for regular subscribers as supportive of its own, continuing claims to popularity:

HUGE RESPONSE TO DICTIONARY OFFER

The Daily Mail's special offer of Nuttalls Standard Dictionary on remarkably generous terms has indeed proved popular.

Thousands upon thousands of applications have been received, and numberless have written voicing their appreciation of the splendid presentation copy.

THE RELAUNCH OF THE *DAILY HERALD* – A DIFFERENT APPROACH TO A POPULAR PRESS

The developments in the *Daily Express* and *Daily Mail* through the 1920s and 1930s were straightforward enough. Their proprietors saw the goal of popular daily newspapers to be first and foremost a commercial proposition, appealing to advertisers to use them to their advantage and using all means to maximize circulation by every trick and gimmick of typography and skilfully targeted writing. To this extent, they never contained any of the tradition of the older popular press which had attempted to propose radical solutions to political and economic problems that contradicted the prevailing economic order and that attempted to fashion a voice for the working people themselves. It is this lack in the early years of the twentieth century which makes the attempts of the *Daily Herald* to forge a compromise between commercial viability and political radicalism all the more noteworthy.

The big newspaper wars in Britain in the 1930s were precipitated by the entry into the commercial battle of the relaunched *Daily Herald*, with a provocative blend of trade union politics and commercial acumen. J.S. Elias, already a successful publisher and printer, ran the commercial side and the TUC was free to include what political emphasis and content was deemed not to be too detrimental to the profits. The *Daily Herald* had started as a strike sheet founded by print workers in 1911 and had been turned into a daily newspaper supporting the position of the trade unions in 1912 by George Lansbury and Ben Tillett. The paper was relaunched on 17 March 1930 and its circulation grew almost immediately from a quarter of a million to a million, beginning to rival the big two, the *Daily Express* and the *Daily Mail*. The circulation spiralled upwards, with the *Daily Herald* reaching two million before the *Daily Express*. Its main attraction for many from a commercial perspective was the provision of a new and comprehensive insurance scheme.

The paper included a competitive range of financial inducements to subscribe to the paper including ones which indicate in their integration into other advertising ventures how well the newspaper was received in the widest commercial circles; for instance a whole-page £1,000 prize competition for Blueband and Pheasant margarine on 18 March 1930.

Reporting its own success in its initial offer for a renewed and extensive version of insurance for subscribers, it writes:

RUSH TO REGISTER FOR £10,000 INSURANCE

DAILY HERALD SCHEME WITH BENEFITS FOR ALL – 18 March 1930

Boots the chemist sold its own brand name to conform with the ideology of the paper as part of a series of 'Milestones in the History of the People' (17 March 1933).

Some of the circulation boosters went beyond a simple call to the avarice of the readership and included strategies that saw the proceeds of recruiting more readers split between the individual canvasser and the Labour Party.

The new version of the newspaper contained explicit calls to the tradition of Labour and trade union politics in the press and attempts to forge a solidarity with its readers based on its adherence to that tradition:

FORWARD!

Today the 'Daily Herald' appears in a new suit. The spirit and purpose behind it remain unchanged.

For years we have been the official exponent of the views of the great British Labour and Trade Union Movement. That high position we are proud to hold today ...

A Wide Field

To give the news is a paper's prime function. But that is not all. We shall publish authoritative articles on politics and economics on literature, on science, on the arts.

Humour and brightness will not be missing from our pages. The world is our province – and the world is not always severe and serious ...

We say to our readers old and new. Here is *your* newspaper. Much has been done in the past. A great deal lies ahead. Let us march. – 17 March 1930

In support of its claims it provided evidence in the form of key articles from eminent left-wing political figures of the time to bolster its credibility and authenticity.

PREMIER WELCOMES THE NEW 'HERALD'
Great Day in History of Labour
FORWARD! (Ramsay MacDonald) 17 March 1933

WHAT MARCH 17 MEANS TO LABOUR
By WALTER M. CITRINE
(General Secretary of the T.U.C.)
... Your Own Paper

By means of the 'Daily Herald' news of interest to all trade unionists can be circulated throughout the land, and those who read it can be sure that the information is genuine and reliable – not distorted or twisted to suit the politics or interests of some capitalistic journal ... We are confident that the workers will give wholehearted support to this their own paper. – 14 March 1930

Yet it still claimed a cross-class, non-partisan popular appeal:

'HERALD' NOW IN THE FRONT RANK

All Classes' Demand For The New National Daily – 18 March 1930

Its political message was often uncompromising and written from such a clear socialist perspective of political involvement that it constituted a radically different choice to either of the daily popular competitors:

DISCIPLINE

We print today a letter from Mr Josiah Wedgewood, M.P. on the burning issue of discipline in the Parliamentary Labour Party. But we find it somewhat hard to discover what it is that he recommends.

What are the limits of individual liberty within an organised Party whose very existence depends on loyalty and discipline?

This is no abstract question, no plaything for theorists. It is vital and urgent, primary and ultimate.

On the answer to it depends the survival of the Labour Government and that whole complex of social progress for which the government stands. – 25 March 1930

Its great skill included being able to take features which had become popularized in the daily press of the early century and give them a slant which tilted them more towards a politically engaged viewpoint. This includes the use of medical opinion on the condition of factory workers in an opinion column which calls on the expert opinion of Dr Marion Phillips:

TALKING IT OVER

Where the Sun is Shut Out!
Factory Workers Who Miss Tonic of Spring
23 March 1930

There was a blend of trade unionism and the traditional fare of popular papers of their time even in its selection of London beauties to fill a column as a glamour feature. Those selected came from the offices and buses of the capital and were identified as the workers that they were. There was no false coyness about their place in the capital's economy.

LONDON'S PRETTIEST WOMEN

WORKING GIRLS AS BEAUTIES – 25 March 1930

After its relaunch the new paper was able to call upon support from a range of sources. Sir Charles Hingham, a leading authority on advertising, was quoted as being extremely impressed by the commercial promise of the new venture:

AMAZED BY SUCCESS OF PAPER'S FINE POPULAR APPEAL – 25 March 1930

As if to underline the efficacy of its commercial operation, the *Daily Herald* contained confident guarantees of the quality of goods advertised in the paper:

GET VALUE FOR MONEY

BUY OUR ADVERTISERS' GOODS – AND YOU WILL

... All goods advertised in the 'Daily Herald' represent honest value at an honest price.

We are absolutely steadfast in refusing an advertisement until we are satisfied that the article is genuine and that its price is equitable. 25 March 1930

The stress of many of the rags-to-riches stories was on the ordinariness of the recipients of good fortune and, sometimes, more interestingly, in a departure from the melodramatic interventions of fate, these stories contained potential for individuals to improve their lot through hard work in a meritocratic society:

PROMOTION FROM THE LOWER DECK

REAL CHANCES FOR EVERY BOY

How to open still wider the road to promotion for all classes in the Navy is to be examined by the Admiralty. – 24 March 1930

There remained also an element of the sensationalist exotica of the day on offer in its rivals:

The Truth Behind the Dope Peril By G.W.L. Day

WORLD-WIDE DRUG SYNDICATES

POISON FLOOD – 18 March 1930

It contained the popular appeal to women readers to be found in all popular newspapers of the era, with features which ranged from the household economy to the latest fashions in an identical manner to the other major popular papers:

At Last

A PERFECT KITCHEN

by Muriel Harris – 18 March 1930

My Wisest ECONOMY

When Penny Wise Is Pound Foolish

I think my own wisest economy is in dressing well...

Employers notice me, underlings respect me, and nobody expects that I shall work for a low salary. – 18 March 1930

Easter Time is Wedding Time

Dress Ideas for a Bridesmaid – 18 March 1930

As part of a wider commitment to explorations of alternatives to military confrontation, the paper manages to merge a socialist policy of international co-operation with the popular and famous author H.G. Wells in a series of articles which proved a veritable coup of political populism: 'The ABC of World Peace' (17 March 1930).

Daily Mirror
THUR
JULY 5
1945

FORWARD WITH THE PEOPLE
No. 12,960   ONE PENNY
Registered at G.P.O. as a Newspaper.

Vote for them

WE reproduce on this page Zec's famous VE-Day cartoon. We do so because it expresses more poignantly than words could do the issues which face the people of this country today.

As you, the electors, with whom the destiny of the nation rests, go to the poll, there will be a gap in your ranks. The men who fought and died that their homeland and yours might live will not be there. You must vote for THEM. Others, happily spared, are unable for various reasons to have their rightful say in this election. You must represent them.

Vote on behalf of the men who won the victory for you. You failed to do so in 1918. The result is known to all. The land "fit for heroes" did not come into existence. The dole did. Short-lived prosperity gave way to long, tragic years of poverty and unemployment. Make sure that history does not repeat itself. Your vote gives you the power. Use it. Let no one turn your gaze to the past. March forward to new and happier times. The call of the men who have gone comes to you. Pay heed to it. Vote for THEM.

Remember the issues. They are national not personal. Your own interest, the future of your children, the welfare of the whole country demand that today you do your duty and

"Here you are—don't lose it again!"

Daily Mirror, 1945 – Forward with the people – popular slogan and layout

RESPONDING TO THE POPULAR COMPETITIVE ENVIRONMENT

The *Daily Herald* of this era continued with its front-page news and its blend of trade union orientated news and impressive commercial panache. The issues of the day in the run-up to the decisive revamp of the *Daily Express* in August 1933 were unemployment, union news from abroad (especially from the United States), labour disputes at home, corrupt practices among landlords and the Irish situation. Inside, political stories carried more weight than showbusiness gossip but there were still many elements to make it a properly miscellaneous popular paper. The City Editor is very informed on the financial pages, as was Bennett with his *Herald* in the United States.

A selection of front-page headlines indicate a distinctive set of news values even at this time of intensifying competition with the *Daily Express* and *Daily Mail*:

THE TRUTH BEHIND THE DEARER BACON PRICES SCANDAL
FOREIGN EXPORTERS POCKET £5,000,000 – August 23

MINERS SHOT FOR THE ROOSEVELT CODE
Men Strike to Assert Their Right To Organise
WOMEN GASSED AND MAN KILLED
OWNERS' GANGS FIRE ON STRIKERS – August 2

US Steel Kings Beaten by a Woman
YOUR WAGE CODE NOT GOOD ENOUGH – August 1

On 4 August they give prominence to a strike among London taxi drivers and print their strike statement.

Yet the *Daily Herald* was also able to reconcile this political content with other features of the commercial popular culture, which was to a large extent driving the newspaper wars:

HOLIDAYS, MUSIC AND £5,000 GO TOGETHER
Holidays and music go together. The 'Daily Herald's £5,000 Free Holiday Music Contest is proving that music is ensuring holiday happiness. – August 3 1933

There is also a chance to share in a £250 prize for holiday snaps in the midst of the hottest holiday season for 33 years.

The subsidized distribution of encyclopaedias was covered as a story in itself and the paper used the familiar device of a credit for the paper from selected recipients:

ENCYCLOPEDIA A 'MIRACLE'
READERS DELIGHTED BY FIRST THREE VOLUMES
As deliveries of the first three volumes of the "Daily Herald" Encyclopedia proceed, praises pour in by every post from readers congratulating themselves on having secured this miracle of modern publishing.

The following are typical of one morning's postbag:–
'I am very pleased with the three volumes. They are beautifully bound. Their structure is the very best I have seen in modern Encyclopedias, and I am looking forward to the completion of my library.' – E.J.B., Chingford

However, in contrast to its competitors, the postbag was also used to make more politicized points and maintain a connection with its ambitions to political radicalism:

This Morning's Postbag
After reading Ronald Martineau's Dixon's article on Wilberforce and the abolition of negro slavery, I thought of a waitress who works 70 hours a week for 16s., a coffee stall assistant who works 85 hours for 25s. a week, and a lorry driver – a married man with two children – who was offered 35s. a week.

The enslavement of our own people still remains.

Let us then, as Wilberforce did, 'persist and keep on persisting,' until we have rid ourselves of these scandals in our midst.

E.H. Maltby

South Harrow, Middlesex – August 1

The trade union element within the content of the paper is never more apparent than in this direct address from one of the paper's founding fathers:

George Lansbury's CALL

Come On, YOUNG MAN

We know that once you, the youth of the country, make up your minds you will transform the chaotic muddle that competitive commercialisation has created into the harmony of co-operation ...

We want you to work now with those who are your elders, to join our Labour Party; to learn all you can and to teach...

So we want you as a comrade in the Labour League of Youth to join up with the local Labour party. We want you as an active colleague. – August 1

THE *DAILY MIRROR* TO 1945 – A NEW POPULAR PARADIGM

The *Daily Express* had a strong cross-class appeal and like the *Daily Mail* this had always been predicated on a middle-brow sensibility to which it was assumed the working classes aspired. The *Daily Mirror* changed this in two ways as it emerged from the Second World War. First, it aimed at providing a plebeian-popular identity for its readership and, second, it allied that particular appeal to support for a specific political party – the Labour Party. The *Daily Mirror* of the war and immediate post-war period was the break into a new paradigm: a daily popular newspaper that articulated the views and aspirations of the working classes and perfected a vernacular style which transmitted that solidarity. The popular newspaper had come home to the people even if it was in an intensely commercialized form.

The *Daily Mirror* had early success as the *Daily Illustrated Mirror* from the early century and had peaked at a circulation of about 800,000 shortly before the First World War. However the challenge was to go beyond its picture-paper status, which was a restriction on its circulation in competition with other popular dailies that were also providing a news service to their readers and thereby a greater range of content that has always been a seller in terms of the popular press.

This success had depended largely on its reliance on illustration and, in particular, photography and was based on an awareness of a continuing popular tradition of poor people decorating their homes with cheap prints. This is indicated in the text accompanying the front-page photograph of the dead King Edward VII on 16 May 1910: 'This last aspect of the earthly tabernacle and soul of the great King, bound to all British hearts by so many ties of duty and affection, will be cherished as a sacred relic in many British homes.'

The *Daily Mirror* was the first of the daily popular papers to experiment with the American-inspired comic strip. It produced its first aimed at younger readers in 1904 with Pip, Squeak and Bubble. It continued to lead the way in this area and developed comic strips to appeal to wider sections of its readership, often with an American popular cultural appeal, such as Mutt and Jeff from 1923.

Its great success was to start with the appointment of Bartholomew as its editorial director in 1934. Bartholomew introduced the heavy black type which was to distinguish the *Mirror* from all its competitors from his first year in charge. The tabloid revolution of 1935–7 had begun but it still needed to find an authentic voice to match its bold appearance. From 1935 Bartholomew brought an awareness of developments in the US tabloid market, particularly New York's *Daily News*. He provided an American formula skilfully adapted to a British cultural context. Dorothy Dix's advice column to women readers was, for instance, syndicated from America. Engel has described its new-found appeal under his stewardship in the following terms: 'In the fuggy atmosphere of a bare-floored pre-war pub, the *Mirror* was the intelligent chap leaning on the counter of the bar: not lah-di-dah or anything – he liked a laugh, and he definitely had an eye for the girls – but talking a lot of common sense' (Engel, 1996: 161).

Key to its development of a demotic printed speech were the columns of Cassandra (Bill Connor). This vernacular had an abrasive, populist political edge which railed against unemployment and appeasement and the complacency of the ruling classes in a language able to provoke debate and stir up passions. The tabloid headline which Christiansen had done much to create in the broadsheet *Daily Express* was to be developed by this language into a weapon of both popular indignation and sensation. The key was its ability to draw the ordinary reader into its project in their language.

The ear for common speech was extended even into the lines of the strip-cartoon characters. Hugh Cudlipp (1953) writes of the concern for accuracy in the work of Jack Monk, who drew the Buck Ryan column. The attention to authentic colloquialisms and low-life slang made the column a microcosm of the broader aims of the newspaper to produce a living representation of the world inhabited by its readers.

It was unashamedly sensationalist and it developed its illustrated range into glamour photography. It pandered to readers' prurience in its 'Pledge of Secrecy' stories. The agony aunt Dorothy Dix was an American and brought her brand of popular psychology to her readership. The question and answer format had long been a part of popular newspapers' appeal and was developed here in breaking middle-class taboos. The paper appealed to the young and in particular it appealed to women. Of particular note is Eileen Ashcroft's 'Charm School' which attracted 60,000 letters in six weeks according to Cudlipp (1953: 85).

Its use of headlines encapsulated much of the change of appeal in the newspaper. Headlines of the 1930s which Cudlipp himself recalls penning include these which were characteristic of the radical new edge to the tabloid journalism of the *Daily Mirror* in the 1930s:

I AM THE WOMAN YOU PITY

POISON-PEN FRIEND'S
ASTONISHING CONFESSION:
I SMASHED A GOOD WOMAN'S LIFE FOR GOOD (Cudlipp, 1953: 83)

MATCH MAKING MAMMIES
SHOO SPINSTER LOVELIES TO GIBRALTAR
TO GRAB A JACK TAR HUBBY

REVELLER VANISHES FOR DAYS –
COMES BACK AS POP-EYED DRAGON
SHOUTING 'WHOOPEE! WHAT A NIGHT!'

BOSSY WIFE GETS HUSBAND'S GOAT –
HE WANTS A VAMP AT 40 (Cudlipp, 1953: 80)

The Crucible of War

It was during the Second World War that the *Daily Mirror* was to transcend the commercialized limitations of a popular newspaper of the early century and become literally the spokesperson of the ordinary people, with a lust for radical change in favour of their interests and against the damaging social and political complacencies of the pre-war era. The size, layout and circulation of all newspapers in the Second World War were restricted by rationing but the content of the *Daily Mirror* despite this hardship came to represent the ordinary people's war against both fascism and the incompetent bureaucrats at home. Without hyperbole Cudlipp can claim it was '... the newspaper of the masses, the Bible of the Services' rank and file, the factory worker and the housewife' (1953: 136).

Much of its credibility derived from the astute identification of the inefficiencies of the bureaucrats and their hindrance of the war effort. Cassandra's crusade against 'army foolery' managed to continually strike a popular chord which was patriotic at the same time as it was disturbing for the wartime leaders. He carried it off because the readers genuinely recognized the problems which he identified in the many cosy preconceptions of hierarchy and protocol in British society.

In the war, its concern to keep in step with what it perceived to be popular opinion led it into conflict with the coalition government which came close to suppressing it in 1942 on the grounds that it was undermining army morale and destabilizing the government through its criticism, its use of the LIVE LETTERS from those in the forces and in particular the work of Cassandra.

Its use of illustration became fundamental to its appeal. Although the strip cartoon 'Jane' had been introduced as early as 1932 it was in the war that she became the forces' cartoon fantasy sweetheart, mirroring the conditions of the war effort at home in a humorous and saucy fashion. In a more sombre style, Philip Zec became known as the 'people's cartoonist', particularly after the controversy of his cartoon that showed a forlorn sailor adrift at sea with a caption by Bill Connor: 'The price of petrol has just been increased by one penny. – Official.' Whether this was aimed at the war-time profiteers or at the inefficiency of the wartime government's petrol distribution policies, it won popular approval for its defence of the heroic armed forces and in its insistence that, unlike in the First World War, their lives were sacred and not to be squandered by high-handed politicians at home.

Its owner Cecil H. King was able to pinpoint how such deep-rooted popular resentment would eventually lead people to break from these patterns from the past and into a brighter future.

> Loyalty to the future involves not only scanning the horizon for the new ideas and ideals which may shape the world, but also the discrediting of the men who made the period 1919–39 such an ignoble page in English history. This is not done to humiliate them, but to impress on the young people growing up (who read our papers), that this is an era which must not recur. (Cecil H. King to Churchill, 3 February 1941, quoted in Cudlipp, 1953: 165–6)

Forward with the People

The *Daily Mirror* was backing the people. It carried this conviction into the post-war election of 1945. On May 11 it adopted the slogan 'Forward with the People'.

In a stroke of populist genius the paper began a campaign of power and subtlety – not mentioning the name of the Labour Party but focusing on the experiences and memories of ordinary people to become a repository of folk memory. The catch-phrase was memorable and convincing: 'I'll Vote for Him' (5 June).

At the general election, the *Daily Express* had a circulation of about 3,300,000 and the *Daily Mirror* 2,400,000, but despite the fact that neither paper was politically affiliated to a party, the *Daily Mirror* better expressed the mood for change that the Labour Party embodied and swept it along to victory.

It continued with its 'Vote For Them' campaign and broadened the popular base of its appeal by including calls from the Church:

2 July

CHURCHES CALL ON PEOPLE OF BRITAIN

The fighting men depend on you – Vote for Them
Rev Bryan S.W. Green, vicar of Holy Trinity, Brompton Road, made a special appeal to women.
'It may sound like a cliche. It need not be. Remember their sacrifices when you vote for brave, adventurous policies which will benefit the whole nation without distinction of class or age; policies that will bring world peace.'

Bishop denounces evils of free enterprise
... The appalling unemployment of the inter-war years was the result of free enterprise in the present century, he [Dr Barnes, Bishop of Birmingham] declared. July 2

The celebrated cartoon heroine of the armed forces, Jane, is also shown to be in tune with the post-war mood as she manages a short holiday for the first time in years. She is off to Paxhaven where her family had a bungalow before the war. It has been requisitioned by the military but now they can get it back. They have also had a car in the garage, laid up since petrol rationing. The next day Jane is trying on the swimming costume which she last used before the Blitz – worried about getting to the coast on the 'basic ration' and her friend quips that the bathing costume is not even a basic ration.

The election slogan begins to gather resonance and to permeate the paper. The people are called upon as a force of experience and a force for change:

<u>THE PEOPLE KNOW</u> July 3

THOSE QUIET DREAMS OF YOUTH

... Let the votes of the people decide. Let his vote decide. To the electors we would say: You know what the fighting man wants. You know which party is likely to give him what he wants. You know the only way to make his future safe. Go then and do your duty. Vote for him. – July 3

The women's page was filled with articles stirring the women voters into action but couched in a playful language of fashion and socializing:

You've got an important
<u>DATE</u> – July 3

These views are further supported in letters repeating the slogan and building upon them in multiple ways. A letter from a mother explains:

The *Daily Mirror* has shown us the way. *We must Vote for Them and for our children.*
– July 4

In stark contrast to much of the conservative individualism of populist appeal in the press of the 1930s or the sublimation of workers into the imperial effort, there is a decisive shift to a collective and a national perspective at this time in the *Daily Mirror*. The people and the nation are merged in a vision of radical change for the benefit of both. An editorial on 4 July reads:

THE ONE OR THE MANY

... When people all over the country go to the polls tomorrow **for whom will they be voting?** Not for this party or that, not for one leader as against another, not to express appreciation or gratitude. They will be voting for **themselves**. They will be voting to express confidence in their own view of the kind of world they desire to live in. They will be voting for the policies which they believe are likely to bring such a world into existence. This election is a **national** issue, not a personal one.

Zec's cartoon of voting day is a repeat of his VE day cartoon of the Tommy bringing back peace from Europe and captioned 'Here you are! Don't lose it again!' It drew on the recent memories of wartime and on the paper's own contribution to the national effort by reprinting on 5 July:

Vote for them 'Victory and peace in Europe'
... Vote on behalf of the men who won the victory for you. You failed to do so in 1918. The result is known to all. The land 'fit for heroes' did not come into existence. The dole did. Short-lived prosperity gave way to long, tragic years of poverty and unemployment. Make sure that history does not repeat itself.

Post-election – A Brave New Popular World

After the election, there was a return to the mixture of features which had brought the *Daily Mirror* such popularity before the war. On 9 July 1945, in a series called 'Readers' Review', a regular column about arguments brings readers' views into the paper. Whether or not the wearing of uniform in the war has improved women's dress sense is the theme of this day's debate!

There are examples of the sensational and bizarre from 10 July:

'MAD ENGLISHMAN' AND HAWK WENT TO WAR
Wounded together, spent 2 years in gaol camp
[with picture]
Lieutenant Gerald Summers with Cressida, the hawk, who accompanies him everywhere, shared two years in a German prison camp with him and never missed his breakfast.

EVA BRAUN TREASURED PHOTOS OF A HANDSOME S.S. MAN
Hitler's mistress may have had secret affair with one of his personal bodyguards
– July 16

Land girl defied armed man in bedroom attack – July 10

Killed his parents, took girl teacher to pictures COURT TOLD – July 10

There is however no let up in the continual highlighting of the incompetence and unreliability of politicians who are represented as letting the people down – particularly in this example which shows the characteristic personal call from popular paper to people to politician:

No house prices ramp, Mr. Willink? Here's proof of it
Despite the protestations of Mr. H.U. Willink, Minister of Health in the Caretaker Government ...
– July 11

Continuing the finger-pointing at red tape and its detrimental effect on the people and the economy, there is a probe into why the first summer of peace is marred by inadequate holiday provision for the heroes of war:

THE HOLIDAY SCANDAL
Will British enterprise continue to be hamstrung? Will the golden opportunity to open up a fine new tourist industry be allowed to slip again next summer? The answer to both questions is 'Yes' – unless we get rid of those bureaucratic Ministers who have hampered British enterprise this season.
– July 19

The day after the election victory for Labour we read how the *Mirror* interprets the choice of Britain: in terms of the choice of the people and their democratic mandate to the politicians who will act on their behalf and listen, by implication, to the people's voice through the newspaper which increasingly could style itself as the popular voice:

BRITAIN TELLS THE WORLD

The British people have spoken clearly to their politicians. They speak no less clearly to the peoples of the world...
Today the British nation walks with pride and dignity among the peoples of the world.
– July 28

The role of women in the war effort and in the new parliament was cemented with the appeal to this readership as part of the paper's core popularity and is highlighted in this extract:

Good luck to these 23 women

The election has proved a triumph for the Labour Party. It has also proved a triumph for the women candidates. In the old House of Commons, there were only fourteen women. And of these, only nine got in at the election in 1935. The rest came in on by-elections later. In the new there will be 23.

That is quite a big increase, but still the proportion of women to men in the House is pitifully small ... twenty three out of 640.

For all that, these women can do a lot. The fourteen women who were in the house before them have proved that, and some of those fourteen are Members again.

There's a hard fight ahead – no use kidding ourselves about that – and all our brains, energy and courage are going to be needed to win it,' whether we're men or women ...

Your effort and interest and support are still needed. Are you ready to give them to the men and women you have put into power? (By Janet Grey, July 30)

After the glow of the election victory the *Mirror* continued to articulate the democratic populism of involvement among the ordinary people and could address them as if the newspaper itself had a role to play in maintaining this involvement. In a piece exhorting people to vote in local government elections on 29 October it writes:

YOUR BELOVED SPOT

Men will always argue about what democracy is. But all are agreed about where democracy begins. It begins with you and your neighbour. It enables you to live and let live by doing together what you cannot do individually ...

Efficient local government is the enemy of bureaucracy. **Efficient local government means efficient political democracy**. The poet whose vision ranged the whole British Commonwealth expressed the truth when he wrote:
'God gives all men all earth to love,
But since man's heart is small
Ordains for each one spot shall prove
Beloved over all.'

You must vote on Thursday, and, thereafter, act in the best interests of your own home, your neighbour, your street, your town. So will you be a faithful citizen of your 'beloved spot'.

The Zenith of a Modern Populism

As in the war years the *Daily Minor* managed immediately after the war to articulate the aspirations of the rising social classes who had emerged from the war with a strong sense of social solidarity and a determination that things would change to the benefit of the ordinary people. For all its overt politics, it was more persuasive in its general tone – the voice it discovered as a conduit to its working-class readership. Popular journalism with the *Daily Mirror* comes to mean a combination of style (including layout), mass circulation and address (rhetorical/content) as never before. The *Daily Mirror* with its astute identification of a representational style and above all the voice to match that constituency was to continue to play a key part in that evolution through the 1950s.

The *Daily Mirror* and the *Daily Express* had both continued to cultivate a readership which transcended class barriers. A.C. Smith claims they both, as the dominant popular papers of the period, had distinctive types of demotic speech (1975: 20). Nevertheless, it was the rhetoric of the *Daily Mirror* which became increasingly proletarian as the newspaper developed its popular base. This was a new form of popular newspaper and in all a new form of popular journalism – written for the masses and self-consciously constructing a voice. Yet Williams has indicated the contradictions in this rhetorical manoeuvre and the paternalism inherent in an appeal to the people and to their political instincts, which was articulated by journalists who were not part of that popular constituency themselves (1970: 18).

Its continued success was rooted in the tradition it had forged for itself, drawing on the memories of the wartime struggle, the sense of a popular-proletarian memory. This was the 'successful projection of personality' of which Fairlie wrote in 1957. He illustrated this by reference to the 'Old Codgers' section of the letters page: 'No other feature in British journalism so superbly creates the atmosphere of a public bar, in which everyone sits cosily round the scrubbed deal tables, arguing the toss about anything which happens to crop up, while the Old Codgers buy pints of mixed for the dads, and ports and lemon for the dear old mums' (Fairlie, 1957: 11).

The language which it used to maintain that sense of readership has been criticized by Smith: '… starting from an authentic populism in 1945, has stylized working class language into parody … ever unbridling the radical conscience that, once, had helped its readers to recognize and accept their own political responsibility' (1975: 238). It was that shift to parody and the willingness of readers to participate in it as a more playful form of identi-fication and retreat from the homogeneity of class identities which was to fuel the next great convulsion of the popular press as it attempted to deal with the disappearance of the people into a rhetoric without a constituency.

The *Daily Mirror* had become too identified with a uniformly working-class readership. Perhaps sensing this, after the Conservatives' election vic-tory of 1959, it dropped the slogan 'FORWARD WITH THE PEOPLE'. The people's paper took a step away from the people it had helped to represent. Its success continued, circulation figures peaking in the mid-1960s, but it was the successful expression of the common people's voice and concerns as a class, the very source of its success and an appeal increas-ingly rooted in the past, which would allow the *Sun* to take the lead with its post-class vulgarian egalitarianism.

7

THE POPULAR PRESS: SURVIVING POSTMODERNITY

MODERNITY AND THE PRESS

The popular press continues many traditions of earlier print culture and indeed elements of communication which predate printing. However, its continuity has been facilitated by an ability to adapt to varying and specific historical circumstances. As we have shifted to a period which has been dubbed 'postmodernity' by academics, artists and even journalists, we have to assess the degree to which popular journalism has been changed by this new phase or to what extent the era has itself been influenced by the popular press. We need to be able to identify whether the popular press has broken with the formation known as modernity or whether it retains a more familiar ambivalent position on the border between this and postmodernity.

The press in general developed in Western Europe and the United States in conjunction with trends which we could call broadly constituent of modernity. These trends included the centring of cultural and economic activity on the human subject and in the press the reporting of these processes in an increasingly professionalized mode. Modernity has come to be defined as belief in, among other things, progress in both social and scientific terms, the triumph of truth over falsehood, reason over superstition and the perfectibility of the human species. The serious political-economic newspapers which developed out of the era of the bourgeois public sphere have a central place in this project.

Modernity saw a subsequent trend towards the inclusion of people as citizens in the processes of their governance from the English to the American and French Revolutions. It also saw the economic development of commodity capitalism as a system of rationalizing economic activity and the place of the human subject in this. As modernity evolved, it became increasingly difficult to envisage humanity without recourse to its place in the economic order of capital and its dependence on a wide range of information, readily available in order for the individual to make rational choices within that political economy, whether those choices were primarily economic or cultural. These political-economic developments of modernity produced both a press which celebrated their achievements and integrated itself within them and also a press which provided a critique of those same developments and attempted to go beyond them. Both the press of the political status quo and the early radical popular press were in contrasting ways located within modernity's belief in progress.

In France, the United States and Britain we have seen how the press played a formative role at different times in liberating societies from the monopoly rule of kings and queens as increasing flows of information hastened the appearance of knowledge-based power structures of government rather than deference and belief-based societies. From the printers of the English revolution to Addison, Steele and Defoe in Britain, Adams and Paine in the United States, Marat and other revolutionaries in France, all employed journalism to move society in this direction, albeit in different ways and at differing speeds.

Of course, this version of the development of the press is a classic liberal perspective which privileges the role of an ever-expanding public sphere. The history of the popular press and its incorporation into the dominant bourgeois norms has a very different trajectory, although one also bound up in the discourses of modernity since modernity includes the teleology of an ever-improving, perfectible social sphere in which suffrage and quality of information for the many inevitably lead to a society better suited to the needs and aspirations of the masses of ordinary people. This populist teleology might be encompassed within certain versions of liberalism. A radical version would insist that it is society itself which must be transformed by those same masses of people and in the image of their collective vision of society. This would entail a radical overhaul of capital and profit and particularly the ownership and control of the press because of its ability to articulate persuasive ideologies and disseminate them to the people. Britain represents a particularly drawn-out struggle between two views of the project of modernity, with the former, the triumph of liberalism, winning out definitively towards the end of the nineteenth century.

We need to consider therefore the place of journalism in enabling discourses of popularity to emerge as part of the tradition of modernity before considering how these discourses function in the contemporary era. Modernity strove to represent a unified if complex reality. One of the ways popular journalism achieved this unified reality was to represent the masses as 'the people' through the pages of the newspaper. This involved closing down many elements of the heterogeneous practices of the ordinary people and stabilizing them into a more homogenized, if idealized, community.

These continuities were better imagined as part of an urban mass and modernity was given momentum by a growth in urban concentration and the ordering of daily urban life and, symbiotically, the daily metropolitan newspaper played a role in allowing this space and community to be imagined. The essential role of urbanization for modernity is eloquently expressed by de Certeau when he writes: 'The city is simultaneously the machinery and the hero of modernity' (1988: 95).

Modernity also has an important political impact within popular journalism which had always to allow for some kind of interchange between the interests and the aspirations of the people and the processes of political decision-making. Hartley stresses the unique function of journalism in forming this popular modernity: '... the only mechanism that was available to hold the two aspects of popular sovereignty together – to link the central socio-political institutions with the dispersed personal practices of private sense-making – was journalism' (1996: 81).

However, to counter this positivistic perspective one might point to Foucault's scepticism which concludes that the distinctiveness of journalism, lay in its particular disciplinary power. This aspect has largely been ignored because of journalism's powerful and persuasive discourse of self-legitimation as a practice which opened up a public sphere for debate and the activities of politicians to scrutiny. Foucault sees the disciplinary effect in terms of the creation of 'opinion':

> It's the illusion of almost all of the eighteenth century reformers who credited opinion with considerable potential force. Since opinion could only be good, being the immediate consciousness of the whole social body, they thought people would become virtuous by the simple fact of being observed. For them, opinion was like a spontaneous re-actualisation of the social contract. They overlooked the real conditions of possibility of opinion, the 'media' of opinion, a materiality caught up in the mechanisms of the economy and power in its forms of the press, publishing ... Basically it was journalism, that capital invention of the nineteenth century, which made evident all the utopian character of this politics of the gaze. (1980: 161–2)

Anything which allows society, or a section of a society such as the ordinary people, to be regarded as a 'whole' permits that medium to wield enormous legitimating power. The gaze of the popular press, increasingly, came to define the people and their political interests, albeit through 'the mechanisms of the economy'.

NEW JOURNALISM'S ROLE WITHIN MODERNITY

The New Journalism discussed in Chapters 5 and 6 was the zenith of the popular press's modernity, narrating the masses as a homogenized, imaginary public. In a similar way to the novel, the newspaper acted as a generic vector of what Jameson has called 'The organic genealogy of the bourgeois collective project' (1991: 18), creating a social grouping as an identifiable market and allowing it a stake in the emergence of a particular society. Nevertheless, popular culture was never as monolithic as that and the popular, conforming as it did to the tastes of the ordinary people and particularly in its propensity to narrow into political radicalism, had to a certain point always disrupted the grand narrative of bourgeois print culture. Furthermore, part of this radical opposition to bourgeois normative influences was articulated in an imprecise, unruly and anarchic impulse. Docker points out how the public sphere was grounded not only in opposition to aristocratic presumptions about the coincidence of wealth, status, sound opinion and taste but also 'in active opposition to the carnivalesque, to the grotesque activities and enjoyments and entertainments of the lower classes in their cultural geography in pubs, inns, fairs, theatres, shows, circuses, forests ...' (1994: 281–2).

He goes on to claim that the bourgeois public sphere enabled its privileged members to break their link with the anarchic carnivalesque and that this became thereafter a repressed desire for the pleasures and escapisms of low life. Because of these tensions the popular is disruptive of the emerging traditions of mainstream journalism of the nineteenth century. Economically it had to be incorporated for this press to survive; culturally it threatened increasingly to overpower the domain of its host, the traditional political-economic space of the serious press. As this successful commercialization of the popular press continues through the twenty-first century, the ambiguities which are located in the tension between the traditional functions of newspapers and the nature of the popular have come to be associated with the crisis in modernity which is often referred to as postmodernity (Dahlgren, 1991: 6–7).

DESCRIBING POSTMODERNITY

With the increasingly intensified incorporation of the popular into commodity capitalism, the globalization of patterns of the capitalist economy and, after 1989, the collapse of plausible alternative systems, we see the erosion of the potential for radical renewal within modernity. This brings the increasing problematization of modernity's teleologies. Habermas sees this more positively – the challenge of postmodernity as a manifestation of the awareness that modernity is an unfinished project. Others interpret it as the end of an era, the end of a faith in progress, the end of ideology or Fukuyama's end of history. We can call both of these trends constituent of postmodernity. Habermas would prefer a reconfiguring of the humanist aspects of a renewed modernity in ways more appropriate to changing economic and cultural perspectives. Yet the way that the repressed other of 'communicative rationality' as expressed in popular genre is articulated in the popular press may be interpreted as one moment in that reassessment.

Postmodernity is a challenge to many assumptions made about the role of the popular press in representing those excluded from direct economic and political power. Postmodernity is described and analysed in terms of a loop of indicators which include the intensification of cultural flows, a crisis in representation and in notions of truth, a collapse of meta-narratives such as class, nation and religion, globalizing forces, the erosion of the divide between popular and elite culture and the intrusion of margins upon the centres of established social and cultural life. The final chapters will attempt to assess the extent to which the popular press in Britain, Germany and the United States is affected by the broader cultural traits of postmodernity and what effect this may have on the discourses of the press in general.

Postmodernity favours market segmentation, fragmentation and volatility rather than the homogenization of modernity's mass culture. This poses a challenge to a popular press's attempts to articulate popular sentiments to a mass-profitable audience. The solution within this postmodern epoch is for the popular press to shift even more to rhetoric as an essential part of its appeal to a large and stable readership at the same time as that mass audience fragments as a tangible community. In addition, economic specialization, referred to by economists as Taylorization, has meant that the popular press is relying increasingly on the genres and traditions of the popular in order to retain an economic identity and less on the parallel traditions of the the economic-political press (Sparks, 1992: 38).

In order to approach this contemporary turn in newspaper development and ponder in what ways it constitutes a clean break with the past or simply a gear change into the future, we need to acknowledge that the discourse of newspapers has two distinct yet overlapping traditions: the first historiographic, the second epistemological. To a large extent the newspaper has narrated the history of the nineteenth and twentieth centuries – instant and increasingly mass history in the making, but to an equal and yet neglected sense it has also provided a philosophical template for these centuries, from a Hegelian evolving spirit of society to Baudrillard's triumph of the simulacrum.

A POPULAR POSTMODERN PRESS

One of the most noticeable features of the current cultural scene is the erosion of the distinctions between popular and high culture and postmodernity's recognition of the ability of the popular to invade all spaces. This does not mean that the popular and the elite have totally colonized each other's spaces, for the debates which rage about dumbing down are indicative that the elite is not prepared to go quietly if at all. Rather than being involved in colonization they are in fact involved in something more akin to switch-flicking, a two-way interchange.

Since this market version of popularity has come to predominate, the popular becomes a key agenda item for postmodernity and therefore changes and continuities in the popular press during an era termed postmodernity may well illuminate broader cultural debates, even if they do take place in that 'introspective world of the press' (Bromley, 1998).

We might consider that the popular press becomes postmodern when its attempts to fulfil the traditional bourgeois functions of the press as a provider of news and political information to a citizenship becomes interchangeable with its function as entertainment. This is a moment of convergence triggered by ever-intensifying communication flows between formats and genres driven by the logic of late capitalism.

For Hal Foster there are two takes on postmodernism: '... a post-modernism which seeks to deconstruct modernism and resist the status quo and a postmodernism which repudiates the former to celebrate the latter: a postmodernism of resistance and a postmodernism of reaction' (1985: xi–xii). Whichever definition is used, it is clear that postmodernity is based upon the cultural consequences of a newly assertive wave of popular culture which refuses to play second best aesthetically, economically or politically.

Postmodernity is further understood as a series of crises in representation and rationality, both key terms for the press. McHale has identified postmodernity in its privileging of the ontological over the epistemological (1989: xii); in other words, it isn't the way you relate a unified reality, but the version of competing realities which you choose to narrate.

Foucault claims in *The Order of Things* that transcendental claims to knowledge and the authority of these claims only made sense within the discourse of the liberal humanism of the eighteenth and nineteenth centuries which has been supplanted by discourses of a post-humanist era of knowledge. The discourse of the enlightenment public sphere and of the role of the journalist belong in this epoch as too does the notion of a progressive popular opinion and its ability to be located outside the discourses of capitalism or at least as a credible enemy within.

The contemporary popular press has reasserted much of the sensationalism and distraction which erode the discursive objectivity of the press, in particular its ability to articulate a set of informed discussions on the nature of contemporary society. Norris underlines this relationship between modernity and the 'truth-telling' interests so close to the core of journalism when he writes:

> For it is among the most basic suppositions in Kant and for thinkers (like Habermas) still committed to the 'unfinished project of modernity' that there exists a close relation between truth-telling interests – including the claims of enlightened Ideologiekritik – and those ethical values that likewise depend upon a free and open access to the 'public sphere' of rational, informed discussion. (1992: 111)

In terms of newspapers, postmodernity's collapse of cultural hierarchies is not only illustrated through debates on 'tabloidization' in the quality press but in concerns over the popular press's erosion of the boundary between politics and entertainment since the boundary between them has always acted as a fulcrum to journalism's own hierarchies and self-definitions. It is no wonder then that such an erosion causes interest and comment as it threatens to demolish a canonical belief in the centrality of political journalism to the genre.

Hartley observes that in postmodernity:

> ... the image of journalism and of its popular readership has changed; it is neither an image of the 'powers that be' nor of their organized or disorganized radical opponents. Currently – and often to the horror of those brought up in the modernist tradition of 'mainstream adversarial journalism' – the image of both readerships and the meanings circulating via popular journalism suggests a different kind of breakfast reading altogether. Here, and now, the emphasis is not on public life but private meaning, and the readership has morphed from:

male to female
old to young
militant to meditative
public to private
governmental to consumerist
law-making to identity-forming. (1996: 15–16)

Perhaps it may be more accurate to represent these binary distinctions in terms of infective flows, reversible and unstable, hopping backwards and forwards when it suits them. Certainly he is right to point out that political resistance has never been unfailingly organized within the popular press.

Journalism's crisis of representation comes when postmodernity's scepticism about the referent begins to infect jounalism's claims to representational truth. In terms of the popular press, rhetoric, up to now simply a vector of the popular, becomes indistinguishable from the claim of the popular press to actually represent the people. It is a popular paper if it presents a persuasive popular rhetoric. As the market comes to dominate more and more, the reduction of the people to market segments accelerates and accentuates this process and the popular is won or lost in terms of style of address.

THE POPULAR AND THE PEOPLE

At one point the popular and the people were close to synonymous terms. Popular art and culture expressed the worldviews of specific groups of ordinary people. The crisis in representation has loosened the hold of the popular on the people. In the popular press we may now only really use the term 'popular' as denoting the ability of a paper to sell to a large readership. The popular press increasingly is only authenticated by its ability to articulate the 'popular' through its rhetoric. Once the rhetoric emerged from the people; now it is a simulacrum standing in for their loss.

Lyotard's 'incredulity towards meta-narratives' (1984: xxiv) claims the discourses of nation, religion and political dogma have lost their ability to persuade, but in terms of the press there is evidence that the contemporary has seen the collapse of the meta-narrative of the 'public sphere' as defined from the emergence of democratic societies in Western Europe. The grand tradition of a press which involved people in a communicative democracy and guided them toward a better future is at least compromised by the developments of newspapers which gear themselves increasingly towards a celebration of consumerist values and the political status quo, not to say anything of the disappearance of an oppositional popular press tradition. The question that we might then ask, paradoxically, is whether the 'popular' in popular culture is also the victim of the collapse of meta-narratives?

Baudrillard's simulacrum – an identical copy without an original – can be applied perhaps to the generation of a popular readership with all the signifiers of community – vernacular, shared tastes, shared habits of media consumption – but without a concrete political community. Newspaper readerships simulate such a community and particularly within the popular press that community is marketed through rhetoric.

If politics and entertainment are blurring and invading each other's spaces, this does not mean that politics has necessarily become entertainment or vice versa. Similarly, if discourse theory helps us to understand the workings and patternings of power in language, this does not lead us inexorably to the conclusion that there is no reality outside the structuring of that language. While we must beware of treating the symptoms of the crisis as a definitive description of reality, there are serious questions for the popular press to answer in terms of the rhetoric which stands in for the people themselves. Is the popular press able to articulate something of the real world of the ordinary people and their political interests unmediated by a simulated rhetoric or does rhetoric go all the way down?

The pressures which have provoked such a generalized crisis in systems of representation and such a proliferation of the reach of popular culture which threaten to turn all discourses of the popular-political into yet another set of empty, depthless signifiers are generally considered to include globalization, commercialization, the intensification of cultural flows and the triumph of the image over narrative (Featherstone, 1993).

GLOBALIZATION

Globalization, although as a process as old as the capitalist system which prompts its logic, has reached a point of radical intensity due to the increasing availability and improved reliability of transport, particularly long-haul air traffic, the corresponding increase in exchange of people and commodities around the globe, increasing information flows via computer and telecommunications technology; these lead to two parallel and paradoxical trends. The first is a tendency to homogenization as brands such as McDonald's, Nike, Benetton, and CNN become global, sweeping national economies and national borders to one side. The second, driven by these flows of increased density of cultural and economic exchange, because they bring diversity and difference more into the everyday experience of people, have a back-lash effect of causing retreats to ethnie and nationalism among groups who do not perceive the benefits of such increased diversity.

The intensification of the importance of place, of location, in the contemporary popular press in Britain illustrates the point made by Featherstone when defining the relationship between postmodernism and globalization:

Postmodernism is both a symptom and a powerful cultural image of the swing away from the conceptualization of global culture less in terms of alleged homogenising processes (e.g. theories which present cultural imperialism, Americanization and mass consumer culture as a proto-universal culture riding on the back of Western economic and political domination) and more in terms of the diversity, variety and richness of popular and local discourse, codes and practices ... (1993: 2)

It may be possible to consider the popular press, especially in Britain and Germany where content is robustly national and even xenophobic, as providing evidence that particular cultural groupings in specific places may react against the 'ontological insecurity' of the instabilities inherent in postmodernity (Giddens, 1987). The Hollywood agenda of the American supermarket tabloids, especially those for export such as the *National Enquirer*, act in a supplementary way to more local popular cultures. They have certainly not supplanted them. Consumption and populism have become reconfigured in terms of a series of tropes of nationhood. Such a 'syntax of solidarity' has been postulated as a crucial element in the construction of a national identity in an era of the uncertainties of postmodern and global trends (Billig, 1995: 165–7).

The three newspapers I have chosen to illustrate these developments in the contemporary British popular market are the *Sun*, the *Mirror* and the *Daily Mail*. The *Sun* is the biggest-selling daily newspaper in the country with a sale of well over three million. It is renowned for its unabashed right-wing populism, although it has recently realigned this to mitigated support for Blair's Labour goverment. It is owned by Rupert Murdoch and expressed all the complexities of appeal of the Conservative Party in power throughout the 1980s and 1990s. In many ways it is still the barometer of the popular vote and remains doggedly resistant to what it perceives as encroaching Europeanization and is implacably hostile to the European currency, the euro. The *Mirror* is now the third largest-selling daily newspaper but it has been chosen for its tradition of left-leaning popular appeal. The *Daily Mail* is a different creature altogether but it must be considered popular in the size of its market: it is now the second-biggest selling daily. If the popular voice that it articulates is not quite the vernacular of the other two then this possibly tells us about the changing nature of the British popular itself and is worth examining for this very reason. It indicates that as popular culture invades other areas of national life the middle market is responding with its own version of accommodation. It is also an adaptation of popular conservatism to the middle-brow which in a different format made Harmsworth's original so successful. For all the differences between their popular approaches, the best analytical perspective is to find the common ground which these newspapers share in their attempt to represent the people.

COMMERCIALIZATION

The willing embrace of commerce in public or creative life is seen as a *sine qua non* of postmodernism. Frederic Jameson has defined it in these terms:

'Postmodernism is the consumption of sheer commodification as a process' (1991: x). Yet popular culture had been commercialized since the late Middle Ages with its professional storytellers, singers, almanac and chap-book sellers. Such an orientation of newspapers, in particular the popular end of the market, to the demands of the political economy is nothing new. Curran (1977) has demonstrated how the press has reflected the capitalist organizational rationale of its political economy throughout the modern era. What is distinctive now is the way in which the balance has shifted in favour of the commercial as absolutely dominant as opposed to simply holding an equilibrium with the informational and political imperatives of previous manifestations of popular press.

From as early as the 1840s, in Britain as well as the United States, newspaper popularity was becoming defined in terms of its market appeal. This became an intensifying momentum as the century progressed. The culmination of this has been an intensified commodification of the newspaper and its satellite supplements, its increasing harmonization of a whole package of offers, accessories and defining identities. This illustrates another characteristic of postmodernity in the celebration of the market as a cultural and economic strategy. Newspapers have always been predisposed in terms of their organization and epistemology to be profoundly marked by economic imperatives even in their primary goal of providing information about events in the real world.

This intensified comercialization means that the popular, instead of being articulated primarily as a political category, becomes a consumer category. As McGuigan has written: 'the popular national daily empowers its audiences, not directly as actors in the public sphere but as consumers' (1992: 178). Popular culture has been commodified since the mid-nineteenth century commercializing of the people and their cultures – a process which took place principally through the medium of the popular press.

We will foreground examples from the British popular press here because it presents a broader range of parallels with the traditions of popular print culture. These newspapers all attract a mass readership and are targeted at a readership which is inscribed in their rhetoric. Even more importantly, they retain at least a nominal choice between popular perspectives which even manage a diversity of opinion. This leaves the possibility that there remains a notion of political involvement via the popular press. These papers are to all intents and purposes resistant to the narratives of Hollywood as globalized news and prefer instead a parochial blend of regional and national popular fare. They retain more diversity and miscellany possibly because they are still part of an extremely competitive market. It is predominantly a daily market of preference where the discourse of antagonistic rivalry drives many of the really demotic and sensationalist aspects of their coverage. They are fighting over the people they want to claim as their own readers.

This celebration of consumption is inscribed in the pages of the popular press and explains much of its success in continuing to exercise market dominance. It is in keeping with the spirit of the age. Yet it depends in this on more historical antecedents. Its success has not sprung from a vacuum. The dominance of a consumerist popular press is based on its ability to continue to carry traditions of popular appeal and legitimate its claims to popularity within a commercial framework. The reader is addressed as an interested consumer and within the context of a particular newspaper. Contrasting the insider share-dealing scandal at the *Mirror* where its editor, Piers Morgan, had been censured by the Press Complaints' Commission for taking advantage of privileged information available to the financial experts on the paper to make a stockmarket killing the *Sun* on 25 February 2000 in its 'Sun Says' column indicates the confluence of appealing to the people and its own financial probity: 'Meanwhile, as we say on our front page today, The Sun will continue to be THE PEOPLE'S PAPER.' This enables the *Sun* to present itself as aligned with the interests of those outside the circle of financial experts and thereby draw a virtuous popular glow around its own integrity and support for the common reader. This casts the paper as a whole in a good light.

This is all the more damning as the consumer-reader is very much to the fore in the specialized letters column in the *Sun*'s rival, the *Mirror*, 'Justice with Jacobs', which covers legal matters with a consumer twist as part of a popular consumer-rights agenda. It has an educational slant of a particular populist and raucous style. Jacobs himself, the consumer champion, is featured with gown and wig pointing his finger from the top of the page – the representation in the pages of the press of a particular sort of popular consumer justice. The comic element of this consumer appeal is enhanced by the rhetoric and concentration on bizarre angles on otherwise dull episodes.

Butcher says he was told a porkie
METRIC MESS SPARKED BY SCALES (The *Mirror*, 30 March 2000)

This is matched by the equally vernacular style of 'Sorted', a column set out as investigative journalism into frauds and consumer rip-offs:

THE SCUMBAG WHO PREYED ON A DISABLED WOMAN
Meet Del ... cowboy builder from hell (The *Mirror*, 18 February 2000)

Quentin Wilson in the *Mirror*, presented as 'the columnist the car industry fears', draws readers and consumer interests into his campaign for cheaper car prices in an on-line buying feature:

Death of the car salesman
YOUR DRIVE FOR FAIRER PRICES IS KILLING THEM (The *Mirror*, 31 March 2000)

The rhetoric employed in these columns is one of resolution within consumer capitalist culture, which speaks of a process of winning battles against the system. In doing so, it distracts from more systemic economic inequalities. The columns point to a more optimistic world of popular consumer power, where people are able to take charge of their own efforts, or a part of them, through the intermediary of their newspaper.

CAMPAIGNS, CONSUMERISM AND THE CONTEMPORARY

Campaigns have continually been used to boost the image of newspapers as active agents in social or political change. This tradition has a contemporary flavour in its further integration into the imperatives of competitive popular capitalism. These campaigns can also be developed implicitly or overtly into part of more politicized agendas.

VOICE OF THE MIRROR

Starter for Ten
THE pressure to bring back News At Ten surely cannot be resisted for much longer. The Mirror campaign was backed by tens of thousands of readers. (The *Mirror*, 23 March 2000)

The emphasis here is not simply on the scale of the support to bring back a popular news programme into the prime time slot as part of an implicit public service broadcasting agenda but the integration of this into identifying the campaign specifically with large numbers of the *Mirror's* readers.

The newspapers' own campaigns can act as self-publicity and as agenda focus. The *Daily Mail* features as the hero of its own campaign in the attempt to find the man who attacked Ruth Lelacheur at the League Cup Final between Leicester City and Tottenham Hotspur in 1999.

WANTED

£2,000 reward to catch soccer thug who savagely attacked a defenceless woman (*Daily Mail*, 30 March 2000)

As if to confirm the effectiveness of the newspaper as crime fighter, the next day it could reveal:

Soccer brawl man is unmasked by the Mail's appeal (*Daily Mail*, 31 March 2000)

There are also ways in which the contemporary popular newspaper can feed back the commercial imperative in a virtuous loop to reinforce the reader as consumer of his/her own generosity, thus integrating and ingratiating at the same time as part of a feel-good factor.

COMMENT

Your generosity
LAST November, this paper launched a campaign to raise £1 million to finance much-needed research into the scandalously neglected disease of prostate cancer – a taboo illness that kills 10,000 men every year.
  Our campaign received the backing not only of doctors and other medical experts but also, inevitably, of politicians ...

But it is you, our readers, who will be making the real difference. We are delighted to thank you for your remarkable generosity – which proves once again that the Daily Mail is the paper that cares. (*Daily Mail*, 22 February 2000)

On the same day there is a feature in 'Good Health', a consumer-oriented section of the paper, entitled 'Thanks a Million', accompanied by a photograph of the handover of the cheque.

Both the *Mirror* and the *Sun* have been involved in campaigns to provide material resources for schools. They are campaigns which ignore the possible political causes of shortages of materials in schools in order to popularize their own contribution to the shortfall through charitable fundraising. This is a covert political strategy which indicates how the issues of education budgets, not covered by and large in the newspapers' mainstream political coverage because they are squeezed out by more celebrity, lifestyle or consumer news stories, become embroidered into consumer campaigning. People's attention is shifted from questions of political priorities and refocused onto the role of the newspaper as popular champion. It is also worth noting that both campaigns are fully integrated into commodity sponsorship which links the newspaper with crisps and biscuits, traditional playground fare for children at school.

In a veritable battle of the snacks, the *Mirror*'s 'Free Maths Stuff for Schools' campaign has tokens jointly sponsored by McVitie's and the *Mirror*, while the *Sun*'s 'Free Books for Schools' campaign has its tokens sponsored by the *Sun* and Walkers Crisps.

In contrast to this, the potential for a newspaper to involve itself in overt political campaigning is illustrated in a feature in the *Sun* which trades on its glory years of the 1980s (Chippendale and Horrie, 1990) when it championed, like no other, the populist consumer agenda of Margaret Thatcher's Conservative Party, who in power introduced a right-to-buy scheme for social housing tenants which changed the face of public housing in Britain and helped to secure the support of those traditional Labour voters who benefited from the sales and were drawn into the Conservatives' hegemony of popular capitalism. It features four corroborating stories of working-class folk sitting on property fortunes:

SUN SPOTLIGHT

MAGGIE'S MADE US MILLIONS ON COUNCIL HOMES

THOUSANDS of council house tenants who bought their homes are sitting on fortunes worth up to £250,000.

They own their homes thanks to Right to Buy legislation introduced by PM Maggie Thatcher 20 years ago.

And last night they chorused: 'Thank you Maggie for making us millions.' (The *Sun*, 24 February 2000)

A commercialized popular press is well placed to authenticate its populist claims by drawing, in this example, on the rhetorical strategy of the all-seeing chorus and the familiar use of an abbreviated first name. A grateful people is constructed around the all-inclusive 'US'. Popular capitalism is celebrated here by the people and they are seen to be articulating their gratitude in the popular press.

This appeal to the readers as consumers is reinforced by its association with the discourse of a nation of consumers; the readership of the newspaper is thus developed as an economic and patriotic community simultaneously. This may be partly involved in the popular columns of consumer complaint but its power is augmented by the potent emotional appeal of the nation-state upon which the newspaper calls so often.

The conflation of readers and economic nation are contrasted to a monolithic EU bloc in the traditionally European-hostile *Sun* on 24 March 2000:

> In a rut
> IF the EU is to prosper, it must learn from America
> Britain is the greatest country in the world but freedom to expand and compete has made America the greatest economy.
> Blair should forget about preaching to Europe and devote his energies to making us as successful as America.

This indicates that part of the power of the discourses of the nation and the newspaper reader as consumer bonded within the interests of that nation is dependent on the nation being far from a simple site of identification. The contemporary popular press draws selectively from the complexity of these discourses which penetrate in multiple ways across all sorts of boundaries. It is an illustration of the 'infection' so characteristic of postmodernity.

THE POVERTY OF IMAGE IN THE PUBLIC SPHERE

Another feature which reinforces the sceptical dominance of postmodernity is the elevation of the power of image over rational argument. This springs as much from the blending of advertising and brand into the news media of the public sphere as from any other technological determinants, such as the proliferation of commodified images through the increased availability of television and other visual media of communication. Habermas (1992) has likened the collapse of rationality in this contemporary promotion of the image to a 'refeudalisation of society' (1992: 231). In his view, this society can only grasp the display of the signifiers of importance rather than have access to democratic involvement. In the popular press it has disturbing implications for the political education of popular readerships if they are merely having these signs presented to them without questioning or debate. Jameson suggests that: 'Depth is replaced by surface or multiple surfaces' (1991: 12). The ephemerality of the popular press makes it an interesting contributor to postmodernity in its constant shuffling of the surface elements of its formulaic approach to content. Which celebrity, which scandal, which populist cause? – all seem to be interchangeable. The constant element is the rhetoric and the ventriloquism of the people themselves.

Unlike previous manifestations of popular political involvement through the press that depended on rational debate, the aesthetic of the contemporary popular press is to instruct the reader into being a more adept reader of contemporary patterns of consumption and identity. Political debate is framed by these. The readers of these papers are not presented with a medium that informs them as active participants in the public sphere but interpellates them as consumer identities with a range of intertextual complexity. It is a virtualization and dispersal of the material people.

The imaginary is mediated through the consumption of popular identities including the identity of the reader of a particular newspaper and its opinions. This links to the rhetorical strength of the popular in the popular press, indicating that for our purposes rhetoric is an imagining device, an image of the idealized reader.

In a feature on the popular press in the *Independent* on 14 July 1998, the *Sun*'s assistant editor Chris Roycroft-Davis claims: 'A reader who wants to be seriously informed would take the quality press ... They are not looking for profound analysis of France. It is easier for them to associate the French with an image like "garlic eaters".' In the same article, David Banks, Mirror Group corporate affairs director, reinforces the changing ambition of the tabloid press: 'We are not trying to educate. On the contrary, we go in the direction people want ... lazy journalism ... common to journal and readers.'

The association of stereotypes and collective images, once transferred to the public discourse of the popular press, can disrupt the press's traditional claim to provide enlightenment. Rather it feeds, through its shifting of surface realities, a propensity for closure around the lowest common denominator. It provides continuities within an idealized and commodified readership. The image phase of postmodernity may be construed in the popular press as an aesthetics of the popular, without a particular aim or purpose outside the commercial articulation of a credible version of the popular voice and enmeshed within the flows of everyday life and its rich cross-currents of intermedia influences.

INTERTEXTUALITY AND SOAPS

Intertextuality with other media had always been a feature of popular tradition within print culture. Chap-book versions of literary masterpieces; woodcut engravings either original or plagiarized from famous paintings to illustrate ballads, broadsides or newspapers; novels reprinted in serial form and through the media explosion into cinema, radio, television and on-line capacity have all provided such multiple connections for popular print. It has now in the contemporary era reached a point of mutual saturation with one category often indistinguishable from any other. This is a particular manifestation of the crisis in representation mentioned above. Individual media of communication lose any specificity to their role which they may have had. In places, the role of the popular newspaper cannot be distinguished from the role of, nor the content of, for instance, the television soap opera. News in the public interest is increasingly defined as news with a public personality in the focus, almost always emanating from the multi-media world of entertainment.

Modleski (1982), among others, provides a progressive and liberationary reading of the soap opera genre itself, suggesting that soaps may be in the vanguard of popular narrative art because they provide multiple, decentred narratives, everywhere breaking the illusion of unity and closure offered to the spectator by classic realism. She claims that they provide the viewer with a multiple perspective on any question which emerges in the plot and resist any dominant reading. Soaps, then, for her, foreground ambiguity and flow. If we consider the way in which the popular press deals with the actors and storylines of the soaps, we can see a very different perspective emerging. The tabloids use this form in a way that transfers the characters out of these open-ended scenarios into ones that close down debates around sensitivities which are anything but progressive. The popular press certainly provides a series of narratives but the overarching popular rhetoric is closed down into reaction not opened up into contestation.

The celebrity is clearly a major element of the popular agenda of these papers. Pages devoted to celebrity gossip in all the tabloids differ only in their strategies to match the content of the stories to the perceptions of their readerships. Despite fears that Hollywood images are about to take over the globe, the content of these pages are overwhelmingly British especially when dealing with the range of indigenous television soaps.

One of the attractions of celebrity news is that it allows the people as readers to be addressed and articulated in terms of consumerist values which are inextricably linked to the newspapers' economic agenda. This is often expressed through the identification of these issues through a particular celebrity story. In such cases the celebrity is presented as consumer and the reader is presumed to be interested in the consumer details as well as the intimate personal details of the famous personalities involved. This is illustrated in a full-page spread and itemization of David and Victoria and baby Brooklyn Beckham's clothes and accessories. From head to foot they are scrutinized on one page, while on the facing page in the *Daily Mail*, 21 March 2000, Jaci Stephen exhorts them: 'Another publicity stunt ... another humourless assault on the media. So will Posh and Becks ever learn to lighten up?' They are censoriously dubbed 'Britain's Most Sensitive Couple' – indicating the ambivalent situation of those in the tabloid limelight: consumerist paragons and spoilt brats. In the illustration there are references to practically every recent headline story about the couple, from the underwear to the haircut, accompanied by judgmental adjectives such as 'ultra-trendy', 'stunning', 'garish' and 'ostentatious'.

The tabloids, with their combination of investigative nous and media-business connections, are the ideal forum for gossip and debate on the TV soap, the most popular genre in Britain. Insider news, behind-the-scenes battles, plot development leaks and the real tragedies of individual actors' personal lives are threaded into an elaborate and extended media narrative whose intertextual elements are difficult to disentangle. This process is characteristic of an intensification of cultural flows identified with post-modernity. It indicates an invasion of the private into the public and vice versa. It blurs the distinction between the political and the trivial and shifts the fulcrum balancing entertainment and information. It does all these things because the popular has become fully integrated with commodified and mediated cultural patterns.

In the *Mirror*, 21 February 2000, Matthew Wright, on his predominantly British media celebrity and showbusiness page, reveals the backstage drama at the celebrations of *Eastenders'* fifteenth anniversary party which blur the script's machinations with the celebrities' real-life disputes:

> Bitterenders
> Eastenders celebrated its 15th anniversary as the nation's grittiest soap with a flash £500-a-head party on Saturday.
>   But I'm sorry to hear that while the stars quaffed champagne a good old-fashioned row was rumbling in the background – the kind the scriptwriters might choose to have spilling out of the Queen Vic at closing time.

Soap plot-lines are revealed and threaded into personal narratives which draw on the readers' familiarity with the stories and characters but are represented in a parallel discourse of participatory wordplay and laughter:

> **NEW GIRLY FOR CURLY**
> Street's pretty police sergeant Emma will mend broken heart
> CORRIE EXCLUSIVE
>
> Corrie's Curly Watts is to cop a police girl lover who mends his broken heart.
>   Curly, played by Kevin Kennedy, falls for attractive sergeant Emma Taylor when she goes on duty in Weatherfield next month.
>   Emma, actress Angela Lonsdale, is quite a catch – and helps ease his pain after being dumped by estranged wife Raquel ...
>   Street writers penned the plot after 18 million fans tuned in at New Year for a one-hour special in which Raquel told Curly he was a dad – then heartbreakingly returned to their daughter Alice and her new life in France.
>   Kevin, 38, put in such a strong performance he convinced bosses he had conquered his booze problems. (The *Sun*, 23 March, 2000)

One actor's off-stage drama is turned by the *Sun* into a soap opera with a different flavour. The *Sun* breaks an exclusive on its front page of 2 March 2000:

> CORRIE LES IN BOOZE CLINIC
> Shattered Coronation Street star Bruce Jones has booked into a top clinic with severe stress .... Bruce, who plays layabout Les Battersby, checked into The Priory last Friday ...
> It is not known how long Bruce – whose TV character was seen overdosing on pills last year – will stay at The Priory.

Collapsing the difference between the fictional narrative of a television soap and the real-life drama of the actor's addiction draws the public sphere into the realm of vicarious private experience:

LES TO THE RESCUE IN CLINIC PUNCH-UP

Troubled Coronation Street Star Bruce Jones was hailed a hero last night after rescuing a woman from a fight.

Bruce, 46, stepped in to calm a violent row between the woman and a male patient at the detox clinic. (The *Sun*, 7 March, 2000)

Weeks later, on 29 March, the *Sun* illustrates how the original tabloid plot-line can generate further interest as the actor emerges to celebrate the success of his son:

Exclusive: Corrie Actor's First Interview Since Going Into Rehab
Coronation Street star Bruce Jones was at his lowest ebb.

Suffering acute stress and the effects of heavy boozing, he had checked in to a £2,500-a-week rehab course to sort out his life.

But the actor who plays Corrie layabout Les Battersby found the perfect boost on a night AWAY from The Priory clinic.

It was the evening he slipped in to the audience to watch his eldest son Jon follow in his acting footsteps by making his stage debut.

At this point, a readership already assumed to be familiar with the spin-off story of Bruce Jones's personal problems, can interpret them as part of the meta-narrative of personal redemption so beloved of narratives in the popular press.

On occasions one has to wonder which audience is being addressed as some of the popular press's intertextualities strain to make their points through ever-more elaborate parodies of other genres. In this case we have the *Sun*'s highest-profile columnist writing a critique of 'political correctness' in the style of a comic character who first emerged in the 1920s – Billy Bunter.

Billy Bunter pulls it off
'Cripes!' said Billy Bunter stuffing another jam tart into his mouth.

'What is it now, you fat chump?' asked Harry Wharton.

The Fat Owl of the Remove was reading the Greyfriars Times.

'I say, you fellows. Just listen to this.'

Bunter began to read out loud. 'Public schools have been warned that they could be sued under new human rights legislation if they ban homosexual relationships between pupils.'

'You're making this up, you spoofing spoofer,' said Wharton. 'You don't want to make Quelch hear you or he'll give you another good whacking.'

'I should be so lucky,' said Bunter.

'Let me see that,' said Wharton grabbing at the newspaper.

'Gerroff!' cried Bunter. 'I haven't finished. There's more. Schools can be challenged on the grounds of degrading treatment for forcing pupils to take early runs followed by cold showers.'

'I say. That's wizard news!'

'And how about this? Head teachers were also advised that pupils could demand the right to challenge the rules on uniform or insist on cross-dressing under article 10 of the human rights convention.'

'Does that mean I can wear my silk ball gown in the quad?' asked Wharton excitedly.

'I suppose so, duckie,' said Bunter.

'Yippee!'

'And here's one for you, my dusky nawab,' said Bunter to Hurree Jamset Ram Singh. 'They could also be guilty of religious discrimination if they force pupils to go to chapel.'

'That is most estimable news,' said Hurree, chair of the Greyfriars Equality Unit.' (Richard Littlejohn in the *Sun*, 31 March 2000)

VOICES OF AUTHORITY

The individual voice and its rhetoricization were common in the modernist version of the popular press and expressed continuity between pulpit and political platform. They also epitomized the missionary fervour of the popular press's political ambitions in a particularly didactic style. This tradition continues into the contemporary postmodern era but with a series of distinguishing characteristics. Despite the cultural preference for the decentring of authorities and the demise of certain meta-narratives, the popular newspapers still maintain a space for a demotic pedagogy which is driven and passionate. In the variety of their address and their underlying themes, they provide a template for the newspapers' identity in profoundly politicized ways but they constitute a politics of narrow-minded common-sense, a reactionary stubbornness. They may constitute part of a characteristically superficial series of positions and may be driven by image and rhetoric but they nevertheless have a persuasive power which indicates that the exploitation of surfaces need not be a trivial affair.

One traditional figure in this process is that of the named columnist/journalist who writes from outside the bounds of accepted convention, stirring up the opinion of the readers and provoking controversy. Just as the novelist of the nineteenth century, as Bakhtin argues in *The Dialogic Imagination*, employed characters such as the clown and the fool to bring private life into the public gaze, popular journalism employs writers who fit this pattern; not rectors, not preachers but intertextual bandits like Richard Littlejohn, Gary Bushell or Jacobs. The masks which they parade are textual: rhetorical masks which fulfil the complex task of achieving popular discourse in the interests of both the media institution in terms of sales and normative closure and the readers in terms of identification with a world of possibility, a world which is opening up to the advantage of the little people – those outside the power bloc.

The popular press, as well as innovating, continues to draw on previous and parallel popular traditions and practices of the journalist. One of these ways is the role of the journalist who, in prying into the area of private experience, becomes a conduit for public interest. Bennett and Stead, Hearst and Pulitzer had all contributed to the evolution of this figure of the journalist as public spy reporting in the interests and for the entertainment and edification of the popular readership. In making private life public, the popular press are reinterpreting the public sphere as one very much constructed through private passions. The popular remains a part of the normative processes of social education.

The case of a bomber's trial in London provides a particular variation. The article is able to exploit the outrages targeted against minorities by a lone attacker to warn of the dangers of allowing liberals to paint a portrait of a Britain which it parodies as full of neo-Nazi cells:

LITTLEJOHN

A 23-YEAR-OLD engineer called David Copeland has pleaded guilty to planting the three nail bombs in Soho, Brixton and Brick Lane, London, last year. He acted alone.

Yet at the time we were told that these atrocities were part of an organized campaign aimed at homosexuals and minorities.

Hysterical politicians and left-wing columnists tried to pretend there was a vast network of neo-Nazis embedded in our British society.

They seized on the bombing as a golden opportunity to advance their own agenda ...

The Government's agenda bears little resemblance to what the people actually want ...

I know from my postbag that most people are sick and tired of being labelled bigots, racists, homophobes, whatever the hell that means.

This is a decent country.

But decent people are being cornered.

There will be a backlash.

Unless they are very careful, the smearmongers will one day get the society they like to pretend already exists.

David Copeland should be seen as a warning not an opportunity. (The *Sun*, 29 February 2000)

In a reversal of what many might perceive to be the reality of the case, Littlejohn manages to suggest that Copeland does not emerge from a society which has embedded racism and homophobia but represents an individual aberration within an otherwise tolerant society. He draws a reassuring picture of a society irritated by slurs against its good name, flattering the readers in a congratulatory tone that they form part of this decent society. He repeats the word 'decent' to underline his point. The sinister warning at the end makes it clear that even decent people can be pushed into extreme reactions. His idiosyncratic voice attempts to bolster a notion of community by portraying the liberals and left-wingers as the hysterics on the margins. This is a complex, yet plausible, attempt to narrate a normative version of the relationship between the ordinary people and extremists of the Left and Right.

In this process of reinforcing common-sense, popular views of normative categories, the *Daily Mail* often uses the ploy of selecting a token representative of a minority group or a marginalized social type in order to present a doubly negative image of them – condemned by their own, as it were. In this case we have a single mother deployed as a voice railing against the alleged mindless promiscuity of single mothers.

A PERSONAL VIEW

by Angela Lambert

I am a liberal and also a single mother but regretfully I have come to the conclusion that feckless mothers must be prevented from having one baby after another ... (*Daily Mail*, 8 March 2000)

A return to older traditions, though this time in a rather empty rhetorical flourish, seems to maintain a tenuous link with the analytical radicalism of old in the *Mirror*:

Brian Reade

COLUMNIST OF THE YEAR

English country pillage

... GROUND rent is an obscenity which confronts millions of house-buyers but being British we laugh it off as a quaint old custom....

It astonishes me how ordinary people are so bogged down with their penny pinching obsessions that they fail to see the bigger picture. While they worship the Royal family and their titled ilk, those people are urinating themselves in private at the loyalty and wealth still lavished on them by mediaeval bumpkins.

So come on, you yeomen of Middle England, discard your prejudices and train your eyes on the thieves, blaggards and scoundrels above.

They are your real persecutors. It's just that you are too busy painting your stucco to realise. (The *Mirror*, 30 March 2000)

There is all the vocabulary of *Reynold's* or Cobbett here but used in a way which issues ultimately in a rather bathetic note indicating how important are the consumerist, house-owning sections of the contemporary 'ordinary people'. It is a skilful reappropriation of the 'old rhetoric' for a new and fully commercialized popular readership.

TWO-WAY EXCHANGES – THE RHETORIC OF DIALOGUE

Another device which rhetorically appeals to a reader in a seemingly informal exchange is the dyadic which constructs a two-way interchange between reader and newspaper. The colloquial nature of the language can range from cosy to aggressive but at both ends of this emotive spectrum we can read a vernacular of personal address. First names, barked commands and vulgar language are typical devices in this strategy. The textualization of an individual voice and its employment to build up a community of two-way dialogues is key. This allows a fragmenting readership to be represented as a mass audience, millions seeking to be involved in a textual dialogue.

The use of first names adds to the impression of the newspaper's informal and hectoring approach to politicians. It permits the newspaper to occupy the high-ground of the watchdog of the Fourth Estate while engaging with them through a jocular jousting. Implicitly, the people are being articulated through a colloquial familiarity with which they are invited to identify. It is a convenient rhetorical strategy to close off larger discussions concerning the bureaucratic and impersonal aspects of politics by promoting instead a pseudo-democracy of personal address. The interpenetration of colloquial and official speech is also illustrative of a certain carnivalesque.

The *Mirror* suggests that the Prime Minister should try to survive on the minimal pension increase for old people and, as if to add to the familiarity of address, the headline is located on the letters' page:

Dear Jo letters page
Try a 10p pay rise, Tony (The *Mirror*, 18 February 2000)

In the run-up to the budget, the *Daily Mail* drops into unusually familiar terms with the Chancellor of the Exchequer: 'Sorry Gordon, taxing the middle classes won't help the poor' (15 February 2000).

The column 'Routledge' is promoted by the slogan which seems to undermine any notion of cosiness between a Labour-supporting newspaper and the Party's apparent obsession with remaining on a consistent media message – 'He's OFF-message and ON the warpath'. This is a hard-hitting political column with an overtly oral tone. Covering the decision to send General Pinochet back to Chile after Spain's attempt to have him extradited from Britain to stand trial for offences against Spanish citizens in Chile during his time as dictator, Routledge bellows: 'In General you got it right, Jack' (The *Mirror*, 3 March, 2000).

A different form of colloquial address issuing from an idealized readership is evident in the *Sun*, covering the races at Cheltenham, on the appearance of the Queen Mother, hovering on the threshold of her 100th birthday. This manages to combine deference and demotic in one highly effective phrase 'You're solid gold ma'am' (17 March 2000).

EXCLUSION AS COMMUNITY

The technique of informal address can be applied to exclude from as well as include into community as illustrated when Tony Blair is pictured with an asylum seeker on a walkabout in South Wales eight months previously who turns out, according to the *Sun*, to be an illegal immigrant:

NICE TRY ALI

But your 'mate' Tony can't give you political asylum (The *Sun*, 28 February 2000)

There is a clear implication that Blair can be cosied up to on a personal level, fitting into broader accusations that he is too soft on immigration. It is reactionary and inflammatory material inciting distrust of the outsider but dressed up in a tone of familiarity and jest. Ali is depicted as cunningly attempting to exploit Blair's weakness. The familiarity is portrayed as contemptuous. Politics dissolve into matters of personal interest and relationships, not providing a softer focus to public sphere debate but detracting attention from the political insinuations of the personal address and the light tone of reporting.

In a direct exhortation to its readers to make their concerns vocal, the *Sun* sets itself up as the champion of unexpressed views. This fits within the tradition of the repressed public of the carnival and the anarchic whose voice is submerged by formal politics and the concerns of the powerful. This silent majority is mobilized textually here in ways which are fanned by fears of foreigners, while at the same time the newspaper can parade its credentials as a very vocal, populist watchdog, keeping an eye on potential slack politicians on behalf of its readers. Hague, the *Sun* readers and the electorate are collapsed into one nexus of concern and the effect is highlighted by the late shift to addressing the Leader of the Opposition as William:

Speak out

Have you noticed something odd about the Tories' campaign against beggars and fake asylum seekers?

There isn't one.

The silence from Hague and his men is deafening.

Why? When The Sun said last week that Britain has had enough, we were spot-on.

Your calls and letters prove how strong public opinion is.

The Tories should be shouting from the rooftops. The Government would have no defence. So is Hague worried about being branded jingoistic, nationalistic or racist?

Is he worried about being called politically incorrect?

Don't be timid, William. This is a real issue that enrages voters.

For goodness sake, ask Tony Blair some difficult questions about it today. (The *Sun*, 15 March 2000)

The strategies of this colloquial tone are extended into commands, written as if emanating from the people themselves. This is the popular as peformative. In their use of commands, newspapers present themselves as having an immediate, performative potential (Halliday, 1978; Fowler, 1991) which they can deploy in the name of the people and their tastes and sensibilities.

TAKE IT OFF, TONY

This was the order given to the Prime Minister in the growing debate about whether he should take time off to support his wife after the forthcoming birth of their fourth child. (The *Mirror*, 24 March 2000)

In debating the issues of popular culture and postmodernity, John Docker asks a question about contemporary culture: 'How can we explain why the "very small minority" is no longer being listened to, is no longer the centre, authority, standards-bearer, keeper of the mind of the race?' (1994: 19). In terms of what might be called a command-culture, the popular press is symptomatic of this erosion of the power of a cultural elite. Nevertheless, any perspective which includes a political-economic analysis would tend to disagree with any strong version of this statement as global ownership patterns confine central cultural authority to a smaller elite of critical decision-makers than ever before. The powerful tool which can be used to obscure this fact and the one which enables a weak version to hold true is that of popular rhetoric. The major popular newspapers are owned and serve the financial interests of some of the wealthiest men in the world. Their readers include a fair proportion of the country's least well-off and most politically marginalized. Through a skilful employment of a rhetoric of the popular, at least this branch of the mass media can legitimate itself in terms of the meritocratic, consumerist imperatives which it claims to be at its heart. The vernacular voice is part of the dyadic attraction of the popular press, drawing the reader into a dialogue conducted in a familiar tone, but it takes its part in a much broader appeal by being integrated into a community which stretches beyond dialogues and into nation. In fact the popular is a very important aspect of the diversification of globalized production which is a part of global capital's sophisticated strategy to maintain a central control. Murdoch and the Springer Verlag are the best examples of that with regard to the news media, producing parochial versions of popular newspapers as a coherent part of their global hierarchy. This is particularly true of the *Bild* newspaper with its different editions for the different German states, thus reflecting the more regional taste for newspaper consumption in Germany. This part of the popular, its ability to close down perspectives to a narrow, national focus becomes part of a global strategy to legitimate certain news media practices at a local level.

THE OUTSIDER – NATIONAL/POPULAR AND DEMOTIC LANGUAGE

One performative function of the popular press is the confirmation of the existence of a national space and indeed a national identity. The vernacular rhetoric of the popular press could simply restrict itself to acting as a method for maximizing market appeal in a voice recognizable to its readership. However it is available for other purposes which, although they are based within the logic of communities of exclusion such as nation and newspaper readership, have a much more politicized rationale. In the contemporary popular press, this rhetoric can be employed to construct a popular view of community defined from the perspective of the threat of the outsider. This is a specific illustration of what McGuigan writes of in terms of the *Sun*: 'The Sun is, arguably, symptomatic of and contributory to a political culture in which popular pleasure is routinely articulated through oppressive ideologies that operate in fertile chauvinistic ground. It is populist in the worst sense' (1993: 184).

A single-theme version of the editorial column 'Sun Says' on 9 March 2000 strikes up the terms of one recent controversial and characteristic debate:

Britain has had enough
SCROUNGERS, illegal immigrants and criminals are sucking this country dry.
The cost of this multi-billion pound racket is staggering.
And it is hard-working taxpayers who are footing this bill ...
They used to say the streets of London were paved with gold.

Today they are paved with East European women and children harassing passers-by for money – and robbing them when they say NO.

But our courts must ALSO hand out maximum sentences to the local crooks here who are cashing in across the country.

The crooked landlords fiddling millions in housing benefit.

The bent employers escaping tax by hiring workers for cash, no questions asked.

BRITAIN HAS HAD ENOUGH

The headline becomes a slogan for a series of campaigning features over the next weeks which orchestrate the popular newspapers' armoury of devices to involve its readership with an agenda the newspaper itself is setting and then selling to the readers as the popular voice. The series of growl words sets the tone of the debate: these people are illegal, immigrant and criminal. The nation is appellated as hard working and once again in terms of its own economic integration through its taxes. Citizens are articulated commercially as primarily tax-paying contributors to the nation as economy. There is a familiar echo of an old folk-story in the allusion to Dick Whittington's London, paved with gold. The second part of the piece works the old rhetoric of crooked landlords and sets them against the foregoing version of upright tax-payers – the ordinary people – but in an era of globalized flows of capital and people which trigger such crises as economic migration. There is no attempt to move beyond the surfaces of populist prejudice here, simply a demonstration of the effectiveness of remaining on the surface and using the popular newspaper as a forum for populist protest. The capitalization stresses the key terms of the debate and orchestrates in the final slogan the readers, the tax-payers and the nation into one bloc of implicit support.

The *Sun*'s series of stories featuring asylum seekers to Britain entitled 'Britain Has Had Enough' is full of devices intended to add to the impression that the popular newspaper is following the impetus of popular reaction and simply attempting to enhance it. All strategies which contribute to that interactivity enhance the popularity of the appeal. The rhetoric of dialogue and the strategies aimed at building an effect of nationalism through the paper are reinforced by the use of interactive feedback from the readers. This promises a kind of popular democratic feedback but it remains one compromised by its agenda having emanated from the press not the people. It remains what Hoggart has termed 'callow democratic egalitarianism' (1958: 178).

One device is the phone-in which promises to not only take opinions but also to call readers back to discuss the issue and canvass opinion:

YOU TELL US

We want to know what you think about the way refugees are treated in Britain. Call us on this number, we'll ring back.

This interactive democratic hotline serves to enhance the performative power of the newspaper when it calls in direct and colloquial questioning of the government of the day: 'Today we demand of the Government: What the hell are you going to DO?' (*Sun*, 13 March 2000).

On the same day there is a sinister carnivalesque version of this inter-activity with a *Sun* journalist being sent to Romania to beg in a cynical comparison which deliberately obscures the motivation and desperation of such economic migration:

BRITAIN HAS HAD ENOUGH

Sun girl begs in Romania and is given just 1p

I TRIED begging in Romania yesterday and discovered why its gipsy scroungers are heading for Britain.

The answer was right there in my begging bowl – 'earnings' of ONE PENNY.

While the grasping nomads of Eastern Europe can wheedle £20 an hour out of soft Londoners, my reward for two hours of humiliating pleading was a worthless two notes.

When it comes to articulating the voice of the ordinary working people, united in outrage, the *Sun* is not shy of asking trade union leader, AEEU general secretary Sir Ken Jackson, to comment: 'It may not worry the chattering classes but it angers working people ... The Sun is right to say enough is enough' (*Sun*, 13 March, 2000). It is unusual for a news-paper traditionally unsympathetic to trade unions to contain such sup-portive comments and perhaps disappointing to read the union leader allowing himself to be used to glibly support the newspaper's approach. It is a cynical deployment of a signifier of the working people and their representatives when for the most part it ignores organized labour groups and parades itself as the one authentic voice and representation of indi-vidual and collective working people. The use of a trade union quote serves to highlight its attempts to broaden its claim to legitimacy on this occasion.

As the interactive campaign gathers pace as part of its engagement with its own construction of the popular, the *Sun* is able to demonstrate its effec-tiveness and thereby the legitimacy of its claims as public watchdog on behalf of the people. The shift to the use of the Home Secretary's surname indicates a stiffening of attitude, the popular semantics of disapproval. The campaign allows the paper to articulate at least the vernacular of a Fourth Estate if not its content or its breadth of coverage:

'Time to kick the scroungers out'

Angry Sun readers jammed our phone lines yesterday demanding: 'Kick the scroungers out.' (The *Sun*, 15 March 2000)

Extracts are printed from the phone calls, with the age and location of the callers, expressing an overwhelmingly hostile attitude to the issue of asylum seekers. The following sequence from this particular week indicates the intensification of the campaign, the simplification of a complex issue through the tabloid techniques of mnemonics and phone democracy and the reliance on an angry rhetoric which claims to include the voice of the people. Indicating the effectiveness of these populist speech acts, the Home Secretary is obliged to respond to the paper's concerns:

STRAW ANSWERS OUR TEN QUESTIONS

YOU THE JURY

IS Jack Straw doing enough to solve the refugee crisis?
If you think yes phone ...
If you think no phone ... (The *Sun*, 15 March 2000)

BRITAIN HAS HAD ENOUGH

17,539 Sun readers lash Straw
17 extracts from phone calls to **YOU THE JURY** (The *Sun*, 16 March 2000)

BRITAIN HAS HAD ENOUGH

35,441 READERS LAY INTO STRAW

'... An amazing 98 per cent of votes ...' (The *Sun*, 17 March 2000)

ASYLUM-SEEKERS' CIG SCAM BUSTED BY SUN

Smoked out ... Polish immigrant sells bootleg ciggies to customer at Hackney market
and (right) offers pack to Sun's Emily Smith

THE Sun today exposes a bootleg cigarette scam fronted by asylum-seekers – which
is robbing Britain of 32.5 BILLION a year ...

That means huge losses in duty – money the government could use to build hospi-
tals and schools.

Another picture features the caption 'Having a laugh at Britain's expense ... Polish
woman flogs cigs to queue'. (The *Sun*, 21 March 2000)

The use of slang appears to endorse the impression that the outrage
expressed by the *Sun* is spontaneous and in keeping with the mood of a
public whose language it claims to share. Immigration is a complex issue
but it is one which the *Sun* seeks to close down through a variety of rhetorical and generic devices to a simple range of targets that can be exploited for
maximum effectiveness in appealing to populist sentiments.

Perhaps the tabloids' call to nation are more rooted in desperation. A
predominantly white, male and patriotic nation hostile to Europe and
sensitive to its past glories stands in for a nation that has ceased to exist –
the community represented as an alibi to stand in for the loss of nationhood which would spell the end for the popular newspaper in Britain as
we know it. The popular press has a vested interest in the survival of at least
a rhetorical version of the nation or its simulacrum. The application of this
rhetoric of the vernacular is a formative aspect of the nation/community in
the popular newspaper. It is doubly effective in being able to combine its
readers and the members of the nation as one community to legitimate its
own claims that it is writing/talking on behalf of a homogeneous community. This is clear in the final extract from this coverage in the *Sun*.

THE SUN SAYS

Danger signs
WHEN The Sun and its readers protest that asylum seekers are making mugs of us,
the chattering classes have a standard response.

'You're prejudiced because you're ignorant of the facts.'

... Our phonelines were swamped yesterday with readers protesting against the disgraceful red carpet treatment handed to the Algerian with two wives and 15 kids.

Today the phones will melt.

Politicians must listen to what ordinary people tell them.

Unless they take heed of public anger over refugees, the door will be open for extremists who are just waiting for the chance to harness the national sense of outrage and helplessness.

This is not an extreme county. Just the opposite in fact.

But even the fairest-minded nation has its breaking point.

And Britain has reached it.

Tony Blair must recognize the danger signals and act – before it is too late. (The *Sun*, 14 March 2000)

COMMUNITY OF RHETORIC OF INCLUSION

A similar dynamic and rhetoric is employed in order to create and reinforce the community of the nation or of the newspaper readership from within. This is grafted onto a second discourse of belonging to increase its effectiveness.

A previously loyal Labour MP resigns and the *Mirror* calls upon the Prime Minister to listen to the community which is layered into readers, ordinary people and the people themselves who are the loyal supporters of the party.

VOICE OF THE MIRROR

Why Blair must listen to Kilfoyle

The loyalty of Peter Kilfoyle to Labour can never be doubted.

So when he attacks the government it had better listen. What he said yesterday echoed the worries about which many Mirror readers have written to us....

... Peter Kilfoyle cannot be ignored. He speaks for too many ordinary people – people who are the backbone of Labour. (The *Mirror*, 28 March 2000)

The *Daily Mail*, without any sympathy for the Labour Party, chooses to construct an ironic stance to the affair using a hackneyed socialist battle-cry to implicitly invite its readers to join in the mockery of a party which it clearly implies is a wolf in sheep's clothing despite its newly acquired media-friendly image:

Old Labour roars into life as rebel ex-minister savages the Chancellor for betraying his party's traditional supporters

WHAT ABOUT THE WORKERS? (*Daily Mail*, 28 March 2000, front page).

The celebrity questionnaire is an informal device with which to promote debate about the state of the nation today:

TRUE BRIT (patterned in Union Jack motif)

As Tony Blair attempts to re-shape patriotism, we asked six very different Britons how they define themselves (*Daily Mail*, 30 March 2000)

From a particularly hostile perspective the Chancellor is accused of launching a propaganda campaign to brainwash the children of Britain into accepting the euro. This is presented as part of a broader strategy of diluting the British way of life. The linkage of such alarming angles on stories with the emotive populist rhetoric of national disenfranchisement plays a large role in reinforcing the paper's leading popular voice in opposition to the introduction of this currency.

NEW BID TO BRAINWASH THE BRITISH

Our millions spent on euro campaign

MILLIONS of pounds is to be spent trying to brainwash Britons into scrapping the £, Chancellor Gordon Brown revealed yesterday.

As part of a giant propaganda campaign, school-children will even be given classroom games to help them 'understand' the euro. (The *Sun*, 10 March 2000)

The key strategies employed by these papers, including the interview, the phone poll and the mimicking of the informality of a popular voice involve the readership in a community dependent on their proximity to the traditions and stabilities of popular genre for their success. The newspapers' ability to gather a community together by drawing on an appeal to those who perceive themselves and their newspaper to be opposed to the interests and indeed outside the power-wielding practices of their political and social superiors adds to the credibility of a popular voice. Even though in the current sceptical climate with its collapse of an identifiable popular politics or even a formal politic, which encourages active involvement, the pastiche and play of surface features of the popular press allow it to be more than simply a simulacrum of the popular. They articulate a representation of a community lost in any real material sense but bonded by their associations with familiar patterns of belief with the public arena, as entertainment, as part of that worldview. It is a triumph of style over content and its continuity becomes part of an explanation for its legitimacy; it becomes an authentic part of that community in its rhetoric.

The appeal of popular rhetoric in the press illustrates how any view of one-way traffic from producer to consumer is not particularly helpful. This rhetoric is certainly agonistic but must act in a much more dialogic way if it is to form a bond with the consumerist-based readership; it must, as always with popular culture, be able to retain a certain credibility around its claims to authenticity but the demands of the political economy of the news media dictate it must also align with the economic status quo. This is hegemony in action, including a vernacular of dissent but one which is structured to preference the institutional winners. This is why the rhetoric employs a voice which does not in the main talk of the people themselves, unless in particularly controlled conditions, within the formats of the newspaper itself, but plays with a ventriloquized voice from which even the people themselves are invited to ironically distance themselves. Part of the new sophistication of the popular press is its ability to incorporate that ironic resistance referred to by Billig (1992) as part of the dialogue itself. The more dialogic it appears, the more successfully will the hegemonic transaction be effected. Rhetoric once again is clearly the key to the success of hegemony even if it includes elements of a particularly postmodern blank irony.

In the popular press we certainly have the 'language games', which Lyotard celebrates in *The Postmodern Condition* but, rather than opening up spaces for diversity and the contestation of rigid hierarchies, the popular press indicates that the postmodern does not open up necessarily very favourably to certain minorities or to outsider groups to the nation-state in this particular set of economic structures but loops back to regressive meta-discourses around sexuality, ethnicity, capitalism and the nation. Without a perspective from the political economy of the popular press, as always with popular culture, we would be perhaps left with a rather empty and celebratory explanation of the appeal of the popular press. The national/popular newspaper functions within a set of activities and intensities which could be called postmodernity but within late capitalism's constraints. Otherness, in these circumstances, is rarely a marketable priority.

Such tendencies could be considered indicative of postmodernity in that there has been an accelerating loss of the legitimacy of nation, class or religious bond as absolute, but the popular newspaper in continuing to appeal to community is using the old rhetoric of national community while in fact addressing a new and virtual community to sell its product. The virtualization of community combined with this overriding economic imperative for the nation to survive, at least as market, are key postmodern trends.

Influential contemporary sceptics such as Stanley Fish and Richard Rorty suggest that we cannot step outside the prevailing habits of belief of our particular generation or lifestyle group and this seems to be corroborated by many of the consensual practices of the popular press which close down the communities of readers into commodified markets. So in the sceptical present we end up with something akin to a carnival of consensus where the stylistic games of inversion, vernacular and utopianism are played out within the restrictive parameters of the status quo, the current common-sense beliefs of the commodified popular which cannot be transcended for fear of losing the market so carefully constructed and re-created, invigorated by the traditional rhythms of carnival and melodrama day after day.

Another important mode of constructing the popular readership is in terms of the schematization and mnemonics of popular knowledge. This tradition of a newspaper providing public information has experienced many forms, from the attempts to report the proceedings of the English parliament in the seventeenth century, the political consciousness-raising of the nineteenth century, through the efforts of reformists to provide a more conservative substance for the reading masses and from the efforts of the popular newspapers and miscellanies of the late nineteenth century to the present. What distinguishes this contemporary form is perhaps its ambivalent and flippant attitude to the stuff of political debate. One moment this is ironic in the extreme and draws on intertextual media references, the next it is deadly serious, sometimes drawing on similar resources. At all times it is a pedagogy of populism – teaching a political agenda to a readership that is clearly not turning to its newspaper as its primary source of information but as a form of politicized entertainment perhaps.

In the run-up to the election of the Mayor of London, the *Daily Mail* utilized a classic popular press strategy in the schematization of politics, '20 Things You Didn't Know':

Let battle commence
20 things about Red Ken that nobody should forget *(Daily Mail*, 7 March 2000)

In colloquial and intertextual fashion the *Mirror*, 8 March 2000, used an actor and his catch phrase to discredit Ken Livingstone:

I DON'T BELIEEEVE IN HIM ANYMORE

TV's Victor Meldrew dumps Ken for Dobbo
ONE Foot in the Grave star Richard Wilson dramatically ditched support for Ken Livingstone as London's mayor last night.
The left-wing TV actor, Red Ken's most high-profile supporter, will campaign instead for official Labour candidate Frank Dobson.

In a different way the *Sun* on 9 March employs one of its daily letters specials, 'The Big Issue', to remind readers through letters of the dangers they perceive in Livingstone's potential tenure, editorially linking its political aversion to Livingstone to readers' views: 'Remember what Red Ken really stands for.' In the wake of Livingstone's eventual victory the *Sun* reverts to its parodic self in poaching from the American television animation South Park's tradition of killing off one of its characters every week to the chorus of 'Oh No They've Killed Kenny', and changes this to

'Oh No They've Elected Kenny', picturing Livingstone framed in a hooded parka like his popular cultural namesake.

A quiz is presented by Brian Reade in the Mirror, 23 February 2000, which relates to the lives of the celebrity Beckhams and links as fun and a set of participative stereotypes with the lives of ordinary people as readers of the *Mirror* – 'Who Rules the Roost ... or who is Hen-Becked?'

'It is the question men are asking each other in factories, offices, gyms and pubs across the land.
Was David Beckham right to ignore the demands of his employers and stay at home nursing a baby while his wife went shopping?
What would you have done in that situation?
Do YOU wear the trousers in your house?'

The light-hearted quiz calls on a shared understanding of everyday life from its targeted readers. It depends upon the imaginary nation and readership simultaneously experiencing a common culture which involves gossip at the workplace about the details of celebrities' lives so copiously reported by the popular press, and the quiz itself functions to harmonize those opinions even if in a parodic, slightly mocking fashion.

The quiz format is again employed in a different format to probe in a flippant fashion the nature of Britain under Tony Blair's government. The *Daily Mail* of 29 March 2000 sets 'a mischievous quiz for you to find your place in the nation':

Are you a Blair Briton?
(20 questions multiple choice answer format)
3 What do you think 'being at the heart of Europe' means?
a) Drinking German beer, Spanish Rioja, and French Champagne.
b) Making concessions to our EU partners so they won't hate us?
c) Carrying the message that Britain is best to those who weren't lucky enough to be born in our 'Other Eden'?

Celebrity links are often used to develop this public knowledge around certain issues often not connected to political affairs at all but part of a broader public sphere extended into the personal issue of diet and nutrition.

In the *Mirror*'s health zone of 23 March 2000, in the nutrition section, we can read:

'Why are so many people becoming ill when they eat ...
What is wheat intolerance?'

It is covered by reference to a series of celebrity victims including television personalities Gaby Roslin, Gillian Anderson and Ulrika Jonsson.

PERSONALITY POLITICS

___

In other areas of popular newspaper practice the dictum that 'the personal is political' does seem to be borne out as issues of maternity are directly addressed through real and fictional characters. In the *Daily Mail*, 21 March 2000, Cherie Blair holds forth on the raw deal facing working women and as a follow-up to this on 23 March, in an article entitled 'What the real Cheries think about Mrs Blair', Seven 45-year-old women called Cherie who are working mothers are interviewed: 'Their opinions make for a fascinating snapshot of women in Britain today ...'

When real-life issues and popular formats or genres coincide the authentification of the popular press as vector of genuinely popular concerns is even more persuasive. Their educational role is better and less dogmatically integrated into the everyday lives of their readers and their consumption patterns of other media. Teenage pregnancy is dealt with in terms of its representation in a soap opera and run against the lives of real teenage mothers:

'I'm a schoolgirl mum like TV Sarah-Louise ... and I wish I could turn back the clock [Caption] REGRETS ... gymslip mum Kathleen Moss, now 14, with daughter Georgia' (The *Sun*, 23 February 2000)

There are pictures of the Sarah-Louise and her mother, Gail from *Coronation Street* above a picture of Kathleen and her mum Pauline posing by a television set with the soap scene. The photo-book approach is completed by a 'Deidre says' special edition, which concludes: 'If Coronation Street has the guts to show us – and our young people – teenage pregnancy as it REALLY is, then it will be worthwhile viewing.'

Letters pages, advice pages, letters specials all tend to be clustered around themes of editorial relevance. The area of sexuality has always constituted a major area of concern in the popular press and its discussion of sexual problems and issues has always had at least a partially educational element. However, there is also the ambiguity of presentation which allows it to have a more hybrid appeal as prurient entertainment. The advice pages on sex must be considered in the context of the overall discourse around sexuality in the newspapers. It forms part of and is supportive of elements of that discourse. Despite concerns about teenage pregnancy, sex still forms a major element of popular appeal from the romantic clichés of the *Daily Mail* to the *Sun*'s Page Three Girl.

The *Mirror* has a celebrity doctor's advice column dressed up as a photo story, 'Miriam's Photo Casebook', with stories such as 'Two-faced best friend', 'Nanny's led astray' and 'Mum-in-law misery'. These are accompanied by a section called 'Miriam's Verdict', incorporating Dr Miriam Stoppard's 'The Advice Line You Can Trust'.

The *Sun* has a rival, raunchier column called 'Dear Deidre', with the more colloquial appeal of stories such as 'Fay's demanding fella', followed by a reply 'Dear Fay'. The incorporation of 'Deidre's Helplines' provides a degree of interactivity once again as part of the newspaper's strategy of involvement and dialogue with its readers as part of its popular status.

POPULAR SCIENCE

Even in its popular science the *Daily Mail*, 1 March 2000, plays on the interrelationship of popular psychology and a character out of a succesful television sitcom, *The Royle Family*:

> Why being idle puts us in a good mood
> It is the scientific study that will bring cheer to Jim Royle and countless other couch potatoes.
> Psychologists have discovered that those who avoid anything active, like the character in the BBC1 sitcom The Royle Family are happier than those who play sport and exercise regularly.

To complete the intertextual effect there is a picture accompanying the article, on the health pages, of Jim Royle played by actor Ricky Tomlinson.

In fact, popular science complete with illustration, is part of the *Daily Mail* tradition going back to its 1896 launch. Part of its mission was to educate the reader in informative yet bright and entertaining ways. In the contemporary paper, the familiar patterns within the miscellany of the popular press become more complex and infected by a broad range of intertextual features. In the following case the mixture is of science and light humour. Rather than an early modern version of didacticism, the learning is definitely there for entertainment and to feed into the discourse of gossip around news.

Greeks hail success on a Plato in the search for a perfect fried potato
Eureka! Great chips (*Daily Mail*, 30 March 2000)

8

INTEGRATING APPROACHES TO CONTEMPORARY POPULAR CULTURE

The public sphere has always functioned as a predominantly serious space, with an emphasis on 'communicative rationality'. Popular journalism has always rivalled that space, particularly in its connections to the traditions of popular culture and its more riotous elements. The popular press as it has developed in the twentieth century has a much closer rapport with laughter and the lighter side of life. This invites comparison with the influential writings of Mikhail Bakhtin on laughter and, in particular, its popular form, carnival. For Bakhtin there are two sides to the laughter of the carnival: first, 'the positive regenerating power of laughter' (1984: 45) and, second, the corrosive laughter which threatens the status quo. Through the ages, Bakhtin says, there has always been a laughing chorus (1984: 474); now it takes the form of the popular press. Its communicative strategies, though effective in the extreme, do not depend on rationality for their appeal, but more on their ability to entertain and employ the discourse of popular culture to make themselves and their interventions more plausible.

The contemporary generalizing of popular culture in postmodernity leads this discussion to a closer consideration of the ways in which two key concepts concerning the effectiveness of popular aesthetics and formats impact upon the popular press and the ways in which these depend also on traditional connections within the genealogies of the popular for their appeal. First, the carnivalesque. We may well compare aspects of popular contemporary newspapers to the carnival, which Bakhtin theorizes in relation to the work of Rabelais. The leading contemporary British popular tabloid emphasizes in its own promotional material that it is a 'fun' newspaper: '... The *Sun* has not only presented itself less as a newspaper and more as a "fun"-paper, but has done so by consciously comparing itself to the broadsheet press. For example, the paper recently parodied the *Financial Times*'s advertising copy-line, "No FT, no comment", with "No Sun, no fun"' (Bromley and Tumber, 1997: 373).

It is through a carnivalesque laughter, strangely suspended between the traditional attractions of the mocking of authority and the conservative exigencies of the political economy that the popular press functions as an institution. A superficial yet obsessive attraction to the the bizarre is part of the appeal of this form of popular journalism. It is what Kelvin MacKenzie and Wendy Turner once coined the 'Cor Doris Look At This' appeal. It belongs quite clearly to the oral tradition of sensational and hyberbolic gossip:

PRIEST BOOTS DOG IN HEAD
Cops arrest cruel Rev (*The Sun*, 29 March 2000)

Another example which highlights the grotesque and bodily humour of the carnivalesque is the following story, accompanied by a photo of the man in question displaying his distended belly and eating one of his curries.

KORMA TRAUMA
Keith gains 5st eating leftovers from his curry firm
CURRY seller Keith Bryson is a lot tikka round the waist – after being forced to EAT the leftovers of his failed delivery firm.
  He said: 'The only way I can pay what I owe and still eat is to work my way through what's left in my freezers.'

Carnivalesque is the temporary suspension of hierarchies of status, taste and behaviour; it allows a utopian glimpse of a community of plenty, freedom and creativity. Its uncrownings and inversions, the transformations into a new existence, unfettered by the exigencies of the everyday, are in the popular press returned into a cycle which redirects these impulses back into a circle of consumption and commodification. The transformations are imaginary via the reflected glories of celebrity; the uncrownings, particularly of celebrities, politicians and sports stars, are returned into a cycle of elevation and reduction. Fortunes are won but the recipients continue within the ethic of financial reward and the stereotypes of wealthy lifestyle so fetishized in all other parts of the popular press.

Celebrity gossip can be successfully mixed with the carnivalesque. In February 2000, in the following example, we see one genre, the gossip of celebrity, transferred into another, the photo-story, in a self-referential parody of the newspaper's own discourses and formats. The protagonists are music superstars Robbie Williams and Liam Gallagher. Self-referentially, the *Sun* launched the story on 22 February that Liam and Robbie were being publicly rude about each other's musical talents. Hostilities escalated on 24 February: 'Liam: I'll break Robbie's nose.' On 29 February we had the culmination in a lookalike photo story of the encounter between the two: 'Deidre's Photo (Fighto) Casebook'. It is because the popular press can maintain and mutate this cultural mode of the carnivalesque that it retains its success, although it is a triumph of genre over content in that it does not allow radical contestations of social or economic hierarchies to emerge.

Throughout history, carnival has served to keep alive alternative conceptions of life and power relations. In the popular press we have a ventriloquized version of the freedom and laughter of Bakhtin's carnival table-talk. It is a carnivalesque which only allows a limited perspective of individual and miraculous change, while mimicking its tone of transgression. Employing a carnivalesque mode explains how the papers retain an authority. They maintain the stance of being on the side of common-sense, against the powerful, on the side of the little man and woman, even if, as media institutions, they belong to structures of the capitalist elite. They articulate that stance in the mocking, deflating language purloined from the common people's armoury.

We have seen the popular press's adroit exploitation of the comic and the carnival of the people's voice, and also the negative aspects and the political implications of their truncated and ventriloquized form of the popular voice. Bakhtin's carnivalesque enabled both social stability and social protest and change (1984: 197). The popular press borrows the people's voice. It borrows the carnivalesque. It embroils them in postmodernity's intensification of cultural and capital flows and exploits the heightened effectiveness of popular culture to close down popular discourses to a restricted political agenda largely supportive of the status quo, using the traditional rhetoric and appeal of the genre to the ordinary people. The desecration and dismemberment typical of the carnivalesque never attack the body of capitalism nor the central ideologies of the status quo with regard to gender, nation, community or capital.

The popular press's version of dialogue is not, as in Bakhtin, opposed to the closure of the authoritarian word, nor is carnival opposed to the official hierarchy of culture; rather they are deployed as strategies to envelop popular traditions within a rhetoric of laughter and ridicule but emptied of anything other than a hollow, ironic resistance to the all-pervasive nature of control. It epitomizes postmodernity's blank irony; parody without a final target. It constitutes a poor deal in the hegemonic bargaining. Yet, viewed optimistically, carnivalesque's resources are still there to be directed elsewhere. Here, as in other genres, it becomes apparent that style is ideologically and politically neutral. It's what you do with it that counts.

Docker claims that we are experiencing 'a culture that in its exuberance, range, excess, internationalism, and irrepressible vigour and inventiveness perhaps represents another summit in the history of popular culture comparable to that of early modern Europe' (1994: 185). If this is so then we can certainly identify the role of the popular press as significant in providing exuberance, excess, range, vigour and inventiveness, but all within a rather restricted political framework and in a mainly parochial series of national settings.

MELODRAMA

In addition to the carnivalesque, a second noticeable feature of the appeal of the contemporary popular press can be seen in its continued appropriation of melodrama. Together they provide the framework of tradition and the patterns of a new aesthetic that enable a mass popular readership to cohere in an era of cultural fragmentation. They provide the reassurance of community and continuity.

Melodrama can be defined as 'the indulgence of strong emotionalism; moral polarisation and schematisation; extreme states of being, situations, actions; overt villainy, persecution of the good, and final reward of virtue' (Brooks, 1984: 11–12). In pursuit of these aims, he also claims, interestingly for our purposes, in exploring the interconnections between melodrama and popular journalism (pace Gripsrud) and particularly this journalism's strong normative streak, that it has as a goal '… to purge the social order …' (1984: 13). According to Brooks, melodrama is one mode of representing a world which has been deprived of divinity. It forms a part of the continuity of popular culture from the French Revolution and is an intrinsic way of modernity's coping with and interpreting the cultural world without the reassurance of religion and monarchy. Late consumer capitalism, with its rough house of winners and losers, is represented within the popular press as a game, a lottery, which throws up life transforming successes. Nevertheless, all that the varied genres and styles of address, in their rhetorical flattening of hierarchy, serve to reinforce is the system's institutional stability.

The melodrama of the popular press of today draws, as its theatrical counterpart of the nineteenth century, upon deep-lying attitudes and archetypes. It plays on the primary relationships and on the roles of characters within traditional story-lines. Parents, scoundrels, saviours, benefactors and judges all figure. In its ability to exploit such popular narratives and their character, the popular newspaper even in its news develops deepseated hopes and fears in a marketable way as a drama of 'pure psychic signs' (Docker, 1994: 252).

Brooks has written that 'With the rise of the novel and of melodrama, we find the entry into literature of a new moral and aesthetic category, that of the "Interesting"' (1984: 13). Yet it is fascinating that he overlooks the newspaper and, in particular, the popular newspaper, which emerged alongside these cultural developments. We could further compare these processes with the rise of the journalist as protagonist: 'It comes into being in a world where the traditional imperatives of truth and ethics have been violently thrown into question, yet where the promulgation of truth and ethics, their instauration as a way of life, is of immediate, daily, political concern' (Brooks, 1984: 15). This begs comparison with the potential of melodramatic forms in the evolution of journalism and particularly in its contemporary popular form, and it also recalls the representational crisis when truth and ethics become suspended as in postmodernity. In this era, the popular, detached from the direct potential of popular political power, has been diverted into a consumer-imaginary, a rhetoric sold to the people to enhance a sense of community embedded within a market economy.

The contemporary popular press provides us with a particularly postmodern version of melodrama – one based for its appeal on the transcendence of the media celebrity and commodity consumerism – and incorporates this within the everyday experience and expectations of the reader. The chief benefactors of the capitalist consumer culture are the media stars whose stories and tribulations play such a part in the success of the papers.

One of the distinguishing features of this version of melodrama which distinguishes it from the nineteenth century form is the blank irony of the decline from grace of celebrity. In earlier periods, such decline and the portrayal of the foibles of the successful and the famous could be glossed in terms of morality. Now the gloss is one of incorporation, a cynicism about the inevitability of political and personal corruption. This popular melodrama highlights a belief that the decline of the famous is a legitimate spectator sport – it is a bleak populism indeed. The implicit moral is that, unlike in carnival, excess, enjoyment and delight have a cost attached to them. There is a mean, puritanical element at work here which is far from a popular celebration.

Brooks claims that in melodrama all 'Conversations become confrontations' (1984: 251). Certainly the agonistic and demotic style of the popular press's dialogues with their readership provide evidence of this as they do also of the theatricalization of their textual display, indicating again as in melodrama: 'The last thing melodrama wanted to do was conceal itself as discourse ... on the contrary, it was eager to call attention to itself as theatricality, as a poetics of excess, as performance, as genre' (Docker, 1994: 69).

The fact that melodrama is politically neutral makes it suited to the ambivalent world of postmodernity with its blank ironies and in particular to the world of the popular articulated both as a rhetoric of the ordinary people and on behalf of ideologies often reactionary to the interests of those same people. Melodrama allows both the energies of the people textualized in the popular press and the interests of the social order to be held in balance.

Grotesque and shocking stories, unforeseen disasters in personal life, are among the most common channels for the melodramatic in the popular press. Since it is aimed at a largely lower-middle-class readership and has the highest female readership from any social class for a daily newspaper, a characteristic *Daily Mail* nightmare is the decline from a comfortable lifestyle, such as the following: 'He had a place at university, a rugby trial for England and a loving family. So how did this middle-class young man end up behind bars for murder?' (*Daily Mail*, 29 February 2000). Another story, which is literally dubbed a 'salutary story', thus highlighting the pedagogic performance explicitly, is the fall from grace of the middle-aged man lured to his ruin by a younger woman. A tale of psychic drama indeed!

At 45, this man had a mid-life crisis, abandoning his respectable family in search of sexual freedom.

What happened next is a stark warning to every middle-aged man.

... 'Looking back, I see a vain, middle-aged man who was prepared to gamble with the affections of the people he loved for his own self-gratification – and I am ashamed.' (*Daily Mail*, 3 March 2000)

Primal stories play their part and are enhanced by the use of emotive language and simple motivations and plot-lines.

BEHEADED

Obsessed father took an axe to the woman next door who had sex with his son (*Daily Mail*, 23 February)

The *Sun*, 23 February 2000, covers the story thus:

'I SWUNG AXE AND STARTED HACKING'

Tormented dad killed sexy neighbour in frenzy

The story is accompanied by likenesses of the protagonists named as:

'BEHEADED, BOY LOVER, BOY'S MUM'

'SHE WAS 34 AND SHE RAPED MY SON AT 15 ... GOD MEANT HER TO DIE'

Below the main story there is a picture of the type of axe used. The *Mirror* on 25 February 2000 runs the same story with parallel melodramatic appeal. The picture captions read:

THE KILLER, THE WIFE, THE SON

EXCLUSIVE: AXE VICTIM'S EX SPEAKS OUT

Lorraine seduced me, deceived me and nearly ruined my marriage ... but didn't deserve her head chopped off.

As in the *Sun*'s coverage, there is a picture of the axe.

COMMENT ON THESE HEADLINES

The *Daily Mail* specializes in stories of random personal tragedy redolent of melodrama: 'If we knew it was meningitis, why didn't the doctor who sent our baby son home to die?' (24 March 2000); 'Agony of mother whose twin son died beside her sleeping friend' (23 March 2000).

The *Sun* and the *Mirror* tend to focus their melodrama in terms of hyperbolic treatment of horror tales with the emphasis on the primal roles of Son, Mother, Baby and Dad:

DANIEL, SIX, DROWNS ON LORRY RIDE 'TREAT' (*The Sun*, 20 March 2000)

SON, 13, FINDS TEACHER MUM KNIFED TO DEATH (*The Sun*, 24 March 2000)

HEARTBREAK NOTE FOUND WITH DUMPED BABY

Take care of me
THIS is the first picture of the newborn baby found abandoned with her teddy bear in a hold-all on Valentine's Day. (The *Mirror*, 16 February 2000)

The story is accompanied by a full page picture of the baby Valentina and a copy of the handwritten note.

DAD'S AGONY AS TODDLER SON DIES UNDER HIS CAR (The *Mirror*, 21 March 2000)

The mirror image of the melodramatic tragedy is the feelgood story. This is crucial in terms of circulation in counter-balancing the gloom and doom of the descent of the great and the good and the grotesque tragedies of ordinary people's lives. The unexpected can also flow in positive ways. In their feelgood stories the popular press continues to tap a rich vein of popular expectation. They provide further evidence of the popular as the repressed alternative to the rationalist bourgeois public sphere. In an era when the dominance of global capital's influence seems to negate any personal-heroic romantic ideal of individual influence other than through the market mechanisms themselves, the melodramatic, as enacted in these popular stories, allows escapism and utopianism to flourish once more. The popular continues in its promise, however attenuated, of an entertaining glimpse of the world we could inhabit; one of plenty, of strong opinions, of victories against the odds and a place for the achievements of the ordinary person, identified through his/her newspaper.

JOY OF MOTHER WHO WAS TOLD THAT GETTING PREGNANT MIGHT KILL HER

My little miracle (*Daily Mail*, 17 February 2000)

MY TINY MIRACLE

Cancer mum's 15oz baby beats the odds to celebrate her first birthday (The *Mirror*, 29 March 2000)

BRAVE BELINDA IS THE BEST MUM UNDER THE SUN

BRILLIANT Belinda Barker was voted Britain's best mum yesterday in the Sun Woman Supermum's contests.
Belinda who showed amazing courage when one baby died and another went blind took the top award. (The *Sun*, 28 March 2000)

The last example had a commercial link as it was jointly sponsored with supermarket chain Safeways.

Contemporary Supermarket Tabloids in the USA

Tabloid-popular newspapers have developed a very different tradition in the United States although it is still one which illustrates the survival of popular genre via the press into the postmodern era. As we have already established, the practices of the tabloid press are inseparable from broadly popular culture and act as a vector of that culture. To varying degrees they eschew what is traditionally viewed as hard news and concentrate on scandal, celebrity, sensation, gossip and visual appeal - the best-selling issue ever of a supermarket tabloid was the *National Enquirer* with Elvis lying in state in his open casket at Graceland.

The centre for the production of America's most profitable, popular tabloids is Florida's east coast, so-called 'Tabloid Valley'. The main titles are the *National Enquirer* and the *Globe*, which devote themselves to the major, that is Hollywood, celebrities. They are followed by the *Star* and the

Examiner – less widely read, more parochial, with characteristically national American sportsmen, politicians and musicians with less of a global appeal. Bringing up the bizarre and cult end of the market we have the *Sun* and the *Weekly World News* which have stories of the weird and wonderful, monsters, the supernatural and the extraordinary.

The stories of these cult tabloids in particular certainly fit with most ancient traditions of broadsheet and almanac. Aliens, monsters, supernatural powers, reincarnation have always been well represented in popular print culture. They contain another aspect of popular tradition in that they are distrustful of government and outsiders and fulfil many of the parochial elements to be found within popular cultural output across the centuries.

In order to explain the place of these newspapers in contemporary society, Elizabeth Bird has written: 'Tabloids, like any kind of cultural phenomenon, exist alongside and because of other cultural phenomena. They complement the star system, the other popular media, the class system, and the gender system. They exist because of television, newspapers, movies, and a vast range of folk narratives and values' (1992: 1–2). She points to Clifford Geertz's definition of culture as a 'web of significance' (Geertz, 1973: 1), and certainly in their ability to tie into the news agendas of Hollywood, music celebrity, gossip about politicians and stories of the bizarre and unwordly they provide a cultural intertextuality and commercial interpenetration that can be described as postmodern.

Iain Calder, as editor-in-chief of the *National Enquirer*, drew attention to a certain postmodern conflation or even confusion of the democratic with the consumerist when he announced the willingness of readers to buy these tabloids: '"This is almost the purest form of democracy. Every single week, people are voting with their pocketbooks"' (Sachs, 1995).

Indeed, as they don't contain conventional news one might claim that they are a particular example the disappearance of the real and illustrate a rupture between traditional and tabloid newspapers in the United States, meaning that a commentator such as *Observer* journalist Peter Preston can write: 'The Enquirer and the rest don't need to worry about mainstream news or sport. They're free to plough a narrower patch of field while the editors of "proper" papers pretend they don't exist' (2000: 7).

In dealing with celebrity stories these tabloids continue to explore the ways in which celebrity is linked to the utopian aspirations of the readers, in the ways described in the nineteenth-century popular presss '"... closely tied to, and constituent of, their dreams"' (Schudson, 1978: 101), but they achieve this in a much more media-intensive fashion. Increasingly the stories cannot be narrowed to straightforward moral absolutes but allow a multiplication of perspectives, narratives and symbolic configurations to circulate. Bird illustrates this in describing some of the heteroglossia attending to the myth of JFK in the American tabloids: '... has become a figure encrusted with narratives that intersect with each other differently according to the reading of different individuals' (1992: 188). Bird argues that much of their appeal lies in the resonance of the tabloids' narratives with older, popular traditions and in particular their vernacular and oral appeal, and that it is the rhetoric of this appeal which provides their hegemonic effect (1992: 196).

Compared to Britain where the tabloids are taken very seriously because of their daily political influence and their apparent empathy with the mundane lives of their readers, the US supermarket tabloids are free to plough their own furrow, largely ignored by the mainstream, and content as long as their circulations hold up. Wendy Henry, fresh from her experiences on British tabloids, articulates this particular reality of the supermarket tabloids, speaking as the *Globe*'s editor: '"None of the political nonsense nightmare that was got into in Britain, with the chattering classes and the Independent and worrying about what the bloody Guardian was saying about you every day"' (Paskal: 1992). 'The lesson from America is that, without the tabloids and their spirit of irreverence, the press becomes a bastion of conformity dedicated to lofty purposes understood only by the few, an instrument for and by the elite – a danger sign for any society' (Taylor, 1992, 17–18). So much so that we have on-line variants of the newspaper, such as *The Onion* or the *Drudge Report*, running stories as parody and gossip because of the fact that the mainstream and tabloid press are strung out between celebrity gossip and turgid economic and political news.

As if to confirm the malleability of popular print culture in the supermarket tabloids, we can read of a realignment of these papers to new commercial trends (Helmore, 2000). As circulation figures are down – *National Enquirer* from 3.4 million in 1994 to 2.1 million last year, the *Star* from 2.8 to 1.8 million, the *Globe* from 1 million to 800,000. David Pecker of parent company America Media is trying to take them upmarket for the sake of advertising credibility. Edward Helmore writes of an era of respectability, more attractive and credible to advertisers, evicting miracle cures and psychic healers.

> He claims there is a new slogan for the Enquirer:
> 'Get it first. Get it fast. Get it Right.'
> Yet the traditional division of news emphasis between the three remains:
> Pecker: 'The easiest way to look at it is, if a big Hollywood story breaks, the Enquirer would do investigative stories, the Star would cover the impact on the celebrity's career, and the Globe would really do the spicy parts of the story' (Helmore, 2000: 10).

BILD-ZEITUNG

Germany provides the best-selling genuinely popular newspaper in the world in the *Bild-Zeitung*. Founded on 24 June 1952 by Axel Springer, originally in Hamburg but soon to cover the whole of West Germany, it was very influenced by the British popular newspapers of the time and combined their uncompromising populism with the tone of the indigenous Hamburg evening newspaper tradition. It was conservative in persuasion but spoke to the average man in the street with an emphasis on local stories, human interest and sensation. Its slogan 'Mit der Heimat im Herzen die Welt umfassen' ('Understanding the world with our homeland in our heart') expresses well the complexity of its appeal to a low-brow, nationalist readership whose worldview is structured by a profound parochialism. By the mid-1960s it had reached a daily sale of four million, a figure it maintains today.

In a similar way to the British tabloids it addresses a local audience. This is even more pronounced in the case of the *Bild-Zeitung* as it has a different edition for each of the German states. This local appeal forms part of the marketing structure of a global media organization and can be contrasted with the US version of tabloid popularity which foregrounds globalized media celebrity and directs this more to a local readership. This paradox exemplified by these two emergent popular print traditions is part of the complexities of postmodernity.

The way in which it directs itself to the local reader has always been through a strong articulation of the vernacular to a very specifically German audience. Dieter Brumm (1980: 127–30) claims that it delivers the templates of conversation for millions of ordinary Germans and presents itself thus as the speech of the speechless. Such linguistic dexterity allows it to live up to a rhetorical appeal to its readers as one of them, a companion.

Despite Gunter Wallraff's exposition of the manipulative tricks of the trade (1977, 1979, 1985) and the well-founded concerns of left-wing critiques of its strategies and effects (Bechmann *et al.*, 1979), the appeal of the paper still lies in its ability to craft a plausible and marketable relationship with the popular. It does this thematically and rhetorically, always emphasizing connections to wider popular cultural concerns and always in an identifiable vernacular.

Its first noticeable feature is its reliance on a solid base of specifically German national appeal. The national appeal of the newspaper is reinforced by an almost exclusive register of German celebrities. Football stars and their marriage problems run side by side with stories of more internationally famous German celebrities such as Claudia Schiffer, Michael Schumacher, Henry Maske, Boris Becker and Steffi Graf. More globally recognized stars are seldom covered with the same regularity or prominence and, as in the British tabloids, this pattern seems to confound any simplistic assumption that globalized media concerns are narrowing down the celebrity agenda to one solely driven by Hollywood agendas.

This impression is reinforced by the mockery directed at the Americans on occasion. On 12 February 2000 the front page included a story headlined: 'Are the Americans too stupid for the Jauch show?' The popular quiz show on German television is reported as being too intellectually demanding for the Americans. This was followed up on 16 February 2000 by 'Der dümmste Mann Amerikas (dumm, dümmer, Amerikaner)' – 'The most stupid man in America (stupid, stupider, American)'.

Bild-Zeitung is a newspaper that relies upon a clear vernacular appeal. This orality is plain in the language of the editorial commentary, 'Bild Kommentare', prominent on page two each day, and its connections to the language of the ordinary people is reinforced by its juxtaposition with the letters of the readers on the selected topics of the day. On page three under the *Bild* logo we read 'Guten Morgen' and then a thought for the day based on a newsy anecdote. This is followed by an appropriate greeting such as 'Schönes Wochenende, einen schönen Tag' ('Have a nice weekend, a nice day').

The ancient vernacular tradition of popular culture finds itself mingled in intertextual fashion in the regular 'TV Sprüche' ('TV Speak') on page four and is based on quotes from TV on political current news. The tradition of the gossip is explicitly referred to on the back page and Katja Keßler each day in her 'hier klatscht' ('here's the gossip') column reinforces the national popular cultural content.

The grotesque and the gothic still play their traditional sensationalist role in the reporting of murder cases. Illustrations of murder weapons and the scenes of crimes, preferably bloodstained, are commonplace.

Again, as in Britain, television soaps of a specifically national variety provide a popular connection to other areas of readers' lives in a commercial media intertextuality. Readers are invited to take part in a national competition to win a part in the top TV soap *Gute Zeiten, Schlechte Zeiten* ('Good Times, Bad Times') in a media variant on the tradition of competitions in the popular press. In a second example, this time employing a version of the phone vote, more usually deployed for political opinion polls, we have a vote for suitable attire for the popular TV presenter Thomas Gottschalk, asking readers (and viewers) to choose whether he should dress in a suit or in a Scottish costume complete with kilt (24 March 2000).

The paper is fully immersed in its role to broker its popularity through an awareness of the interest in all things consumerist and commercial in its readership. It is full of tricks and tips aimed at the idealized 'little man' on the German street. Stories and features in February and March 2000 included how to act if the rent is too high, how to get the most back from your taxes, outraged debate about the increases in petrol prices, including a story of a man who has to steal petrol in order to be able to drive to work, how to get the best deal on a used car and the best stock market tips for Germans.

The traditional element of popular science is often represented, but in a parodic fashion very different from the earnest popularizing of another age of popular newspapers. Mars sends greetings from the heart – allegedly a picture of the planet on Valentine's Day; does the Earth have hiccoughs with illustrations of volcanoes (28 February 2000); or the intertextually illustrated story of the microchip which can, as in the film *Total Recall*, create a record of our memories (18 March 2000) are illustrative of this trend.

There are then a series of ambiguous positions around the carnivalesque, the melodrama and the popular voice articulated in the popular press. They can either be inclusive and positive as Docker (1994) tends to suggest, opening up momentary alternatives to the dominance of economic patterns. They can be manipulative and pejorative of both the political actor and the political process, as we have seen in discussions on vernacular and demotic address. For these to be simultaneously true the popular voice cannot have been incorporated in any truly representative way but must have been grafted onto the discourses of global news media. This gives the popular press its authentic feel; it retains at least the echo of the people and their interests outside these power blocs, whether this is articulated within the discourses of populist political engagement or within the discourses of escapist fantasy and melodrama.

A negative history of the popular press in Britain is narrated briefly by Raymond Williams:

> first, the emergence of an independent popular press, directly related to radical politics, in the first decades of the nineteenth century; second, the direct attack on this, and its attempted suppression, in the period up to the 1830s ...; and third (and most important as a way of understanding our own situation) the indirect attack, by absorption but also by new kinds of commercial promotion, which aimed not at suppressing the independent popular press but at replacing it, in fact by the simulacrum of popular journalism that we still have in such vast quantities today. (Smith, 1975: 204)

Although Williams's concerns for a properly functioning political press are still of relevance, his analysis of the popular press dramatically underestimates the economic and normative linkage of any press that has claimed to represent the people. Perhaps we must see the early nineteenth-century British radical/popular press as an exception rather than as an ideal type. The radical Unstamped in Britain is divorced from many of the traditional features of popular print.

The popular as representative of the people, certainly in the contemporary era, only has currency when that is reflected in a mass appeal. Authenticity is now economically marked, not by some reference to a set of criteria unrelated to number. That battle was lost with the liberalization of the newspaper markets in Europe and in the United States. We may bemoan the inability of the newspaper to genuinely and consistently campaign on radical popular issues, but if we expect that we are perhaps looking in the wrong place for pure action. The press as an economic agent can only modulate its popular appeal through economics. This does not stop it being representative of many areas of ordinary, everyday life and popular culture – but then again these were never absolutely radical at any point in their history.

An approach rooted in the rhetoric of popular culture may resolve this potential antagonism in a slightly different way but still in terms of the complex negotiation of a variety of features, including its ability to talk representatively on behalf of the people, despite its involvement in larger economic processes which are inimicable to them as a class or interest group.

Genre, rhetoric and the traditions of popular culture provide a complex but dynamic view of how the content and politics of the popular press play their part in authenticating their appeals to the people. These rhetorical aspects are crucial in the negotiation of the hegemonic site of the popular in the press.

The traditional narrative elements and characterizations, coupled with the colloquial and strong demotic appeal of the language, enhance the apparent participatory nature of the popular press as it is conducted in a complex refraction of popular tastes. These tastes are harnessed in a set of commercial, commodified imperatives within the political economy of the newspapers. But their popularity does not mean that they are liberationary in any sense. The paradox is that the forms and genres may have subversive potential – that is their popular appeal – but, within the political economy, these forms and genres are what is surrendered in order for the power bloc to maintain its hegemonic control in this play of give and take to stabilize the system. Peter Golding argues that '... "tabloidisation" is, in fact, at least partly the process by which the popular is incorporated into the political' (1999: 62).

The popular press enables a deep structure to cohere where there is a diminution of direct political involvement but in its images of politics and in its rhetoric it provides a disturbing aestheticization of the people to counterbalance the personalization and even trivialization of politics at its core. Its version of vernacular, carnivalesque and melodrama play a part in making such politics attractive and therefore marketable.

I would argue with Bromley and Tumber (1997: 365) that although the popular press is different from its broadsheet neighbour, particularly in its tradition of popular miscellany and its prioritization of entertainment, this does not lessen the political impacts, in particular its normative influence through its narratives of nation and community. In fact, its incorporation of its idealized readership into a discourse apparently divorced from main-stream political-economic coverage, makes its worldview all the more powerful for it is located within the rhetoric of the everyday and the common-sense of popular culture.

It is connected to everyday life through the vernacular and their inclusion into broader cultural patterns of media consumption such as TV celebrity, soap storyline, music and film stars and popular memory, through on iconography of the nation (Conboy: 99). These are the bridges between the trivial and the serious, which include the personalization of the public space as well as the commercialization of the private domain. Popular tabloid newspapers in Britain are different from their broadsheet cousins but their miscellany contains a politics – one suited to a consumer-oriented, popular cultural postmodernity.

This popular press, then, is resistant to many aspects of the political elite and quick to point a corrective finger at deviant behaviour, but it lacks a corresponding politics that is able to define any alternative approach. It maintains a cool, ironic detachment from the overtly political elements of the traditional bourgeois public sphere. Its deployment of popular cultural devices and genres such as the carnivalesque and the melodramatic, allied to a strong grasp of a vernacular address, allow these papers to employ popular cultural forms for hegemonic ends. The *Sun* can still claim, with a reasonable amount of authority, that it is 'THE PEOPLE'S PAPER', as it does as a banner on its front page. This claim no longer resides in ownership but exclusively in representation and rhetoric – it represents and refracts the views of the people in a deliberately populist format and agenda. It may be a 'parody of a newspaper' as McGuigan has called the *Sun* (1992: 185) but this may not be as negative a term as he intends. This parodic approach constitutes a timely and commercially successful solution to the problem of mass popular readerships in contemporary Britain.

The newspaper is, as a genre, always attempting to edit down a range of worldviews, to structure them so as to cohere to an institutional and a cultural framework of expectation. It is involved in arresting the heteroglossic flows which always attend to democratic communication. In postmodernity, its ability to achieve this feat is strained. Yet popular newspapers still achieve it through their ability to draw upon and develop a rhetoric of demotic conformity. Tabloidization, dumbing down and other debates are simply anxieties that a slippage of control – hegemonic since the victories of the capitalist press in the mid nineteenth-century – is occurring. They are really debates about the function of newspapers at this particular time of representational crisis. The impact of the popular press on the broadsheets in the so-called tabloidization debate is further proof of the ability, so marked in postmodernity, of popular forms to infect bourgeois forms. The fact that the debate reaches the content of and direction of the broadsheets means that they are continuing to redefine the popular as an expanding discourse and even to redefine the broadsheets' space as a political medium.

The popular cultural rhetoric of parody, pastiche, blank irony, the mingling of the cultural and the commercial, the public and the private are all forms of what Jameson terms 'infection', "the very prototype of what we may call the postmodern mode of totalizing" (1991: 373). The apparent ability of the popular press to export this to broadsheet newspapers is a sign of its resilience and effectiveness as well as a symptom of postmodernity.

Is the disturbing phenomenon in contemporary popular print journalism not that it has lost sight of its need to bring its readership, as the people, a diet of political news, but that it has lost sight of the linkage between the people and the popular? There remains simply a voice, an echo, an aural version of Baudrillard's simulacrum. Perhaps postmodernity's critique's obsession with the visuality of image has led to a neglect of voice. Recognizing these aspects of the 'orality' of the popular press leads us to conclude it is based just as much on the articulation of an image.

How, then, does the popular perform as a discourse and how does the popular press arrest the loosening of that embrace which Foucault has observed is so characteristic of discourses (Foucault, 1974: 49)? The popular press is still dependent on rhetorical appeal to legitimate its claim to popularity and to represent the people and their interests, particularly as articulated against the power bloc. This is manifest in two distinct but interconnecting ways. First, there is the attempt to further stylize the popular, vernacular voice. Second, the newspaper seeks to integrate itself and its discourses with an ever-expanding number of other popular discourses and genres to add legitimacy to its own rhetoric of popularity. The growth of consumer capitalism has meant that more and more genres are now available for popularization and the newspaper has moved adeptly to colonize them as it has always moved rapidly to incorporate the interests and speech of the masses. Key aspects of this include:

- Hybridity, as ever it was, is the key to their success and the consistency of their voice, their rhetoric.

- The people are interpellated as consumers or as a nation. This approach combines the new mode of integrated consumerist identity and lifestyle with a more resilient version of older modernist configurations of national community.

- Celebrity and consumerism are used as conduits to everyday concerns of illness, crime, heartbreak.

Politics is covered in a watchdog sort of way but confined very much to a perspective of the status quo and the occasional bout of aggressive agenda setting. Politics is often, in addition, presented in an adversarial fashion with either/or choices or presentations, which further serve to contract choice back to two already delineated options. Phone-ins and campaigns are extensions of the popular rhetoric of appeal to the readers as democratic processes, initially perfected by the American mass-selling dailies and continuing restricted to their conservative agenda.

In conclusion, we must reassert that the contemporary tabloid newspaper remains a challenge to bourgeois notions of the public sphere, particularly in its political manifestations. That it maintains a continuity with its predecessors both in terms of the popular newspaper and more broadly popular culture and aligns itself with contemporary configurations is not simply a last-gasp effort to rescue a place for itself in the coming decades but part of a longer more intrinsic strategy for the popular to graft itself onto whatever other current cultural and political discourses are constructing the people. Thus the ability of the popular newspaper to articulate its readers in a rhetoric acceptable to them is part of its tradition and also part of the challenge that exists forever within this hegemonic tension of exchange.

The idea of an infinite re-exploration of this readership and the implication that the readership is in fact a key element in the creative resources of this press has a familiarity to readers who appreciate the 'hall of mirrors' of postmodernity, the recycling of previous paradigms and styles in cycles of simplicity and elaboration. David Harvey has observed that: 'During phases of maximal change, the spatial and temporal bases for reproduction of the social order are subject to the severest disruption ... it is exactly at such moments that major shifts in systems of representation, cultural forms, and philosophical sentiment occur' (1989: 239).

The popular press, with its reliance on narratives that draw on established genres and scripts, is a key and subtle purveyor of normative assumptions to a mass audience. Therefore it is inevitable that major shifts in how an era is narrated and how its aesthetics are constructed will have an influence on the content, rhetoric and impact of the popular press itself as part of that mainstream of integrated popular experience. In addition, the press is passing through one of those phases of 'maximal change'. This is demonstrated by the effects on the popular press and the press in general of the intensified economic effects and cultural shifts percolating through from popular culture and everyday life. To this extent, beating in tune with the common experiences of its readers, the popular press is as problematically authentic as it ever was.

BIBLIOGRAPHY

Agger, B. (1992) *Rethinking Popular Culture*. Sussex: Falmer Press.

Altschull, J. Herbert (1990) *From Milton to McLuhan: The Ideas Behind American Journalism*. Longman.

Anderson, B. (1986) *Imagined Communities*. Verso.

Arnold, M. (1887) 'Up to Easter', *The Nineteenth Century*, no. CXXIII, May: 627–48.

Bakhtin, M.M. (1984) *Rabelais and His World*, trans. H. Iswolksky. Indiana University Press.

Bakhtin, M.M. (1996) *The Dialogic Imagination,* ed. M. Holquist, trans. C. Emerson and M. Holquist. University of Texas Press.

Bechmann, R., Bischoff, J., Maldaner, K. and Loop, L. (1979) *Ideologie als Ware*. VSA.

Bellanger, C., Godechot, J., Guiral, P. and Terrou, F. (1969) *Histoire de la Presse Francaise, vol. 1*. Paris: P.U.F.

Belsey, C. (1993) *Critical Practice*. London: Routledge.

Bennett, T. (1986) 'The politics of the popular', in T. Bennett, C. Mercer and M. Woolacott, *Popular Culture and Social Relations*. Oxford: Oxford University Press.

Bennett, T., Mercer, C. and Woollacott, M. (1986) *Popular Culture and Social Relations*. Oxford: Oxford University Press.

Berridge, V.S. (1976) 'Popular journalism and working class attitudes, 1854–86: a study of *Reynold's Newspaper, Lloyd's Weekly Newspaper* and the *Weekly Times*'. PhD thesis, University of London.

Berridge, V.S. (1978) 'Popular Sunday papers and mid-Victorian society', in G. Boyce, J. Curran and P. Wingate (eds), *Newspaper History from the Seventeenth Century to the Present Day*. London: Constable. pp. 247–64.

Bessie, S. (1938) *Jazz Journalism*. New York: Dutton.

Beutin, W., Ehlert, K., Emmerich, W., Hoffacker, H., Lutz, B., Meid, V., Schnell, R., Stein, P. and Stephan, I. (1993) *A History of German Literature. From the Beginnings to the Present Day*. London: Routledge.

Bhabha, H. (1990) *Nation and Narration*. London: Routledge.

Billig, M. (1992) *Talking of the Royal Family*. London: Routledge.

Billig, M. (1995) *Banal Nationalism*. London: Sage.

Bird, S. Elizabeth (1992) *For Enquiring Minds: A Cultural Study of Supermarket Tabloids*. Tennessee, TN: University of Tennessee Press.

Blickle, P. (1984) 'Social protest and reformation theology', in P. Blickle, H.-C. Rublack and W. Schulze, *Religion, Politics and Social Protest*. London: Historical Institute and Allen and Unwin.

Blickle, P., Rublack, H.-C. and Schulze, W. (1984) *Religion, Politics and Social Protest*. London: German Historical Institute and Allen and Unwin.

Bode, C. (1959) *The Anatomy of American Popular Culture 1840–1861*. CA: University of California Press.

Booth, M. (1965) *English Melodrama*. Herbert Jenkins.

Boyce, G. (1978) 'The long road to objectivity and back: the kinds of truth we get in journalism', in G. Boyce, J. Curran and P. Wingate, *Newspaper History from the Past to the Present*. London: Constable.

Boyce, G., Curran, J. and Wingate, P. (eds) (1978) *Newspaper History from the Past to the Present*. London: Constable.

Boyd, D.H. and MacLeod, (1977) *Newsletters to Newspapers*. WV: West Virginia University Press.

Brake, L., Jones, A. and Madden, L. (eds) (1990) *Investigating Victorian Journalism*. London: Macmillan.

Bromley, M. (1998) 'The "tabloiding" of Britain: "quality" newspapers in the 1990s', in H. Stephenson and M. Bromley (eds), *Sex, Lies and Democracy*. Harlow: Longman.

Bromley, M. and Tumber, H. (1997) 'From Fleet Street to cyberspace: the British "popular" press in the late twentieth century', *European Journal of Communication Studies*, CA: 22 (3): 365–78.

Brooks, P. (1984) *The Melodramatic Imagination*. Columbia University Press.

Brown, L. (1985) *Victorian News and Newspapers*. Clarendon Press.

Brumm, D. (1980) 'Sprachrohr der Volksseele?', in M.W. Thomas (ed.), *Porträts der deutschen Presse*. Spiess.

Brummett, B. (1991) *Rhetorical Dimensions of Popular Culture*. Alabama: University of Alabama Press.

Burke, P. (1978) *Popular Culture in Early Modern Europe*. Temple Smith.

Burke, P. (1981) 'The "discovery" of popular culture', in R. Samuel (ed.), *People's History and Socialist Theory*. London: Routledge & Kegan Paul.

Capp, B. (1979) *Astrology and the Popular Press: English Almanacs. 1500–1800*. London: Faber & Faber.

Carr, E.H. (1986) *What is History?* Harmondsworth: Penguin.

Chartier, R. (1991) *The Cultural Origins of the French Revolution*, trans. L.G. Cochrane. Duke University Press.

Chippendale, P. and Horrie, C. (1990) *Stick It Up Your Punter: The Rise and Fall of the Sun*. Mandarin.

Chiswick, H. (1991) *The Press in the French Revolution*. Oxford: Oxford University Press.

Clark, C.E. (1994) *The Public Prints: The American Newspaper in Anglo-American Culture 1665–1740*. Oxford: Oxford University Press.

Clarke, T. (1955) *Northcliffe in History: An Intimate Study of Press Power*. Hutchinson.

Cobbett, W. (1816) *Political Register*, vol. 31, 2 November.

Cobbett, W. (1819) *Political Register*, vol. 34, 24 April.

Cobbett, W. (1820) *Political Register*, vol. 35, 27 January.

Colley, L. (1994) *Britons: Forging the Nation*. London: Vintage.

Conboy, M. (1999) 'The Ethnic Origins of Readerships', in V.E. Beitter (ed), *The New Europe at the Crossroads*.

Connell, I. (1991) 'Tales from Tellyland', in P. Dahlgren and C. Sparks (eds), *Communication and Citizenship*. London: Routledge.

Connell, I. (1992) 'Personalities in the popular media', in P. Dahlgren and C. Sparks (eds), *Journalism and Popular Culture*. London: Sage.

Cranfield, G. (1978) *The Press and Society*. Harlow: Longman.

Crouthamel, J.L. (1989) *Bennett's New Herald and the Rise of the Popular Press*. Syracuse University Press.

Crystal, D. (1991) *Dictionary of Linguistics and Phonetics*. Oxford: Basil Blackwell.

Cudlipp, H. (1953) *Publish and Be Damned*. London: Andrew Dakers.

Curran, J. (1977) 'Capitalism and the control of the press 1800–1975', in J. Curran, M. Gurevitch and J. Woollacott (eds), *Mass Communication and Society*. London: Edward Arnold and Open University Press.

Curran, J. (1978) *The Press as an Agency of Social Control in Newspaper History*.

Curran, J. (1991) 'Rethinking the media as a public sphere', in P. Dahlgren and C. Sparks (eds), *Communication and Citizenship*. London: Routledge.

Curran, J. and Sparks, C. (1991) 'Press and popular culture', *Media, Culture & Society*, 13: 215–37.

Dahlgren, P. (1991) 'Introduction', in P. Dahlgren and C. Sparks (eds), *Communication and Citizenship*. London: Routledge.

Dahlgren, P. (1992) 'Introduction', in P. Dahlgren and C. Sparks (eds), *Journalism and Popular Culture*. London: Sage.

Dahlgren, P. and Sparks, C. (eds) (1991) *Communication and Citizenship*. London: Routledge.

Dahlgren, P. and Sparks, C. (eds) (1992) *Journalism and Popular Culture*. Sage.

Darnton, R. (1996) *Forbidden Fruit*. HarperCollins.

Daspit, T. and Weaver, J.A. (1999) *Popular Culture and Critical Pedagogy*. Garland Press.

de Certeau, M. (1988) *The Practice of Everyday Life*. CA: University of California Press.

Dickens, A.G. (1976) *The German Nation and Martin Luther*. Edward Arnold.

Docker, J. (1994) *Postmodernism and Popular Culture*. Cambridge: Cambridge University Press.

Douglas, G.H. (1999) *The Golden Age of the Newspaper*. Westport, VI: Greenwood.

Dunnett, P. (1988) *The World Newspaper Industry*. Croom Helm.

Dyck, I. (1992) *William Cobbett and Rural Popular Culture*. Cambridge: Cambridge University Press.

Eaton, S., Hawkins, A., Laing, S., Merricks, L. and Walker, H. (1986) *Disorder and Discipline: Popular Culture from 1550 to the Present*. Aldershot: Temple Smith.

Ellyard, E. (1971) 'Readerships of the periodical press: mid-Victorian Britain', *Victorian Periodicals Newsletter*, 13: 5–22.

Emery, M. and Emery, E. (1992) *The Press and America: An Introspective History of the Mass Media*. Prentice Hall.

Engel, M. (1996) *Tickle the Public: One Hundred Years of the Popular Press*. Englewood Cliffs, NJ: Gollancz and Prentice Hall.

Ensor, R. (1968) *The Oxford History of England: Vol X1V: 1870–1914*. Oxford: Oxford University Press.

Epstein, J. (1976) 'Feargus O'Connor and the *Northern Star*', *International Review of Social History*, 21: 51–97.

Fairlie, H. (1957) 'Brilliance skin deep', *Encounter*, 8–14 July.

Featherstone, M. (ed.) (1993) *Global Culture. Nationalism, Globalization and Modernity*. London: Sage.

Fiske, J. (1994) *Reading the Popular*. London: Routledge.

Fletcher, A. and Stevenson, J. (1985) *Order and Disorder in Early Modern England*. Cambridge: Cambridge University Press.

Foster, H. (1985) 'Introduction', in H. Foster (ed.), *Postmodern Culture*. Pluto. pp. xi–xii.

Foucault, M. (1974) *The Archaeology of Knowledge*, trans. A.M. Sheridan-Smith. London: Tavistock.

Foucault, M. (1980) 'The eye of power', in C. Gordon (ed.), *Power/Knowledge*. Brighton: Harvester Wheatsheaf. pp. 161–2.

Foucault, M. (1989) *The Order of Things*. London: Routledge.

Fowler, R. (1991) *Language in the News*. London: Routledge.

Friedman, J. (1993) *Miracles and the Pulp Press during the English Revolution*. University College Press.

Frow, J. (1993) 'The concept of the popular', *New Formations*, 18 (Winter): 25–38.

Fukuyama, M. (1992) *The End of History*. Avon Press.

Gans, H.J. (1977) *Popular Culture and High Culture*. New York: Basic Books Inc.

Geertz, C. (1973) *The Interpretation of Cultures*. New York: Basic Books Inc.

Giddens, A. (1987) *Social Theory and Modern Sociology*. Cambridge: Polity Press.

Giroux, H. and Simon, R. (1989) *Popular Culture, Schooling and Everyday Life*. Bergin and Garvey.

Golby, J.M. and Purdue, A.W. (1984) *The Civilisation of the Crowd*. London: Batsford.

Golding, P. (1999) 'The political and the popular: getting the measure of tabloidisation', in *Moving On: Changing Cultures, Changing Times*. Proceedings of the AMCCS Conference, Sheffield Hallam University.

Golding, P. and Fergusson, M. (1997) *Cultural Studies in Question*. London: Sage.

Goodbody, J. (1985) 'The *Star*: its role in the rise of popular newspapers 1888–1914', *Journal of Newspaper and Periodical History*, 1 (2): 20–9.

Gordon, I. (1998) *Comic Strips and Consumer Culture 1890–1945*. Smithsonian Institution.

Gough, H. (1988) *The Newspaper Press in the French Revolution*. London.

Gramsci, A. (1971) *Selections from the Prison Notebooks*, trans. and ed. Q. Hoare and G. Nowell Smith. Lawrence & Wishart.

Gripsrud, J. (1992) 'The aesthetics and politics of melodrama', in P. Dahlgren and C. Sparks (eds), *Journalism and Popular Culture*. London: Sage.

Gurevitch, A. (1990) *Medieval Popular Culture*. Cambridge: Cambridge University Press.

Habermas, J. (1984) *The Theory of Communicative Action, vol. 1*. Beacon Press. pp. 82–101.

Habermas, J. (1992) *The Structural Transformation of the Bourgeois Public Sphere*. Cambridge: Polity Press.

Hall, S. (1981) 'Notes on deconstructing the "popular", in R. Samuel (ed.), *People's History and Socialist Theory*. London: Routledge & Kegan Paul.

Halliday, M.A.K. (1978) *Language as Social Semiotic*. Arnold.

Hardt, H. (1979) *Social Theories of the Press: Early German and American Perspectives*. London: Sage.

Harris, M. and Lee, A.J. (eds) (1986) *The Press in English Society from the Seventeenth to the Nineteenth Century*. London and Toronto Associated University Presses.

Harris, T. (1995) *Popular Culture in England 1500–1850*. Basingstoke: Macmillan.

Harrison, S. (1974) *Poor Men's Guardians*. Lawrence and Wishart.

Hartley, J. (1996) *Popular Reality*. London: Arnold.

Harvey, D. (1989) *The Condition of Postmodernity*. Oxford: Basil Blackwell.

Hayes, T. (1992) *The Birth of Popular Culture*. Duquesne University Press.

Helmore, E. (2000) 'Alien concepts. Something strange is happening to US tabloids. They are trying to go upmarket', *Guardian* (Media Supplement), 9 October.

Herd, H. (1952) *The March of Journalism*. Allen & Unwin.

Hoggart, R. (1958) *The Uses of Literacy*. Harmonsworth: Penguin.

Hollis, P. (1970) *The Pauper Press*. Oxford: Oxford University Press.

Horkheimer, M. (1947) *The Eclipse of Reason*. Oxford: Oxford University Press.

Hughes, H.M. (1940) *News and the Human Interest Story*. University of Chicago Press.

Hughes, Catherine (1986) 'Imperialism, illustration and the Daily Mail: 1896–1904', in M. Harris and A.J. Lee (eds), *The Press in English Society from the Seventeenth Century to the Nineteenth Century*. London and Toronto Associated University Presses.

Humphreys, A. (1990) 'Popular narrative and political discourse in *Reynold's Weekly Newspaper*', in L. Brake, A. Jones and L. Madden (eds), *Investigating Victorian Journalism*. Basingstoke: Macmillan.

Inglis, F. (1990) *Popular Culture and Political Power*. Brighton: Wheatsheaf Books.

James, L. (1976) *Print and the People*. London: Allen Lane.

Jameson, F. (1991) *Postmodernism, or the Cultural Logic of Late Capitalism*. London: Sage.

Jeannery, J.-N. (1996) *Une Histoire des Médias des Origines a Nos Jours*. Paris: Seuil.

King, B. (1980) *The New English Literatures*. Basingstoke: Macmillan.

Lee, A.J. (1976) *The Origins of the Popular Press 1855–1914*. London: Croom Helm.

Lee, Alfred M. (1937) *The Daily Newspaper in America*. New York: Macmillan.

Lindemann, M. (1969) *Deutsche Presse bis 1815*. Berlin: Colloquium.

Lyotard, J.-F. (1984) *The Postmodern Condition*. Manchester: Manchester University Press.

MacKenzie, J.M. (1986) *Imperialism and Popular Culture*. Manchester: Manchester University Press.

McGuigan, J. (1993) *Cultural Populism*. London: Routledge.

McHale, B. (1989) *Postmodernist Fiction*. London: Routledge.

Mercer, C. (1986) 'Complicit pleasures', in *Popular Culture and Social Relations*. Milton Keynes: Open University Press.

Miller, T. and McHowl, A. (1998) *Popular Culture and Everyday Life*. London: Sage.

Modleski (1982) *Loving with a Vengence: Mass-Produced Fantasies for Women*. Methuen.

Mott, F.L. (1961) *American Journalism: A History of Newspapers in the US through 250 Years 1690–1960*. Basingstoke: Macmillan.

Mukerji, C. and Schudson, M. (1986) *Rethinking Popular Culture*. University of California Press.

Nerone, J.C. (1987) 'The mythology of the penny press', *Critical Studies in Mass Communication*, 4: 376–404.

Neubauer, H.-J. (2000) *The Rumour: A Cultural History*. Free Association Books.

Neuburg, V.E. (1977) *Popular Literature*. Harmondsworth: Penguin.

Nordin, K.D. (1979) 'The entertaining press: sensationalism in eighteenth century Boston newspapers', *Communication Research*, 6 (3): 295–320.

Norris, C. (1992) *Uncritical Theory*. London: Lawrence & Wishart.

Nowell-Smith, G. (1987) 'Popular Culture', *New Formations*, 2, Summer.

Ong, W. (1982) *Orality and Literacy: The Technologizing of the Word*. Methuen.

Oriad, M. (1993) *Reading Football*. University of North Carolina Press.

Palmer, M.B. (1983) *Des Petits Journaux aux Grandes Agences*. Aubier.

Palmer, R. (1979) *A Ballad History of England*. London: Batsford.

Paskal, C. (1992) *Columbia Journalism Review*. May/June.

Pennypacher, S. (1909) 'Sensational journalism and the remedy', *North American Review*', 190, November: 586–93.

Perkin, H. (1991) *The Structured Crowd*. Brighton: Harvester Press.

Preston, P. (2000) *Observer*, 20 August.

Read, D. (1961) *Press and People 1790–1850*. Edward Arnold.

Reay, B. (1998) *Popular Cultures in England 1550–1750*. Harlow: Longmann.

Robertson, R. (1993) 'Mapping the global condition: globalization as the central concept', in M. Featherstone (ed.), *Global Culture. Nationalism, Globalization and Modernity*. London: Sage.

Rollins, H.E. (ed.) (1969) *The Pack of Autolycus*. Boston, MA: Harvard University Press.

Root, R.L. (1987) *The Rhetorics of Popular Culture*. Greenwood Press.

Sachs, A. (1995) 'Mud and the mainstream: when the respectable press chases the *National Enquirer*, what's going on', *Columbia Journalism Review*, June, 1995.

Said, E. (1994) *Culture and Imperialism*. Vintage.

Samuel, R. (ed.) (1981) *People's History and Socialist Theory*. London: Routledge & Kegan Paul.

Schiach, M. (1989) *Discourse on Popular Culture*. Cambridge: Polity.

Schiller, D. (1981) *Objectivity: The Public and the Rise of Commercial Journalism*. Philadelphia, PA: University of Pennsylvania Press.

Schudson, M. (1978) *Discovering the News: A Social History of American Newspapers*. New York: Harper.

Shattock and Wolff (1982) *The Victorian Press: Samplings and Soundings*. Leicester: University of Leicester Press.

Shephard, L. (1962) *The Broadside Ballad*. Herbert Jenkins.

Shephard, L. (1973) *The History of Street Literature*. London: David & Charles.

Sloan W.D. and Williams, J.H. (1994) *The Early American Press* 1690-1783. Greenwood Press.

Smith, A.C. (1975) *Paper Voices*. London: Chatto & Windus.

Smith, Anthony (1986) *The Ethnic Origins of Nations*. Oxford: Basil Blackwell.

Sparks, C. (1988) 'The popular press and political democracy', *Media, Culture & Society*, 10: 209-23.

Sparks, C. (1992) 'Popular journalism: theories and practice', in P. Dahlgren and C. Sparks (eds), *Journalism and Popular Culture*. London: Sage.

Spufford, M. (1981) *Small Books and Pleasant Histories*. Cambridge: Hambledon Press.

Stead, W.T. (1896) 'Government by journalism', *The Contemporary Review*, 653-74.

Steele, J.E. (1990) 'The 19th century *World* versus the *Sun*: promoting consumption (rather than the working man)', *Journalism Quarterly*, 67 (3): 592-600.

Stevens, J. (1991) *Sensationalism and the New York Press*. New York: Columbia University Press.

Storch, R.D. (1982) *Popular Culture and Custom in Nineteenth Century England*. Croom Helm.

Street, J. (1997) *Politics and Popular Culture*. Cambridge: Polity.

Taylor, S.J. (1992) *Shock! Horror! The Tabloids in Action*. Black Swan.

Thomas, M.W. (1980) *Porträts der deutschen Presse*. Berlin: Spiess.

Thomas, W.I. (1908) 'The psychology of the yellow journal', *American Magazine*, March: 491-6.

Thompson, E.P. (1979) *The Making of the English Working Class*. Harmondsworth: Penguin.

Vincent, D. (1993) *Literacy and Popular Culture*. Cambridge: Cambridge University Press.

Wallraff, G. (1977) *Der Aufmacher. Der Mann der bei Bild Hans Esser war*. Cologne: Verlag Kiepenhauer und Witsch.

Wallraff, G. (1979) *Zeugen der Anklage: Die 'Bild' - Beschreibung wird fortgesetzt*. Cologne: Verlag Kiepenhauer und Witsch.

Wallraff, G. (1985) *Bild-Störung. Ein Handbuch*. Cologne: Verlag Kiepenhauer und Witsch.

Whitby, G. (1982) 'The penny press and the origins of American journalistic style', in *Studies in Journalism and Mass Communication: A Review from the Texas Journalism Education Council Annual Conference*.

Wiener, J. (ed.) (1988) *Papers for the Millions: The New Journalism in Britain 1850-1914*. New York: Greenwood Press.

Williams, F. (1957) *Dangerous Estate: The Anatomy of Newspapers*. London: Arrow.

Williams, K. (1998) *Get Me a Murder a Day: A History of Mass Communication in Britain*. Arnold.

Williams, R. (1961) *The Long Revolution*. Harmondsworth: Penguin.

Williams, R. (1970) 'Radical and/or respectable', in R. Boston and K.P. Boston (eds), *The Press We Deserve*.

Williams, R. (1970) 'The press and popular culture: an historical perspective', in G. Boyce, J. Curran and P. Wingate (eds), *Newspaper History: From the Seventeenth Century to the Present Day*. Constable & Company. Routledge and Kegan Paul.

Williams, R. (1976a) *Communications*. Harmondsworth: Penguin.

Williams, R. (1976b) *Keywords*. Fontana.

Yeo, E. and Yeo, S. (eds) (1981) *Popular Culture and Class Conflict 1590-1914*. Brighton: Harvester.

INDEX